The Medieval Natural World

The Medieval Natural World

Richard Jones

PEARSON

Harlow, England • London • New York • Boston • San Francisco • Toronto • Sydney
Auckland • Singapore • Hong Kong • Tokyo • Seoul • Taipei • New Delhi
Cape Town • São Paulo • Mexico City • Madrid • Amsterdam • Munich • Paris • Milan

PEARSON EDUCATION LIMITED
Edinburgh Gate
Harlow CM20 2JE
Tel: +44 (0)1279 623623
Website: www.pearson.com/uk

First published in Great Britain in 2013 (print and electronic)

© Pearson Education Limited 2013 (print and electronic)

The right of Richard Jones to be identified as author of this work has been asserted by him in accordance with the Copyright, Designs and Patents Act 1988.

Pearson Education is not responsible for the content of third-party internet sites.

ISBN: 978-1-4082-4889-8 (print)
      978-1-4082-4890-4 (PDF)
      978-0-273-79201-7 (eText)

British Library Cataloguing-in-Publication Data
A catalogue record for the print edition is available from the British Library

Library of Congress Cataloging-in-Publication Data
A catalog record for the print edition is available from the Library of Congress

10 9 8 7 6 5 4 3 2 1
17 16 15 14 13

Cover image: Kitab al-Hayawan d'al-Jahiz (fourteenth century, Syria) © Veneranda Biblioteca Ambrosiana – Milano/De Agostini Picture Library

Print edition typeset in 10/13.5pt ITC Berkeley Oldstyle Std by 35
Print edition printed and bound in Malaysia, CTP-PJB

NOTE THAT ANY PAGE CROSS REFERENCES REFER TO THE PRINT EDITION

Introduction to the series

History is narrative constructed by historians from traces left by the past. Historical enquiry is often driven by contemporary issues and, in consequence, historical narratives are constantly reconsidered, reconstructed and reshaped. The fact that different historians have different perspectives on issues means that there is also often controversy and no universally agreed version of past events. *Seminar Studies* was designed to bridge the gap between current research and debate, and the broad, popular general surveys that often date rapidly.

The volumes in the series are written by historians who are not only familiar with the latest research and current debates concerning their topic, but who have themselves contributed to our understanding of the subject. The books are intended to provide the reader with a clear introduction to a major topic in history. They provide both a narrative of events and a critical analysis of contemporary interpretations. They include the kinds of tools generally omitted from specialist monographs: a chronology of events, a glossary of terms and brief biographies of 'who's who'. They also include bibliographic essays in order to guide students to the literature on various aspects of the subject. Students and teachers alike will find that the selection of documents will stimulate discussion and offer insight into the raw materials used by historians in their attempt to understand the past.

Clive Emsley and Gordon Martel
Series Editors

For Ione and Adela

Contents

Publisher's acknowledgements   x
Abbreviations and editorial notes   xii
Chronology   xiii
Who's who   xvii
Glossary   xxii

PART ONE   ANALYSIS   1

1   THE NATURE OF THINGS   3

2   UNIVERSAL MODELS   12

3   ON THE HEAVENS   25

4   METEOROLOGY   37

5   IMAGE OF THE WORLD   48

6   MAN AND NATURE   62

7   ON ANIMALS   73

8   ON PLANTS   85

9   ON MINERALS   96

10   THE BOOK OF NATURE   106

PART TWO DOCUMENTS   115

1   Psalm 104 (Vulgate Psalm 103) (*c.* 1000–300 BC)   116
2   Extracts from Plato's *Timaeus* (*c.* 360 BC)   117
3   Aristotle's *Metaphysics*, Bk 5, Ch. 4 on the various meanings of
    'nature' (*a.* 322 BC)   119
4   *Physiologus* on the partridge (second–fourth century)   120
5   St Augustine of Hippo, *De Genesi ad litteram* on the relationship
    between Christian and non-Christian conceptions of the cosmos
    (*a.* 430)   120
6   Isidore of Seville, *De natura rerum*, Ch. 11, 'The elements of
    the world' (*c.* 612)   121
7   Extracts from the *Qur'an* (610–632)   122
8   Al-Jāhiz, *Kitāb al-Hayawan* on differences between
    scholarly and popular questioning of natural phenomena
    (*c.* 800–850)   123
9   Al-Jāhiz, *Kitāb al-Hayawan* on the nuisance of flies
    (*c.* 800–850)   124
10 Dicuil, *Liber de Mensura Orbis Terrae* on Iceland (825)   124
11 John Scotus Eriugena, *Periphyseon* or *De divisione naturae*,
    Bk 3, ll. 3257–77, on the structure of the universe (860)   125
12 Captain Buzurg ibn Shahriya of Ramhormuz, *Ajaib al-Hind*
    on the hermaphroditic hare (*c.* 950–1000)   126
13 Avicenna, *Danishnama-i 'ala'i* on the senses (*a.* 1037)   126
14 Al-Birunī, *Kitāb-al-Saydanah fi't-Tibb* on barley (*a.* 1048)   127
15 Physiologus ascribed to Theobald, abbot of Monte Cassino,
    'Concerning the ant' (1022–1085)   128
16 Baudri of Bourgueil, *To Countess Adela*, ll. 1042–1064 on
    astronomy (*a.* 1130)   129
17 *Bestiary* on the partridge (twelfth century)   130
18 William of Conches, *Dragmaticon*, Bk 6, Ch. 22 on smell
    (1147–1149)   131
19 Hildegard of Bingen, *Physica* on gemstones (1151–1158)   132
20 Rabbi Petachia of Ratisbon, *Travels* on the flying camel
    (1170–1187)   132
21 Extracts from the Anglo-Norman and French bestiaries of
    Philippe de Thaon, ll. 307–48 (*c.* 1120) and Gervaise, ll. 282–304
    (*c.* 1200) concerning the Idrus and the Crocodile   133
22 The Owl: Hugh de Fouilloy's *De avibus* (*c.* 1132–1152) and the
    anonymous *The Owl and the Nightingale*, ll. 56–100
    (late twelfth century)   135

23   Farid al-din 'Attar, *Mantiq al-tair* on the spider (*c*. 1130–*c*. 1229)   137
24   Bartholomew the Englishman, *De proprietatibus rerum*, Bk 14,
      Chs 9 and 10 on the mountains of Ethiopia and Mount Etna (*a*. 1240) 138
25   Gauthier de Metz, *The Myrrour of the World*, Pt 2, Ch. 4 on Inde
      (*c*. 1245)   139
26   Matthew Paris, *Historia Anglorum* on unseasonable weather (*c*. 1274) 139
27   *Seneschaucy*, Ch. 7 on the duties of the cowherd (*a*. 1276)   140
28   Albertus Magnus, *De natura locorum*, ll. 43–62 on planetary
      influence (*a*. 1280)   141
29   Albertus Magnus, *De mineralibus* on silver (*a*. 1280)   141
30   Meteorological observations attributed to Roger Bacon for
      February 1270   142
31   Marco Polo, *Divisament dou monde*, Bk 3, Ch. 9 concerning
      pygmies (1298)   143
32   Meteorological observations of William Merle (1344)   143
33   *Mandeville's Travels* on monstrous races (*c*. 1360)   144
34   Edward of Norwich, *The Master of Game* on greyhounds
      (1406–1413)   145
35   *The Secrete of Secretes*, 'On the condition of Man'
      (fifteenth century version)   145

      REFERENCES   147

      INDEX   165

Publisher's acknowledgements

We are grateful to the following for permission to reproduce copyright material:

Text

Document 3 reprinted by permission of the publishers and the Trustees of the Loeb Classical Library from ARISTOTLE: VOLUME XVII, METAPHYSICS, Loeb Classical Library Volume 271, translated by H. Tredennick, pp. 219, 221, 223, 225, 227, 229, 231, 233, Cambridge, Mass.: Harvard University Press, 1933. Loeb Classical Library ® is a registered trademark of the President and Fellows of Harvard College; Document 5 from *On Genesis (Works of St Augustine) (Book 13)*, New City Press (Augustinian Heritage Institute 2002) pp. 186–7; Document 6 from *Isidore of Seville, De natura rerum: Traite de la nature*, 28, Bibliotheque de l'Ecole des Hautes Etudes Hispaniques (Fontaine, J. 1960) pp. 213–6; Document 13 from *Avicenne, Le Livre de Science*, Les Belles Lettres/UNESCO (Achena, M. and Masse, H. 1986) pp. 56–7; Document 16 from Baudri of Bourgueil: To Countess Adela, *Journal of Medieval Latin*, 11, pp. 91–2 (Otter, Monika 2001). By permission of Brepols Publishers; Document 17 from *Bestiary*, Boydell Press (Barber, Richard 1992) pp. 151–3; Document 19 from *Hildegard von Bingen's Physica*, Healing Arts Press (Throop, Priscilla 1998) pp. 137–8, published by Healing Arts Press, a division of Inner Traditions International, 1998. All rights reserved. http://www. Innertraditions.com. Reprinted with permission of publisher; Document 22 from *The Owl and the Nightingale, Cleanness, St Erkenwald*, Penguin (Stone, B. (trans) 1971) pp. 182–4, translated and introduced by Brian Stone (Penguin Classics 1971, Second edition 1988). Copyright © Brian Stone, 1971, 1988; Document 27 from *Walter of Henley and Other Treatises on Estate Management and Accounting*, Clarendon Press (Oshinsky, Dorethea 1971) pp. 283–5. By permission of Oxford University Press (www.oup.com); Document 29 from *Albertus Magnus, De Mineralibus*, Clarendon Press (Wyckoff, D. 1967) pp. 200–1. By permission of Oxford University Press (www.oup.com); Document 33 from *Mandeville's Travels: Text and translations*, series 2, 101, The Hakluyt Society (Letts, Malcolm 1953) pp. 141–2; Document 34 from *Edward of Norwich, The Master of Game*, University of Pennsylvania Press (Baillie-Grohman, William A. and Baillie-Grohman, F. (eds) 2005) pp. 113–4, reprinted with the permission of the University of Pennsylvania Press.

Plates

The publisher would like to thank the following for their kind permission to reproduce their photographs:

Plate 1: The Pierpoint Morgan Library, New York. MS M.722. Purchased in 1927; **Plate 2:** The Bodleian Library, University of Oxford, MS. Rawl d. 939, fol. 4v; **Plate 3:** Copyright © The British Library Board. Cotton Tiberius B.V. f56v; **Plate 4:** Bibliothèque nationale de France, MS FRANCAIS 2810; **Plate 5:** © The Trustees of the British Museum; **Plate 6:** National Gallery / Bridgeman Art Library; **Plate 7:** Copyright © The British Library Board. Sloane MS278, fol 48v; **Plate 8:** Bibliothèque nationale de France, MS FRANCAIS 616; **Plate 9:** Musée Condé / Bridgeman Art Library; **Plate 10:** The Bodleian Library, University of Oxford, MS. Bodl. 130, fol. 26r.

All other images © Pearson Education

In some instances we have been unable to trace the owners of copyright material, and we would appreciate any information that would enable us to do so.

Abbreviations and editorial notes

Abbreviations

a.	*ante*
b.	born
c.	*circa*
C	century
d.	died
fl.	*floruit*

Dates

Unless specifically stated to the contrary, all dates in this book should be read to mean AD. Dates are expressed according to the Christian calendar even when providing chronological information regarding the Islamic world. The beginning of the Islamic calendar is reckoned from the emigration of Mohammed from Mecca to Medina, 622 in the Christian calendar. Because the Islamic calendar is strictly lunar, however, the Islamic year is approximately eleven days shorter than the Christian year; thus calculating equivalent dates is not a simple case of mathematical subtraction. This is further complicated by the fact that the start of the Islamic year is taken as the first day of the first month Muharram, which is rarely coincident with 1 January. Several calendar converters can be found on-line.

Original titles

Works are referred to throughout in their Latinised Greek, Latin, Latinised Arabic or medieval French forms. English translations are provided in parentheses. Where translations of titles are not given in the text, these can be found in the Chronology section at the beginning of the book.

Chronology

This chronology seeks only to order and highlight *some* of the more important works of scholarship dealing with nature. Consequently its coverage is selective rather than comprehensive. It necessarily includes those texts of the Classical period upon which medieval writers drew most heavily. These works were occasionally transmitted directly; more usually, however, they were transmitted indirectly through Arabic and Hebraic translations, which in turn were rendered into Latin primarily during the twelfth and thirteenth centuries. This handlist also includes a representative sample of the most influential original works of scholarship composed during the middle ages, together with a selection of the more popular textbooks, manuals and literary works that dealt with the theme of nature.

a. 435 BC	Empedocles, *Physis* ('On Nature')
a. 370 BC	Hippocrates, *Aphorisma* (*Aphorisms*), *Prognostica* (*Prognostications*), *Regimen* (*Health*) and others
c. 360 BC	Plato, *Timaeus*
a. 322 BC	Aristotle, *Libri naturales* ('Books on Nature')
a. 287 BC	Theophrastus, *Historia plantarum* (*Enquiry into Plants*) and *De causis plantarum* (*On the Causes of Plants*)
70	Dioscorides, *De materia medica* (*On Medical Matters*)
77	Pliny the Elder, *Naturalis historia* (*Natural History*)
C2–4	*Physiologus* (The 'Naturalist')
a. 168	Ptolemy, *Almagest, Tetrabiblos* (*Book of Four Parts*)
a. c. 210	Galen, *Megategni* (*Great Arts*), *Pantegni* (*All Arts*), etc.
early C3	Solinus, *De mirabilibus mundi* (*The Wonders of the World*)
C4	Calcidius, partial translation of Plato's *Timaeus*
a. 423	Macrobius, *Commentarii in somnium Scipionis* (*Commentary on Cicero's Dream of Scipio*)
a. 430	Augustine of Hippo, *De civitate dei* (*The City of God*), *De Genesi ad litteram* (*The Literal Meaning of Genesis*) and many other works

early C5	Martianus Capella, *De nuptiis Philologiae et Mercurii* (*The Marriage of Philosophy and Mercury*)
c. 524	Boethius, *Consolatio philosophiae* (*The Consolation of Philosophy*)
c. 612–13	Isidore of Seville, *De natura rerum* (*The Nature of Things*)
c. 630	Isidore of Seville, *Etymologiae sive origins* (*Etymologies or Origins*)
c. 703	Bede, *De natura rerum* (*On the Nature of Things*)
c. 725	Bede, *De temporum rationale* (*On the Reckoning of Time*)
a. 800	al-Batrīq, translations of Hippocrates and Galen
C9	pseudo-Aristotle, *Kitāb sirr al-asrār* later *Secretum secretorum* (*The Secret of Secrets*)
a. c. 856	Rabanus Maurus, *De naturis rerum* (*The Nature of Things*) or *De universo* (*On the Universe*)
a. c. 877	John Scotus Eriugena, *Periphyseon* or *De divisione naturae* (*The Division of Nature*)
a. 900	al-Battāni, *Kitāb al-Zij* or *De motu stellarum* (*The Motion of the Stars*)
a. 925	al-Rāzī, *Kitāb al-Asrār* (*The Book of Secrets*)
a. 930	Bald, *Leechbook*
a. 976	al-Khwārizmī, *Māfātih al-ʿUlūm* (*The Keys of the Sciences*)
c. 1011	Byrhtferth of Ramsey, *Enchiridion*
a. 1037	Avicenna, *al-Qānūn fiʼ al-Tibb* (*The Canon of Medicine*)
a. 1048	al-Bīrunī, *Taʼrikh al-Hind* (*Chronicles of India*)
a. 1050	Gariopontus of Salerno, *Passionarius* (*Book of Diseases*)
1058	Avicebron, *Fons vitae* (*Fountain of Life*)
a. 1087	Constantine the African, translations of medical works from Arabic including Hippocrates and Galen
c. 1112–21	Lambert of St-Omer, *Liber Floribus* (*Book of Flowers*)
a. 1123	Marbode, *Liber de lapidibus* (*Book of Stones*)
a. 1125	Philippe de Thaon, *Li bestiaire* (*The Bestiary*)
a. 1130	Adelard of Bath, *Quaestiones naturales* (*Natural Questions*)
1147–49	William of Conches, *Dragmaticon philosophiae* (*A Dialogue on Natural Philosophy*)
1160	Eugene of Palermo, translation of Ptolemy's *Almagest*
1161	Matthaeus Platearius, *De simplici medicine* (*On Simple Medicine*) or *Circa instans*
1170	Roger of Salerno, *Practica chirugia* (*Surgical Practice*)
1175	Gerard of Cremona, translation of Ptolemy's *Almagest*
a. 1179	Hildegard of Bingen, *Physica* (*Natural Sciences*)
c. 1180–90	Alfred de Sareshel, translation of Nicolas of Damascus' *De Plantis* (*On Plants*)
a. 1187	Gerard of Cremona, translations of Avicenna, al-Rāzī, al-Khwārizmi and others
1190	Maimonides, *Dalālat al-Hāʼirīn* (*The Guide to the Perplexed*)

a. 1193   Burgundo of Pisa, translations of the works of Galen

a. 1198   Averroes, commentaries on Aristotle

a. 1200   Ibn al-'Awwam, *Kitāb al-Filāhah* (*Treatise on Agriculture*)

a. 1214   Maurus of Salerno, *Anatomia Mauri* (*Anatomy of Maurus*)

a. 1217   Alexander Neckam, *De naturis rerum* (*On the Natures of Things*)

1217–35   Michael Scotus, translations of *Liber astronomiae* (*Book of Astronomy*),
Averroes' commentaries and others

c. 1225   Arnold of Saxony, *De floribus naturalium rerum* (*The Flowers of Nature's
Things*)

a. 1240   Bartholomew the Englishman, *De proprietatibus rerum* (*On the Properties
of Things*)

a. 1244   Thomas de Cantimpré, *De natura rerum* (*The Nature of Things*)

1245   Gautier de Metz, *L'image du Monde* (*Image of the World*)

a. 1250   Frederick II, *De arte venandi cum avibus* (*The Art of Hunting with Birds*)

a. 1253   Robert Grosseteste, *De luce* (*On Light*) and many other treatises concerning
astronomy, cosmology, sound, colours, time, tides and geography

c. 1258–66   Translation of *Tactinium Sanitatis* (*Maintenance of Health*)

1262   Judah Cohen and Isaac ben Sid of Toledo, *Alfonsine Tables*

a. c. 1264   Vincent of Beauvais, *Speculum maius* including *Speculum naturale*
(*Mirror on Nature*)

a. 1267   Brunetto Latini, *Li livres dou tresor* (*The Book of the Treasure*)

a. 1274   Thomas Aquinas, *Summa theologica* (*Summary of Theology*) commentaries
on the works of Aristotle

a. 1275   Gershon Ben Shlomah, *Shaar ha-Shamayim* (*The Gate of Heaven*)

1275   William of Saliceto, *Chirugia* (*Surgery*)

c. 1277   Guido Bonatti, *Liber astronomicus* (*Book of Astronomy*)

a. 1280   Albertus Magnus, reworking of Aristotle's *Libri naturales*

a. 1284   Alfonso the Wise, *De septennario* (*On the Seven*)

1292   Roger Bacon, *Compendium philosophiae* (*Compendium of Philosophy*)

1298   Marco Polo and Rustichello of Pisa, *Divisament dou Monde* (*Division of
the World*) or *Livre de merveilles dou monde* (*Book of Wonders of the World*)

a. 1307   Pietro die Crescenzi, *Opus ruralium commodorum* (*Book of Practical
Agriculture*)

1316   Mondino de'Luzzi, *Anatomia* (*Anatomy*)

1328   John of Milan, *Regimen sanitatis Salernitanum* (*The Salernitan Rule of Health*)

1330   Friar Jordanus, *Mirabilia Descripta* (*The Wonders of the East*)

1351   Konrad of Megenburg, *Das Buch der Natur* (*The Book of Nature*)

a. 1359   John Buridan, *Quaestionaes octavi libri physicorum* (*Questions on the Eight
Books of Physics*)

1372   al-Damīrī, *Kitāb hayāt al-Hayāwan* (*Lives of Animals*)

a. 1382   Nicole Oresme, *Le livre du ciel et du monde* (*The Book of Heaven and Earth*)

1391   Gaston Phoebus, *Livre de chasse* (*Book of Hunting*) *a.* **1400**   Juliana Berners, *Treatyse Perteynynge to Hawkynge, Huntyng*

a. **1410**   Edward of Norwich, *The Master of Game*

     1410   Benedetto Rinio of Venice, *Liber de simplicibus* (*Book of Medicinal Herbs*)

a. **1411**   Nicolò Falcucci, *Sermones medicales septem* (*Seven Medical Lectures*),
          Liber de materia medica (*Book of Medical Matters*)

Who's who

Adelard of Bath (*c.* 1080–*c.* 1150): Scientist and scholar heavily influenced by contact with Arabic scholars. Author of several works on astrology, cosmology and natural philosophy. These included the wide-ranging *Quaestiones naturales*, which sought to reconcile Neoplatonic and Aristotelian ideas; a treatise on the astrolabe; and a short treatise on birds.

Albertus Magnus (*c.* 1200–1280): Dominican friar and scholar of such renown that he enjoyed the title 'great' during his own lifetime. A key figure in the revival of Aristotle's natural philosophy through his commentaries on and extensions to the greater part of the philosopher's corpus. He was regarded as an authority on physics and chemistry, geography and astronomy, botany and zoology, physiology and mineralogy. His work was also influenced by Arabic scholars such as Avicenna and Averroes.

al-Birunī (973–1048): Moslem scholar and author of *c.* 150 texts, of which only 22 survive. These cover *inter alia* astronomy, physics, medicine, ethnography and geography, and all aspects of what would now be described as the natural sciences.

Alexander Neckam (1157–1217): Augustinian canon and abbot of Cirencester who taught in Paris and later Oxford. His most extensive work *De naturis rerum* provided a commentary on the Book of Ecclesiastes arranged in five books, of which the first two were dedicated to the working of the natural world.

Aristotle (384–322 BC): Athenian philosopher and student of Plato. Author of the *libri naturales*, the most important works on natural philosophy in the medieval period. Aristotle's ideas were formative for Moslem and, after their translation into Latin, European scholars alike. His works were condemned by the Church in 1270 and 1277 and banned from the curriculum at the University of Paris.

Augustine of Hippo (354–430): Bishop, saint and early Church father. Augustine did much to reconcile Neoplatonic conceptions of the creation of the cosmos with the Biblical narrative in Genesis, identifying a place for natural philosophy in the discussion of theological matters in *De Genesi ad litteram*.

Bartholomew the Englishman (*a*. 1203–1272): Franciscan friar, probably studied in Oxford under Robert Grosseteste, taught in Paris and later Magdeburg in Saxony. His encyclopaedia *De proprietatibus rerum*, arranged in 19 books, was compiled *c*. 1245. It drew on a wide range of patristic, Neoplatonic and newly translated Aristotelian works. It was a Paris textbook by 1284.

Bede (*c*. 675–735): Monk of Monkwearmouth, historian and scientist, author of *De natura rerum* 'On the nature of things' and *De temporibus* 'On times' *c*. 703, the latter reworked and expanded in *De temporum rationale* 'On the reckoning of time' *c*. 725. His scientific innovations included empirical observation of timing of the tides and moon phases, informed by a network of correspondents around England, and the use of astronomical observation and mathematical calculation to establish the timing of Easter.

Boethius (*c*. 480–*c*. 524): Member of the royal court of the Ostrogothic King Theodoric. Author of *Consolatio philosophiae*, written when facing execution, a work that presented an archetype for later Neoplatonic writers such as Bernard Silvestris and Alan of Lille.

Calcidius (C4): Translator of the first 53 chapters of Plato's *Timaeus*, giving the Latin west its most comprehensive account of natural philosophy until the 'rediscovery' of the works of Aristotle.

Constantine the African (d. *a*. 1097–1098): Benedictine monk of Monte Cassino and associated with the medical school at Salerno. He was responsible for translating the key Arabic translations of Hippocrates and Galen into Latin.

Dioscorides (*c*. 40–*c*. 90): Author of *De materia medica*, a medical treatise that dealt with the properties of plants and offered the basis for the medieval herbal tradition.

Frederick II (1194–1250): Holy Roman Emperor and great patron and promoter of the translation movement. Author of *De arte venandi cum avibus*, demonstrating careful firsthand observation of bird behaviour.

Galen (129–post 216?): Roman physician, whose works were translated into Arabic by the ninth century where they would form the basis of Islamic medicine. His works were also key to the establishment of the medical school at Salerno.

Gerard of Cremona (*c*. 1114–1187): Lombard scholar and the most prolific translator of texts in Arabic (found in the library of Toledo) to Latin. These included Ptolemy's *Almagest*, most of Aristotle's *libri naturales*, the medical works of Galen and Avicenna's *al-Qānūn fi' al-Tibb*.

Gershon ben Shlomah of Arles (*fl.* 1242–1275): Rabbi and author of *Sha'ar ha-Shamayim*, one of the most important Judaic encyclopaedic works of the middle ages, drawing heavily from Arabic authorities and Aristotle.

Hildegard of Bingen (1098–1179): German Benedictine abbess and author of *Physica*, a short encyclopaedia on natural science and *Causae et curae*, a cosmologico-medical manual.

Hippocrates (*c.* 460–*c.* 370 BC): The 'father' of medicine. The first to articulate the idea that ill health stemmed from an imbalance of the body's four humours. His ideas were built upon by Galen and adopted by Arab and Christian scholars alike.

Ibn Rushd (Averroes) (1126–1198): Spanish Moslem philosopher who wrote influential commentaries on the works of Avicenna and Galen, but notably Aristotle, reviving interest in Greek philosophy in the west. A strong opponent of Neoplatonism.

Ibn Sīnā (Avicenna) (*c.* 980–1037): Moslem philosopher and physician whose *al-Qanun fi'l-Tibb* became the standard medical textbook in both the Latin west and the Islamic world until the early modern period. His philosophical stance has been described as 'Aristotelian Neoplatonism'.

Isidore of Seville (*c.* 560–636): Bishop of Seville best known for his *Etymologiae*, which quickly became one of the most popular and influential encyclopaedias of the medieval period. Arranged in 22 books, this work covered cosmology, physiology, zoology, botany, agriculture and mineralogy. It was through this work that much classical learning was transmitted to the Latin west. Less well known is his *De natura rerum*, an explanation of natural phenomena, later reworked by Bede in the early eighth century.

John Scotus Eriugena (*c.* 815–*c.* 877): Irish scholar who succeeded Alcuin of York as head of the palace school of Charles the Bald. His greatest philosophical accomplishment was *Periphyseon* or *De divisione naturae*, a work condemned in the thirteenth century as heretical.

Konrad of Megenburg (1309–1374): Bavarian scholar, author of the first natural history to be written in German, *Das Buch der Natur*. Based on Thomas of Cantimpré's *De natura rerum*, but substantially revised and restructured, containing a number of significant original contributions.

Marbode (*c.* 1035–1123): Bishop of Rennes and author of the *Liber de lapidibus*, a popular versified lapidary.

Moses ben Maimon (Maimonides) (1135–1204): Spanish Jewish philosopher and court physician to Saladin, author of *Dalālat al-Hā'irīn* completed in *c.* 1190.

Plato (429–347 BC): Athenian philosopher and author of the cosmological work *Timaeus*, which presents a systematic account of the creation of the universe and its constituent parts. The first 53 chapters were translated into Latin and commented upon by Calcidius in the fourth century, allowing its transmission into medieval Europe where it remained unchallenged as the foundation for all natural philosophy until the 'rediscovery' of Aristotle in the twelfth and thirteenth centuries. Traces of *Timaeus* can be found in a great number of later works.

Pliny the Elder (23–79): Civil servant and author of *Naturalis historia*, a vast compendium in 37 books, which covered all aspects of the natural world including geography and ethnography, physiology, zoology, botany, pharmacology and mineralogy. Widely consulted in the middle ages, it was through this work that much classical learning passed into the medieval world.

Physiologus (C2–4?): 'The naturalist', an anonymous Greek author who probably wrote in Alexandria. It has been suggested that his eponymous work comes second only to the Bible in the profound influence it has had on subsequent Christian thought. The work, which used animals for the purpose of Christian allegory and moralising, formed the basis and provided the model for later bestiaries.

Ptolemy (*c.* 90–*c.* 168): Astronomer, astrologer and geographer. The astronomical measurements found in *Almagest* became the basis for all later medieval astronomy. His astrological treatise, *Tetrabiblos* or *Quadripartitum*, was also highly influential.

Rabanus Maurus (*c.* 780–856): Abbot of Fulda and Archbishop of Mainz. Author of *De rerum naturis* also known as *De universo* probably written in the 840s in 22 books. Books 6–13 deal specifically with the natural world: the parts of Man and the human body, animals, astronomy, time and the calendar, waters, oceans, rivers, and floods, the regions of the earth, and physical geography. The rest of the work is dedicated to a range of topics which includes geology and agriculture.

Robert Grosseteste (*c.* 1170–1253): Bishop of Lincoln who had previously taught at the University of Oxford and who contributed original work in the natural sciences including on the movement of planets, sounds, tides and optics, as well as commentaries on the works of Aristotle.

Roger Bacon (*c.* 1219–1292): Franciscan friar, scientist and philosopher who taught at Oxford and Paris. His *Opus maius* dealt with mathematics, optics and astronomy. A pioneer of experimental science, he was scathing about the intellectual capacities of his contemporary Albertus Magnus and the over-reliance of most scholars on ancient authorities.

Solinus (C3–4): Author of the *Collectanea rerum memorabilium*, otherwise known as *De mirabilibus mundi*. Essentially a reworking and abridgement of Pliny's *Naturalis historia*, its brevity and focus on the fabulous creatures ensured its popularity in the middle ages.

Theophrastus (371–*c.* 287 BC): Author of two botanical treatises, *Historia Plantarum*, which offered a classification based on how they reproduced, their habitat, size and uses, etc., and *De causis plantarum,* which deals with taxonomy together with the practicalities of growing plants as well as detailed commentaries on their germination and growth. Influential only in later centuries after translation, when heavily borrowed by medieval scholars.

Thomas Aquinas (*c.* 1225–1274): Dominican friar and student of Albertus Magnus. Advocate and key disseminator of Aristotelian natural philosophy through his commentaries on Artistotle's *Physica, Meteorologica, De generatione et corruptione* and *De caelo*. Used Aristotelian natural philosophy to inform on theological matters, but not vice versa.

Thomas of Cantimpré (1201–1272): Augustinian canon and later Dominican friar. Author of *Liber de natura rerum*, an encyclopaedic treatment in 20 books of all aspects of the natural world, which would be heavily drawn upon by Albertus Magnus, Bartholomew the Englishman and Vincent of Beauvais.

Vincent of Beauvais (*c.* 1190–1264): Dominican friar and author of the *Speculum maius*, the first part of which, the *Speculum naturale*, provided the most comprehensive account of thirteenth-century natural philosophy and history. In 32 books with over 3,700 chapters.

William of Conches (*c.* 1090–1154+): French scholar and part of the so-called 'School of Chartres' who provided glosses of Plato's *Timaeus* and Boethius' *Consolatio philosophiae*. His major work *De philosophia mundie*, revised as *Dragmaticon*, covered physics, astronomy, geography, meteorology and medicine in four books.

William of Moerbeke (d. 1286): Flemish Dominican, the greatest of the thirteenth-century translators, who is credited with over 50 translations or revisions from Greek to Latin, including large parts of the Aristotelian corpus.

Glossary

Abrahamic religions: Monotheistic religions that trace their origins to Abraham and his descendants. The three main religions are Judaism, Christianity and Islam, which all consequently share the Old Testament as a sacred text.

Agronomy: The science of agriculture giving the word agronomist, an 'agricultural writer'.

Anatomy: Relating to the structure of a living body (human, animal, plant).

Augustinians: Community of clerics following the short Rule of St Augustine, leading semi-monastic lives having taken religious vows but retaining responsibility for the pastoral care of lay congregations.

Benedictines: Order of monks following the Rule of St Benedict, a monk of Monte Cassino, written 530–560. The earliest and most influential of the monastic traditions in the Latin west.

Candlemas: The feast of the Purification of the Virgin Mary celebrated on 2 February.

Cathars: A Christian heretical sect, also known as the Albigensians, because of their strong hold in southern France during the twelfth and thirteenth centuries. Accused by the established Church of being Manichaean due to their dualistic convictions (see Manichaeism).

Celestial sphere: In a geocentric conception of the cosmos, those parts of the universe which begin at the orbit of the moon and which stretch to the outer orbit of the fixed stars or firmament. Constituted of the fifth element or quintessence, ether, and regarded as constant, perfect and incorruptible.

Church Fathers: The most influential writers of non-canonical texts during the first few centuries of Christianity, whose works helped to define theological doctrine. They divide into three time-frames relative to the adoption of the Nicene Creed at the Council of Nicaea in 325: ante-Nicene writers such as Origen; Nicene writers such as St Augustine; and post-Nicene fathers such as St Jerome, St Basil and St Ambrose.

Complexion: The combination of qualities (hot/cold, dry/moist) found in all living bodies and which determine their nature. Used as a synonym for 'temperament'.

Computus: The science of calculating astronomical phenomena and movable dates in the calendar, particularly Easter.

Cosmology: The theoretical science of the universe and the laws which govern and explain its workings.

Cryptozoological: Creatures now considered by modern science to be legendary or mythical. They include: the bonnacon (probably based on the European Bison); the griffin (a lion-like animal with the head and wings of an eagle); and the manticore (a lion-like animal with a human face, occasionally horned or winged).

Cynegetic literature: Works which deal directly with hunting.

Deferent: In Ptolemaic astronomy, the point around which the epicycle rotated. See 'epicycle'.

Demiurge: The Creator of the universe in Platonic philosophy (see Gnosticism).

Divination: Predicting the future through magical or supernatural means. Includes aeromancy (observation of meteorological phenomena, cloud forms, the flight of birds, etc.); geomancy (signs read from the earth); pyromancy (fire signs); and necromancy (prediction through communication with the dead).

Dominicans: Emerging from the preaching activities of Dominic and his followers in southern France during the late twelfth and early thirteenth century, a mendicant 'Order of Preachers' surviving on the alms of others. By combining elements of both monastic obedience and ascetic observance, few religious lives were stricter than that of the Dominican friar.

Eccentric: In Ptolemaic astronomy, a circular orbit which was not centred on the earth, meaning that planets would appear to move faster or slower depending on proximity or distance of their position on their orbit from the earth. In contradistinction to concentric orbits, which all share the same centre.

Elements: The essential building blocks of the cosmos. Found in combination in all physical forms, comprising earth, water, air and fire.

Enlightenment: Conventionally covering intellectual developments from the middle decades of the seventeenth century through to the end of the eighteenth, the period of seismic change during which philosophy was freed from its earlier theological constraints and when the foundations for modern western thought were laid down. Spurred by the scientific discoveries in the sixteenth and seventeenth centuries, Enlightenment thinkers emphasised rationalism and reason, empiricism and the scientific method, over the natural philosophies of the Ancients and the doctrines of the Church.

Epicurean physics: Based on an atomist view of the world composed of indivisible atoms and vacuum developed by Democritus (d. 460 BC). Atoms combine chaotically (without design) to form the material world. Revised by Epicurus (d. 270 BC) following Aristotle's criticism of the original theory. Contrast with Stoic physics.

Epicycle: Astronomical term for the small circle around which planets rotated, which has its centre on a larger circle, and which was used to explain planetary stations and retrogradation.

Equant: A point in space around which a celestial body, travelling along an eccentric orbit, would move at a constant velocity. See 'eccentric'.

Exegesis: Explanation and interpretation of the written word particularly, in a Christian setting, the Bible and other sacred texts.

Firmament: In Ptolemaic astronomy, the eighth sphere of the heavens on which the stars were fixed.

Forests: A legal term for an area under Forest Law, in which royal monopoly over the hunting of animals (venison) and use of timber and underwood (vert) was protected. A medieval Forest is not necessarily heavily wooded.

Franciscans: Mendicant Order following the Rule of St Francis established in the early thirteenth century. The rule imposed strict regulations upon the receipt of alms, fasting and preaching.

Geocentrism: The concept of the universe which revolves around the earth.

Gnosticism: A key component of Gnostic religions is their belief that the world was not created directly by God but through an intermediary, the 'Demiurge', a false or inferior god. Because of this, the material world was imperfect. Salvation could only be gained through superior knowledge of the ultimate godhead, the monad, a knowledge that was independent of faith. For this reason Gnosticism was attractive to, and able to unite, both pagan and early Christian thinkers.

Heliocentrism: The concept of a universe which revolves around the sun.

Humours: The main fluids of the body – blood, phlegm, yellow bile and black bile – and associated with the temperaments – sanguinity, plegmatism, choler and melancholy – respectively. The basis of Hippocratic medicine.

Julian calendar: A year calculated as 365.25 days achieved by adding a leap year every four years. Because of slight inaccuracies, however, the calendar gained approximately three days every four centuries. This was resolved in 1582 by Pope Gregory XIII.

Kinematics: System of mechanical motion whereby the movement and position of one object affects the movement and position of another.

Liberal Arts: The basis of Classical and medieval education, made up of the Trivium (grammar, rhetoric, and logic) and the Quadrivium (arithmetic, geometry, music and astronomy).

Manichaeism: Gnostic religion originating in Babylonia in the third century. A dualistic religion that believed in a spiritual world of light and a material world of darkness.

Mazdaism (Zoroastrianism): Pre-Islamic Gnostic religion originating in Persia in the sixth century BC. A central theme in Zoroastrianism is the unequal struggle between a beneficent god and a god of evil. Although dualistic, the ultimate victory of the former ensures that it leans more towards monotheism than polytheism. Because of this it would later influence Judiasm, Christianity and Islam.

Metaphysics: The philosophical study of the first principles of nature – e.g. being, substance, time and space – which lie outside or beyond the realm of science.

Monstrous races: Otherwise known as the 'fabulous tribes', sub-human creatures thought to inhabit the edge or the opposite side of the inhabited world. These include the Antipodes (opposite-footed people), a term which eventually came to stand for the region as well as the people; the one-eyed Cyclopes; Cynocephali or Dogheads (human figures with canine faces); Essedones (a cannibalistic tribe found in Scythia); Androgyni or Hermaphrodites; Pygmies; Sciapodes (possessing a single large foot used as a sun-shade); and Tigolopes (semi-human creatures with webbed feet and tails).

Morphology: The form and shape of an object or living thing.

Mozarab: A Christian living in Islamic Spain between the eighth and eleventh centuries, who despite not converting, adopted Arabic language and Moslem culture. From the Arabic word *musta'rib* 'Arabicised'.

Neoplatonism: Originating in the works of Plotinus in the third century, a philosophical paradigm which combined the ideas of Plato, Aristotle, Pythagoras and the Stoics and which distinguished between the eternal world accessed by thought and the physical world experienced through the senses. Influenced the writings of the early Christian fathers and Islamic scholarship.

Numerology: The study of the hidden (often theological or symbolic) meaning of numbers. Medieval numerology built upon and extended that developed by Pythagoras.

Organistic: Of or relating to an organism or an organised structure, applicable in both senses to the living or animated cosmos conceived by Plato.

Ostrogoths: Germanic tribe that established a kingdom in Italy during the late fifth century.

Pedology: The science of soils.

Physics: Used in this book in its general sense of natural science.

Physiology: The functioning of a living body.

Planetary station: A planet which appears to remain motionless and fixed in place over a period of time.

Pluralism: Tolerance of a range of ethnic or cultural groups in one place and the acceptance of the coexistence of alternative ideas and cultures.

Pre-Socratic philosophy: A term used to encompass Greek philosophical thought as it developed in the sixth and fifth centuries BC whose exponents largely rejected mythological readings of the workings of the world in favour of more rational explanations. While never presenting a coherent natural philosophy, ideas which formed at this period remained influential through the later reworkings of Plato and Aristotle.

Precession: The process, caused by irregularities in the rotation of the earth around its polar axes, which results in the apparent slow retrograde motion of stars.

Prognostication: The act of foretelling a future event.

Retrogradation: The period during which a planet appears to move contrary to its natural orbit.

Scholasticism: The intellectual mode, which dominated western thought between 1000 and 1500, based on critical reasoning that sought to reconcile and remove contradiction between Christian theological dogmas and class-ical philosophies. The apogee of medieval scholasticism is often considered to be St Thomas Aquinas' *Summa theologica*.

Stoic physics: Greek philosophy which stressed living in accordance with natural circumstance and thus dealt directly with determinism and human freedom of action. In the natural sciences, Stoicism divided the elements between the active – fire and air – and the passive – earth and water. They did not sanction the existence of void in contradistinction to Epicurean physics.

Sublunary sphere: Otherwise known as the 'terrestrial sphere'. As an Aristotelian term of reference, that part of the cosmos in a constant state of flux through the processes of generation and decay. Constituted of the elements. Includes the lower atmosphere up to the orbit of the moon.

Taxonomy: Systematic classification of animals, plants, etc.

Temperament: See 'Complexion'.

Vapour: Any gaseous or moist exhalation or humour. A synonym for 'fumosity'.

Part 1

ANALYSIS

1

The Nature of Things

The attempt to explain nature – and by so doing order and control the material world – has been one of humanity's greatest intellectual challenges. It has been an enterprise that has historically defined who we are and continues to do so into the modern era. Despite the size and complexity of the task, this has never discouraged people from trying. Every age and culture has made its own contribution (Glacken, 1967). The middle ages were no different. How people came to understand nature during this long period, sandwiched as it were between the great age of philosophy that preceded it and the ages of science and discovery that would follow, is introduced here. It is a subject, however, that demands clear definition if it is not to become unmanageable.

From the outset we must be clear that what might now be labelled the 'natural world' had no currency for Classical or medieval scholars. The phrase is never encountered because, as either a physical entity or a mental construct, its existence was simply not acknowledged. Modern western society has no problem with the idea because it has found a philosophical rationale for separating it from us, nature from culture (Thomas, 1984). But this division, false or otherwise, has a relatively short historical pedigree and enjoyed little or no validity before the seventeenth century. Indeed in other parts of the world such disaggregation has yet to occur (Pilgrim and Pretty, 2010). To compound this potential conceptual problem, the line which would now be drawn between the natural and the supernatural worlds would itself only begin to be demarcated towards the end of the middle ages; and even then it would remain a rather imprecise division (Bartlett, 2008).

The middle ages, then, had no natural world to explain. What it had instead, and what it wrestled with, was the more encompassing concept of nature. For the ninth-century scholar John Scotus Eriugena nature was 'the general term for all things that are and all things that are not' (Sheldon-Williams, 1987). Nature seen in this way seems to imply that it was everything and everywhere. But as C.S. Lewis sagely counselled, '"Everything" is a subject on which there is not much to be said' (1967: 37). That medieval scholars devoted so much time to its study and wrote so copiously on the subject is indicative of the fact that by the middle ages nature had come to be much more closely delineated. Viewed against the broader intellectual landscape of the period, Eriugena's position reveals itself to be unusual: for most medieval commentators nature had become something quite specific and far from universal (Hackett, 2005). So when scholars wrote about nature (*natura*), what did they understand it to mean? What did it encompass?

As might be expected of a word viewed as one of the most complex in the language (Williams, 1976: 67), the semantic development of the term 'nature' has had a long and convoluted history. For pre-Socratic thinkers nature did indeed encapsulate everything that they knew of or believed in. A single word, *Physis* (giving us the modern word '**physics**'), was sufficient to express this totality. The parameters of nature began to narrow with Plato, who distinguished between a creative power existing outside and beyond nature, and the created, nature itself. For Plato, then, nature resided exclusively in the tangible and visible universe, the 'realm of forms' (Lewis, 1967: 37). This would be the view held by medieval Neoplatonists down to the eleventh and twelfth centuries. With the 'rediscovery' of the works of Plato's student Aristotle, however, the medieval period was provided with a different configuration of nature's scope. For Aristotle, Platonic nature was too static. It was not physical substance that mattered (as Plato had emphasised) but the principle of change. Nature was not found in the realm of forms but in the realm of motion, of generation and corruption, in the cycles of life and death that characterised earthly existence [**Doc. 3**]. Aristotle thus had the effect of further restricting nature's locus. Now excluded were those parts of the created universe which were considered to exist in an unchanging form. For Aristotle this was the **celestial sphere** (beginning at the moon and extending across the planetary orbits to the fixed stars) whose study belonged more appropriately to mathematics. Also excluded was that which was unchangeable and existed in and of itself – God, the prime mover – the subject of **metaphysics**. The middle ages drew upon and further extended these Platonic and Aristotelian positions. From both Plato and Judaic traditions, the Christian Church developed the idea that God was the creator of nature and in so doing insisted on nature's subordinate and subservient place in the greater scheme of things. And following Aristotle, some (but by no means all) later commentators had come to restrict their discussions on nature to terrestrial and atmospheric phenomena below the orbit of the moon.

If, by these philosophical and theological stages, nature's place became progressively more restricted, its range of meanings, and how the concept of nature itself was understood, became ever more complex. Aristotle provided seven definitions of nature in his *Metaphysica* (*Metaphysics*; Tredennick,

Physics: Used in this text in its general sense of natural science.

Celestial sphere: In a geocentric conception of the cosmos, those parts of the universe which begin at the orbit of the moon and which stretch to the outer orbit of the fixed stars or firmament. Constituted of the fifth element or quintessence, ether, and regarded as constant, perfect and incorruptible.

Metaphysics: The philosophical study of the first principles of nature – e.g. being, substance, time and space – which lie outside or beyond the realm of science.

1947: 219–23) [**Doc. 3**], Eriugena offered nine and, writing in the twelfth century, Alan of Lille advanced eleven in his glossary of biblical words *Liber in distinctionibus dictionum theologicalium* (*Book of Definitions of Theological Words*; Migne, 1855: col. 871A–D). But amongst these various nuances, two senses of nature came to dominate medieval thought: nature as the 'essential quality or character *of* something' and nature as 'the inherent force which directs either the world or human beings or both' (Williams, 1976), the latter sometimes, and always strikingly, personified as Nature with a capital N (Park, 2004).

These two ideas lay behind all discussion of nature in the middle ages. And they provide the main strands of the thread by which explorers of nature's medieval maze might extricate themselves from its many unfamiliar turns and false endings. Of the two, that dealing with qualities and characteristics, captured in the Latin phrase *natura rerum*, 'the nature of things', is the more visible and most easily grasped. The many scholarly tracts which deployed this phrase in their titles – borrowed directly it should be noted from the first-century BC poem of Lucretius, *De rerum natura*, which set out the principles of **Epicurean physics** and philosophy (Rouse, 1953) – mark out the route by which medieval ideas on nature developed over the course of the seventh to thirteenth centuries: Isidore of Seville's *De natura rerum*, a treatise written at the request of King Sisibut of Spain to quell popular superstitions relating to natural phenomena reawakened by the solar and lunar eclipses of 611–612 (Fontaine, 1960); Bede's *De natura rerum*, an early eighth-century reworking of Isidore's text heavily supplemented with material taken directly from Pliny the Elder's *Naturalis historia* (Kendall and Wallis, 2010); the mid-ninth-century *De naturis rerum* of Rabanus Maurus, a work in 22 books (the number of books in the New Testament), otherwise known as *De universo* (Schipper, 2004); Alexander Neckam's *De naturis rerum* written before 1217, a work of natural philosophy and biblical exegesis (Wright, 1863); Arnold of Saxony's compilation of texts in *De floribus naturalium rerum* (Stange, 1905–7); and Thomas of Cantimpré's encyclopaedia *De natura rerum*, achieved by *c.* 1244 and written as a **Dominican** preacher's manual but so voluminous it was certainly no pocket book (Boese, 1973).

If these works represent the core of the surviving corpus of general writings on nature which have come down to us from the middle ages, they are complemented by other texts. Medieval scholars were great compilers and orderers of information. Several compendious encyclopaedias were written during the period: from the seventh century there was Isidore of Seville's *Etymologiae* (Barney *et al.*, 2006), and from the twelfth century Hildegard of Bingen's *Physica* (Throop, 1998). The encyclopaedic tradition reached its apogee during the thirteenth and fourteenth centuries: Bartholomew the Englishman's *De proprietatibus rerum* – the nature of things in all but name

Epicurean physics: Based on an atomist view of the world composed of indivisible atoms and vacuum developed by Democritus (d. 460 BC). Atoms combine chaotically (without design) to form the material world. Revised by Epicurus (d. 270 BC) following Aristotle's criticism of the original theory. Contrast with Stoic physics.

Dominicans: Emerging from the preaching activities of Dominic and his followers in southern France during the late twelfth and early thirteenth century, a mendicant 'Order of Preachers' surviving on the alms of others. By combining elements of both monastic obedience and ascetic observance, few religious lives were stricter than that of the Dominican friar.

Stoic physics: Greek philosophy which stressed living in accordance with natural circumstance and thus dealt directly with determinism and human freedom of action. In the natural sciences, Stoicism divided the elements between the active – fire and air – and the passive – earth and water. They did not sanction the existence of void in contradistinction to Epicurean physics.

Benedictines: Order of monks following the Rule of St Benedict, a monk of Monte Cassino, written 530–560. The earliest and most influential of the monastic traditions in the Latin west.

Franciscans: Mendicant Order following the Rule of St Francis established in the early thirteenth century. The rule imposed strict regulations upon the receipt of alms, fasting and preaching.

Augustinians: Community of clerics following the short Rule of St Augustine, leading semi-monastic lives having taken religious vows but retaining responsibility for the pastoral care of lay congregations.

Cathars: A Christian heretical sect, also known as the Albigensians because of their strong hold in southern France during the twelfth and thirteenth centuries. Accused by the established Church of being Manichaean due to its dualistic foundations (see Manichaeism).

(Seymour *et al.*, 1975); Vincent of Beauvais' *Speculum naturale* in 32 books and over 3,700 chapters; and Konrad of Megenburg's *Das buch der natur*. These were aimed at a scholarly audience and were designed to enable information to be extracted quickly and easily. From the same period, heavily abbreviated encyclopaedias, written in a more literary style, enjoyed equal popularity among lay readers and within elite circles, of which Gauthier de Metz's *L'image du monde* (printed by William Caxton in 1481; Prior, 1913) and Brunetto Latini's *Li livres dou tresor* (Carmody, 1948) represent model exemplars.

It was common too for nature to be discussed, and its workings elucidated, in the form of dialogues and questions. The model, like *natura rerum* literature, had Classical roots, in this case the **Stoic**-influenced *Naturales quaestiones* of Seneca (Corcoran, 1971–2). Works of natural philosophy using this didactic device became more common in the twelfth century, including the so-called 'Salernitan Questions' emanating from the medical school of Salerno in southern Italy (Lawn, 1979), Adelard of Bath's *Quaestiones naturales* (Burnett, 1998) and William of Conches' *De philosophia mundi*, later revised as *Dragmaticon* (Ronca and Curr, 1997).

These were all works written in the Christian tradition, their authors and compilers (with the odd exception) vocational churchmen and members of open and closed monastic orders: **Benedictines** such as Bede, Hildegard and Rabanus; the **Franciscan** Bartholomew, the **Augustinian** canons Alexander and Thomas, and the Dominican Vincent; Isidore was bishop of Seville, Gauthier a priest, and William part of a group of intellectuals that came to be associated with Chartres. The hold of Christianity over medieval Europe should never be underestimated. Indeed, much that was original with regard to medieval thinking on nature stemmed directly from the need to reconcile pre-Christian philosophy with new religious doctrines, a task begun by early doctors of the Church – in the west Augustine, Ambrose and Jerome, and in the east Basil and John Chrysostom (Glacken, 1967) – whose thoughts and writings can be detected in much that would follow [**Doc. 5**]. But Christianity's hold was not total. Medieval Europe accommodated significant populations of Jews and Moslems, particularly in Spain after the Islamic conquests of the early eighth century. Any assessment of medieval nature must, therefore, take account of these non-Christian voices. It might be noted, too, that the presence of heretical Christian groups such as the **Cathars** ensured that, in and of themselves, Christian views of nature were far from internally consistent across the period (Biller, 2010).

But despite this **pluralism**, and perhaps against first expectations, one discovers that writings on nature irrespective of their religious and cultural milieux do not radically diverge from one another. This is, in part, explained by the fact that all three of the main religious groups in Europe shared a common sacred text, the Old Testament. Genesis provided the basis for the cosmological models for Jews, Moslems and Christians alike; while the Book of Psalms provided each religion with its poetic glorification of nature [**Doc. 1**]. In other part it is explained by the common inheritance of the natural philosophies of Plato and Aristotle shared by medieval scholars irrespective of religion. Indeed, perhaps the greatest narrative in the development of medieval ideas on nature relates to the early dominance of Platonic (more precisely Neoplatonic) interpretations of nature and their replacement with Aristotelian models. Different parts of Europe and its hinterland adopted these ideas at different times, of course, and this is important to bear in mind when considering what may have been influencing later writers on nature. The availability of Greek texts in Arabic translation, for instance, ensured that Aristotle was more quickly embraced in the Islamic territories than in the Latin west where knowledge of Greek had all but been lost; but by the thirteenth century Aristotle's ideas had become the prevailing view everywhere. For example, Hebrew encyclopaedias of this period, such as Judah ben Solomon ha-Cohen's *Midrash ha-Hokhmah* and Shem-Tor ibn Falaquera's *De'ot ha-filisofim* (*Opinions of the Philosophers*) drew heavily on Aristotle via the earlier commentaries of the Spanish Moslem Ibn Rushd, known in the west as Averroes (Harvey, 2000). And similar intellectual cross-fertilisation is again in evidence in Gershon ben Schlomah of Arles' *Sha'ar ha-Shamayim*, which cites a large number of Greek, Arabic and occasional Latin authors, as well as fellow Jews (Bodenheimer, 1953: 20–34).

It was in those places where pluralistic society was tolerated, and where scholars of all religious backgrounds were brought together, that much of the effort on bringing Greek works on nature first into Arabic and then into Latin was concentrated: in al-Rahman III's court at Cordova where a substantial library was established in the tenth century; at Toledo where scholars such as Gerard of Cremona, helped by the **Mozarab** Galippus, translated many Arabic works during the twelfth century; at the medical school of Salerno; and in the trilingual Sicilian court of Frederick II in the next century where people such as Michael Scotus (previously himself assisted by the Jew Abuteus Levita when in Toledo), Theodore of Antioch and Jacob Anatoli would continue the translation of Arabic and Hebrew texts (Lindberg, 1978).

Cross-cultural cooperation of this sort in the translation of key sources of natural philosophy, building on the theological commonalities uniting the three medieval **Abrahamic religions** help to account, then, for why the matter of nature appears to have been treated in such a similar way in sources of Christian, Jewish or Moslem origin. If alike, however, they were not identical. Christian scholars were careful to draw upon the pre-Christian ideas of Plato, Aristotle and others, only to the extent that they did not contradict Biblical teaching. And they were equally careful in their handling of material

Pluralism: Tolerance of a range of ethnic or cultural groups in one place and the acceptance of the coexistence of alternative ideas and cultures.

Mozarab: A Christian living in Islamic Spain between the eighth and eleventh centuries, who despite not converting, adopted Arabic language and Moslem culture. From the Arabic word *musta'rib* 'Arabicised'.

Abrahamic religions: Monotheistic religions that trace their origins to Abraham and his descendants. The three main religions are Judaism, Christianity and Islam, which all consequently share the Old Testament as a sacred text.

emanating from the Islamic world. Jewish and Moslem scholars did likewise in accordance with their religious precepts. Such nuances need to be continuously borne in mind since, for the sake of brevity here, these crucial variances of usage and interpretation have largely had to be glossed over, or left unremarked upon, in the text where the emphasis (some might argue undue emphasis) has been placed on shared ideas rather than difference.

The sheer number of medieval written sources dealing with nature appears to offer a firm foundation upon which an assessment of the attitudes and understandings of the age can be based. What has been so far cited has not strayed beyond general works. Yet to these could be added many hundreds of manuscripts dealing (often in great detail) with particular parts of nature whether the stars, human **anatomy**, animals, plants, stones and metals. With their inclusion an abundance of material becomes a super-abundance. Nevertheless it is perhaps wise to remember the words of St Bernard of Clairvaux:

Anatomy: Relating to the structure of a living body (human, animal, plant).

> Believe me who have experience: you will find much more labouring amongst the woods than you ever will amongst books. Woods and stones will teach you what you can never hear from any masters.
>
> (James, 1998: 156)

For however profound, extensive and enduring the testimony of the 'masters' and however transient and now lost the physical realities of medieval nature are (even if archaeology is now helping to redress this imbalance), any enthusiasm for what these scholars report, and any temptation to read this as a universal truth, must be tempered with the acknowledgement that these men and women belonged to an educated and literate minority. It must be questioned just how representative their picture was of medieval nature when set against the views held by those (the greater majority) who lived beyond their rarefied intellectual circles in which they moved [**Doc. 8**]. How did Piers Ploughman view nature as it surrounded him and how did he come to understand it through the daily encounters he had during the course of his labours? Can we ascribe to him either an innate feel for nature, or more likely one learned from experience, comparable to Alexander Neckam's weasel who 'educated by nature, knows the virtues of herbs although it has neither studied medicine at Salerno nor been drilled in the schools at Montpellier' (Wright, 1863: 2, 123; Thorndike, 1929: 2, 200). Of course, identifying this other voice is no easy task since the witness of the medieval peasant – heard *sotto voce* at best – tends to be received through the distorting filter of elite texts wherever it has not been silenced altogether for lack of available evidence. Yet it is clearly important to try to establish just how far down through the ranks of medieval society scholastic ideas may have percolated and, moreover, how these ideas might have been received and whether or not they were subsequently reconfigured, if we are not to present a skewed picture of nature in the middle ages. Despite strict social hierarchies, medieval social groups did not exist in isolation. There was considerable intermixing and contact whether at mass, or in undertaking the agricultural activities on the manor, or in the manorial courts. These offered opportunities for knowledge transfer, not just from the learned to the unread, but also from those that worked directly with nature to those who wrote about it. One should approach medieval sources, therefore, with one eye on the possibility that 'folk' attitudes to the natural world may have become integrated into the scholarly or pseudo-scholarly writings at our disposal. Examples of both the peasant contribution to medieval knowledge of nature and their apparent familiarity with ideas presented in scholarly texts are presented throughout this text as and when the evidence allows. But the treatment of this vital exchange of ideas should not be considered exhaustive, and readers are encouraged to search for other examples which might either reinforce or contradict what is presented here.

What follows is an attempt to distil and present the most widely held views about nature in the middle ages, to trace their origins and to chart their development. Temporal focus is given to the period between the seventh and the fourteenth centuries: its beginning marked by the near contemporary appearance of the first great medieval encyclopaedia, Isidore of Seville's *Etymologiae*, and the foundation of Islam whose scholars would do so much to alter medieval attitudes to nature; its end chosen for no more than convenience and succinctness, to exclude the explosion in scientific developments that characterised the fifteenth century and beyond. However, as will become plain, these terminal dates must necessarily remain porous. The geographic and cultural focus of the book concentrates firmly on Christian Europe, with evidence drawn primarily from English and French sources, supplemented by occasional references to works originating in other parts of the Latin west – Spain, Italy, Germany. Hebraic and Islamic texts are brought into the discussion, but essentially only where these add to our understanding of Latin sources, or where they help to identify the particularities or commonalities of approach taken to the reading of nature in different cultural contexts. Readers should not expect to find, however, a balanced account of the ways that the natural world was interpreted by the three great medieval scholarly traditions.

All that is offered here, then, is a primer. But as such it follows a long tradition. In his preface to *De temporum rationale*, Bede recalled that 'Some time ago, I wrote two short books in a summary style which were, I judged, necessary for my students.' These were *De natura rerum* and *De temporibus* (Kendall and Wallis, 2010). Bede himself admitted that they were found wanting: '[w]hen I undertook to present and explain them to some of my brethren, they said that they were more concise than they would have wished' (Wallis, 1999: 3). Undoubtedly, the same charge, multiplied a hundredfold, can be levelled at this text. Nor was Bede the only one to write for students; so too did the thirteenth-century English encyclopaedist Bartholomew. He concluded his monumental work with the following observation:

> . . . in the varied material contained in this book, truly little or nothing have I set down of my own. Rather I have brought together truth and followed the words, meanings, sayings and comments of holy saints and philosophers, so that the simple need not [consult] endless books . . .
>
> (Seymour et al., 1975: 1395)

Again this text cannot begin to claim such utility although it is to be hoped that it offers pointers to the wider literature. But its structure and content has certainly been influenced by this and other similar medieval works: what is presented here, for instance, is largely derivative; wherever possible medieval authorities have been allowed to speak for themselves. Moreover, in beginning with discussion of the universe, and thereafter progressing sequentially from celestial bodies, stars and planets, meteorological phenomena, the world, humans, animals, plants, and concluding with metals, minerals and stones, it follows one of the widely used medieval conventions, one ultimately based on two of the age's greatest universal models, the theory of the **elements** and the Chain of Being (see Chapter 2). Far from encyclopaedic in its length or breadth, however, its brevity more closely mirrors the shorter works of Isidore of Seville and Bede, and the few diagrammatic representations that it contains also borrow heavily from archetypes contained in early manuscripts of these works.

Elements: The essential building blocks of the cosmos. Found in combination in all physical forms, comprising earth, water, air and fire.

Over the last decade, the question of nature has begun to enjoy greater prominence on the academic agenda within the Arts and Humanities. Environmental history is becoming a mainstay in the university curriculum. In many ways this represents a return to medieval practices. Undergraduates in the Faculty of Arts at the University of Oxford in the fourteenth century would have been intimately familiar with the greater part of the Aristotelian corpus known as his *libri naturalis*. Three terms were devoted to the study of his *Physica* (*Physics*, i.e. *Nature*) in eight books – the foundation of all later medieval natural science – through the Latin translation of James of Venice. For two and a half terms they explored the four books of *De Caelo* (*On the Heavens*) and for one term the four books of *Meteorologica* (*Meteorology*), both through the translations of William of Moerbeke. A term was devoted to the two books of *De generatione et corruptione* (*On Generation and Corruption*) and another to the three books of *De anima* (*On the Soul*). They were required to read each book of the *Parva naturalia* ('Short Treatises on Nature') in a few weeks, and the first ten books of *De animalibus* (*On Animals*) together with *De progressu animalium* (*On the Progress of Animals*) and *De motu animalium* (*On the Motion of Animals*) in six. They would have been acquainted with *De partibus animalium* (*On the Parts of Animals*) and *De generatione animalium* (*On the Generation of Animals*) even though these were not formally taught. Completing their education in the natural sciences, undergraduates were required to know *De plantis* (*On Plants*) – believed to be an Aristotelian work but actually written by Nicholas of Damascus – and Alfredus of Sarashel's translation from the Arabic of *De vegetabilibus* (*On Vegetables*; Weisheipl, 1964: 173). Today's students, feeling pressurised by what they may feel to be unduly heavy workloads and looming deadlines, might usefully reflect on the intense intellectual demands made of their medieval predecessors. In short, this introductory text aims simply to offer some early assistance to those now embarking on similar studies, studies that will require those sources mentioned here in passing to be explored in greater depth than has proven possible in what follows.

Further reading

On *De natura rerum* literature, readers are encouraged to read Kendall and Wallis' recent translation of Bede's *On the Nature of Things* and the commentaries provided for each chapter; so too Wright's introduction to *Alexander Neckam, De naturis rerum*. On the translation movement Lindberg provides an excellent account in *Science in the Middle Ages*.

2

Universal Models

The theoretical model which underpinned the medieval scheme of nature was beautiful in its simplicity. Yet the ramifications which flowed from it were far-reaching and profound. Despite the near infinite range of shapes and forms to be seen in nature, the material world was universally understood to be composed of just four elements – earth, water, air and fire. These essential building blocks came to dominate not only everything that was written about nature but also how people worked with it, whether they were growing crops or treating medical conditions.

The theory of the elements has its origins in **pre-Socratic philosophy**. In his poem *Physis* (roughly translated as *On Nature*), Empedocles (*c.* 495–435 BC) developed the notion of four unchanging and indivisible 'roots' from which all things were made (Leonard, 1908: 15–52; Janko, 2004). Observable change in the physical world could be accounted for by the constant mixing and separation of these 'roots' under the influence of two further forces, respectively love and strife. However, this model did not transfer directly to the middles ages but rather arrived through its later reworking by Plato. The foundational work was *Timaeus* (Taylor, 1929) **[Doc. 2]**, made available to the Latin west via the partial translation of the fourth-century writer Calcidius, giving 'the middle ages its most systematic account of natural philosophy until the further translations of the twelfth century' (Lindberg, 1978: 53). Here Plato (the first to use the term 'element') laid out his vision of the creation and working of the universe. He accorded primacy to the element fire, which made all tangible things visible, and earth, which gave everything their substance. These were bound together by two intermediary elements air and water. Plato was clear that these elements were not equivalent to their physical counterparts; pure elements were unalterable while their earthly equivalents could be shown to change from one to another in what he described as 'cyclical transformation' through various physical processes such as solidification, liquefaction, disintegration, inflammation, coalescence and condensation (Taylor, 1929: 48).

Pre-Socratic philosophy: A term used to encompass Greek philosophical thought as it developed in the sixth and fifth centuries BC whose exponents largely rejected mythological readings of workings of the world in favour of more rational explanations. While never presenting a coherent natural philosophy, ideas which formed at this period remained influential through the later reworkings of Plato and Aristotle.

A thousand years later Platonic thought guided Isidore of Seville's treatment of the elements [**Doc. 6**]. In a very short passage the Spanish bishop not only captured the philosopher's vision but rendered it palatable for his Christian audience. In so doing he clarified the hierarchical relationship of the elements that was implicit in *Timaeus* and the key concept that the elements did not exist in isolation but were all present in all things:

> [the elements] are said to be joined . . . among themselves with a certain natural logic, now returning to their origin, from fire to earth, now from earth to fire, since fire ends in air, and air is condensed into water, and water thickens into earth; and in turn earth is loosened into water, water rarefied into air, and air thinned out into fire. For this reason, all the elements are present in all, but each one has taken its name from whichever element is more abundant in it. The elements are assigned by Divine Providence to the appropriate living beings, for the Creator himself has filled heaven with angels, air with birds, water with fish, and earth with humans and the rest of the living things.
>
> (Barney *et al.*, 2006: 272)

Underlying this elemental hierarchy was the notion of their relative weights and densities. This was the scheme which Bede used as the basis for his discussion of their relationship in *De natura rerum*. Because earth was the heaviest element and could not be held up by the others, it assumed the lowest position within the created cosmos. Water, as the element lighter than earth but heavier than air, occupied the second rung on the elemental ladder. Air was naturally located above water (Bede uses the analogy of air introduced under water in a vessel which immediately bubbled to the surface) and fire as the lightest element of all naturally desired to ascend to the highest position (Kendall and Wallis, 2010: 75–6). This arrangement went unchallenged throughout the middle ages.

An otherwise unknown scholar named Marius, writing on the elements at the end of the twelfth century, laid out the basic premises upon which elemental theory was then based: since created things contained *all* the elements, no element could exist in its primary state; everything that existed derived its being and characteristics from the exact proportion of each of the four elements it contained. Marius tabulated 145 possible mixtures of these four elements arising from their combination in equal or unequal proportions, the latter divided into the simple categories of 'more' or 'less', and then further subdivided into the presence of 'much', 'moderate' or 'small' amounts of each. Marius asked his student to categorise milk against this scheme:

> It is known immediately that milk is liquid, thick, and greasy – exceedingly liquid, somewhat less thick than liquid, but more so than it is greasy. And

water is liquid, earth is thick, air is greasy. We cannot find fire in it visibly, but we can prove by experience that it is present, for man is warmed up as a result of drinking milk. Therefore it can truly be said that there is less of fire than anything else in milk. And so I might answer that milk is similar to that kind of mixture in which there is much water, less earth, still less air, and least of all fire.

(Dales, 1972: 198–9)

In response to the question of how a finite number of combinations might account for the near infinite variety of composite bodies visible in nature, Marius noted that 'by increasing or decreasing the parts, you will undoubtedly find them innumerable'.

Marius' work was in the vanguard of those based in Neoplatonist tradition but which were just beginning to exhibit signs of influence from Aristotelian thought. In particular, the mid-twelfth-century translations by Gerard of Cremona of Aristotle's *De caelo* (*On the Heavens*), especially books three and four (Guthrie, 1953: 257–369) and *De generatione et corruptione* (*On Generation and Corruption*; Joachim, 1930) gave the Latin west a more developed model of the elements. Most importantly they questioned the Platonic view that the celestial zone was composed of the purest parts of the four elements. In *De caelo* Aristotle argued instead that the four elements belonged to and together comprised only the **sublunary** or terrestrial zone which stretched from the earth to the moon. The celestial or supralunary zone was made up of a fifth element, the quintessence, or ether (Guthrie, 1953: 8–18). This would have an immediate and profound impact on medieval thought, a reconfiguration that was evident at the turn of the thirteenth century in Daniel of Morley's *Philosophia* (*Philosophy*, *c.* 1140–*c.* 1210), whose Aristotelian content had been taken from the author's contacts with Arab scholars (Thorndike, 1929, II: 176). Furthermore, Aristotle attached greater significance to the qualities associated with the four terrestrial elements – hot, cold, dry and moist. These properties acted on the terrestrial elements through the influence of the celestial bodies (the sun in particular), leading to a constant process of generation and decay, resulting in the changeable and corruptible state of flux that characterised the material world and visible nature. In contrast, ether possessed none of these properties and in their absence the celestial sphere remained permanent, regular and unchanging. The natural movement of ether was circular, that of the four other elements rectilinear.

The effect of the Aristotelian model of the structure and workings of the cosmos coloured how nature subsequently came to be understood. It was implicit in the title of Bartholomew the Englishman's *De proprietatibus rerum* and other such works: it was the *properties* of things, not the things themselves which now most mattered. In this scheme, each element was held to encapsulate two of these qualities: fire was hot and dry, earth dry and cold,

Sublunary sphere: Otherwise known as the 'terrestrial sphere'. As an Aristotelian term of reference, that part of the cosmos in a constant state of flux through the processes of generation and decay. Constituted of the elements. Includes the lower atmosphere up to the orbit of the moon.

water cold and moist, and air moist and hot. It was the oppositions and the counterbalances provided by these differing qualities that necessitated the combination of the four elements in all substances. If unrestrained by the presence of other elements, each individual element would destroy everything in which they were found through the extremes of their qualities. Water thus acted as a correcting influence over fire and vice versa. However, without the mediation of air and earth, which both shared common but different qualities with fire and water, these two opposing elements would also destroy themselves through their natural antipathy for one another.

Texts which dealt with this co-relationship of the elements, the idea that lay at the heart of both Platonic and Aristotelian cosmologies, were often accompanied from an early date with diagrammatic representations that most commonly took the form of a wheel or *rota*. Six diagrams of this type were included in eighth-century manuscripts of Isidore of Seville's *De natura rerum* (Figure 1), resulting in its alternative title, the *liber* or *libri rotarum* (the Book or Books of Wheels), as used by Cuthbert in his 'Letter on the Death of Bede' (Kendall and Wallis, 2010: 138). Schema such as these became particularly useful as the elemental principles that they depicted began to be extended out to encompass other aspects of nature's working. Concordances, for example, were identified between the elements and their qualities with the seasons, with cardinal points and wind directions, and with human temperament and the life cycle. Of these diagrams those contained in Byrhtferth's

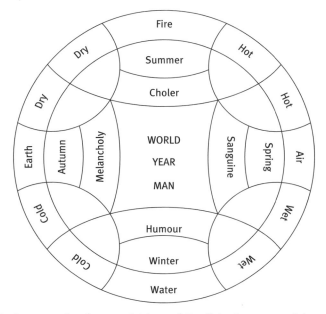

Figure 1 An example of a *rota*: Isidore of Seville's depiction of the microcosm and macrocosm taken from Bibliothèque Nationale de France, MS lat. 6413, fol. 5v, eighth century.

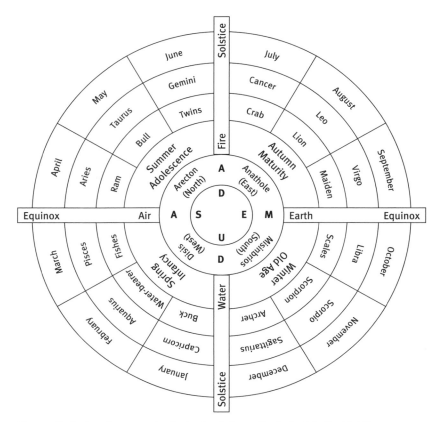

Figure 2 A simple cosmological wheel from Byrhtferth's *Enchiridion* (Bodleian Library MS Ashmole 328, p. 85, mid-eleventh century) highlighting concordances between the cardinal directions, the elements, the life cycle, the months and seasons together with the spring and autumn equinoxes and the summer and winter solstices.

early eleventh-century *Enchiridion* are some of the most developed of their kind (Crawford, 1929) (Figure 2); but they would be used too by William of Conches in the mid-twelfth century (Ronca and Curr, 1997) and would be artistically portrayed in fifteenth-century manuscripts of Bartholomew the Englishman's popular encyclopaedia.

The power of the elemental qualities to effect real change in the physical world found its most explicit early statement in Aristotle's *De generatione et corruptione* (*On Generation and Corruption*):

the 'elements' must be reciprocally active and susceptible, since they 'combine' and are transformed into one another . . . hot and cold, and dry and moist, are terms, of which the first pair implies *power to act* and the second pair *susceptibility*. 'Hot' is that which 'associates' things of the same kind (for 'dissociating' which people attribute to fire as its function *is* 'associating things of the same class, since its effect is to eliminate what is foreign), while 'cold' is that which brings together, that is 'associates', homogeneous and heterogeneous things alike. And moist is that which, being readily adaptable in shape, is not determinable by any limit of its own: while 'dry' is that which is readily determinable by its own limit, but not readily adaptable by its shape.

(Joachim, 1930: 329b)

According to Bartholomew the Englishman, writing in the mid-thirteenth century, hot and cold were active qualities, 'able to work', while dry and moist were passive, 'able to suffer'. Heat was considered more active than cold, but the effects of both on material bodies could be complex and seemingly contrary. Heat, for instance, might both prompt dryness and moisture as in the case of the salting of meat: the hot salt drove away moisture from the surface of the meat but retained it at its core. It could soften (the melting of metal) and harden (the boiling of an egg). It might make bodies lighter as was the case when water was turned into steam, or make them denser by encouraging the release of light **vapours**. It could make things sweet (the ripening of fruit for example) or sour through dehydration and much more besides. The passive qualities acted in different ways. Dryness could make objects rough (the difference between dry and lubricated surfaces) and slow in movement through friction. Its ability to convert airy and watery matter to earth meant that it could make substances thicker. But it could waste and destroy solid objects by turning them into smoke and gases. It could dissolve and separate moisture (for instance the use of lime on cadavers), whereas by drawing moisture to the surface it could make objects appear wet. It could make substances lean and hard but also soft and tender by driving away the moisture that bound them together (contrast the hardness of desiccated wood with the softness of old and decaying timber) (Seymour *et al.*, 1975: 133–40).

Vapour: Any gaseous or moist exhalation or humour. A synonym for 'fumosity'.

Examples such as these, drawn from real life, demonstrate the extent to which the theory of the elements pervaded medieval thinking. In *Physica*, Hildegard of Bingen wrote:

With earth was the human being created. All the elements served mankind, and sensing that man was alive, they busied themselves in aiding his life in every way. And man in turn occupied himself with them.

(Throop, 1998: 9)

The same idea reappears in her *Causae et curae* (*Causes and Cures*): 'The elements . . . are subject to humans, and as they are touched by humans' deeds

Humours: The main fluids of the body – blood, phlegm, yellow bile and black bile – and associated with the temperaments – sanguinity, plegmatism, choler and melancholy – respectively. The basis of Hippocratic medicine.

so they perform their tasks' (Berger, 1999: 38). The elements, then, were not simply a matter for scholarly consideration but guided everyday practice from agriculture to medicine. For the latter it was an essential component and the basis from which another complementary theory of the **humours** evolved.

The humours, it was held, were born from the elements. This was the imagery used by the great translator of Greek medical texts Constantine the African and quoted by Bartholomew the Englishman for whom the humours were 'the children of the elements' (Seymour *et al.*, 1975: 147). Like the elements, humoural theory already had a long history by the start of the middle ages. Its origins lay in the works of the Greek physician Hippocrates, three of whose works – *Aphorisma*, *Prognostica* and *Regimen* (Jones, 1943) – had already been translated into Latin by the third quarter of the eleventh century by Constantine. Hippocratic medicine posited that since the human body was composed of the four elements it too was affected by their qualities. These were carried in the four principal fluids found in the body – blood, phlegm, black bile and yellow bile. These fluids or humours corresponded with the four elements and their qualities. Thus blood was warm and moist, phlegm cold and moist, black bile cold and dry, and yellow bile warm and dry. In its natural state, the body tended towards warm and moist, giving it its natural sanguine **complexion**. The precise degree of warmth and mois-

Complexion: The combination of qualities (hot/cold, dry/moist) found in all living bodies and which determine their nature. Used as a synonym for 'temperament'.

ture was held to be different among the two sexes however. Women were considered to be naturally more cold and dry than men, explaining why they menstruated since they were too cold to burn off excessive humours in the way that men could do. Superfluities of any kind were potentially unhealthy, producing phlegmatic, melancholic (black bile) or choleric (yellow bile) temperaments, as indeed was an over-abundance of sanguinity.

The other great authority on the humours from which the medieval world drew was the Roman of Greek descent, Galen. His work was widely known in the Arabic world from an early date through the translations of al-Batrīq (d. *c.* 800), but only became available in the west through translation in the eleventh century. Again it was Constantine who led the way, translating an abbreviated version of the *Megategni*, a work that was widely consulted in the medical school at Salerno to which he appears to have had close associations. Extracts of Galen's work had also transmitted more directly through the works of Dioscorides (e.g. *De materia medica*; Osbaldeston, 2000) although their influence on European thought was only really given impetus after their incorporation into the curricula of the emerging universities where they were studied alongside Avicenna's *al-Qānūn fi al-Tibb*. Galen proposed a slightly different conception of the humours which he associated much more closely than his predecessors had done with the four qualities themselves. One might contrast, for example, Isidore of Seville's Hippocratic explanation 'just as there are four elements so there are four humours, and each humour resembles its element: blood resembles air, [yellow] bile fire, black bile earth, and phlegm water' (Barney *et al.*, 2006: 109) with the Galenic influence visible in discussion of the same by the Jewish scholar Moses Maimonides in *Dalālat al-Ḥā'irīn*: 'sometimes a humour is absorbed which is too warm, too cold, too thick, or too thin' (Friedländer, 1903: 256).

Despite the tensions which these two humoural systems posed, Hippocratic and Galenic ideas dominated medieval medicine and help to explain many entries found in later encyclopaedias and, as we shall see, herbals (see Chapter 8). But they were not necessarily followed dogmatically. In typically original fashion, Hildegard of Bingen combined the two whilst also adding others of her own, producing an intriguing and unique take on the subject. She rejected, for example, the equality of the humours and instead implied a hierarchy consisting of two inferior humours analogous to water and earth (the 'foamy' and the 'tepid') and two superior humours associated with fire and air ('dry' and 'moist'). The peculiar proportions attributed to each humour – 'the pre-eminent humour outweighs the next one to it by one fourth and by one half of one third' – it is suggested, represents a poor attempt to recon-stitute the cosmic ratios found in Plato's *Timaeus* (Berger, 1999: 134).

At the heart of humoural theory was an acknowledgement that the external environment exerted a power over the internal workings of the body (Arikha, 2007: 12). This was made explicit in one of the most important early Hippocratic texts, often attributed to Polybus, the son-in-law and pupil of Hippocrates himself, *De natura hominis* (*On the Nature of Man*; Jones, 1943: 2–41). Here shifts in humoural balance were directly associated with the seasons and with diet. Plants and cereals took up various qualities – acid, sour, sweet and salt – from the soil in which they were grown and these in turn might detrimentally affect the temperament of those who ate them. It was diet, age and lifestyle which largely accounted for individual ailments. Illness among the general population was attributed to atmospheric change experienced across the year, with each humour associated directly through analogy to the seasonal conditions which most closely matched their qualities, a theme also developed in *De humoribus* (*Humours*; Jones, 1943: 62–95). Thus phlegm was linked to winter (cold and wet), blood to spring, yellow bile to summer and black bile to autumn.

Links between the body and the wider environment were paralleled and extended in a second philosophical paradigm, the notion of the microcosm and the macrocosm. This conceptualisation of the world held that Man was a direct if miniature reflection of the whole universe. The idea was so seduc-tive – once more because of its simplicity and for its power to explain both physical and metaphysical phenomena – that this model found general acceptance across a broad range of cultural and religious milieux. It appears

Gnosticism: A key component of Gnostic religions is their belief that the world was not created directly by God but through an intermediary, the 'Demiurge', a false or inferior god. Because of this, the material world was imperfect. Salvation could only be gained through superior knowledge of the ultimate godhead, the monad, a knowledge that was independent of faith. For this reason Gnosticism was attractive to, and able to unite, both pagan and early Christian thinkers.

Manichaeism: Gnostic religion originating in Babylonia in the third century. A dualistic religion that believed in a spiritual world of light and a material world of darkness.

Mazdaism (Zoroastrianism): Pre-Islamic Gnostic religion originating in Persia in the sixth century BC. A central theme in Zoroastrianism is the unequal struggle between a beneficent god and a god of evil. Although dualistic, the ultimate victory of the former ensures that it leans more towards monotheism than polytheism. Because of this it would later influence Judiasm, Christianity and Islam.

Organistic: Of or relating to an organism or an organised structure, applicable in both senses to the living or animated cosmos conceived by Plato.

to have been present at a very early date in Hindu sacred writings such as the *Riga veda* (literally 'praise/verse knowledge'), from where it permeated the **Gnostic** religions – **Manichaeism** and **Mazdaism (Zoroastrianism)** – of Persia during the third to seventh century. In Jewish, Christian and Muslim thought, however, microcosm and macrocosm grew more directly from a common Platonic root. With access to Plato's *Philibus* and *Timaeus* and the later Neoplatonist treatises of Plotinus (*c.* 205–270) known as the *Enneads*, this conception of universal structure quickly became established in Hebrew and Arabic scholarship. Nothing at the time in the Latin west could compare with the treatment of this subject found in the tenth/eleventh-century philosophical-scientific encyclopaedia written by a secretive scholarly collective known as *Ikhwan al-Safa*, or the Brethren of Purity, based at Basra in Iraq. This included two 'epistles' entitled 'Man as a Little World' and the 'World as a Big Man'. At around the same time Avicenna used microcosmic and macrocosmic relationships as the basis for his medical treatments laid out in his *Canon*. The slow adoption of microcosm and macrocosm in northern Europe almost certainly stemmed from a lack of access to these key Greek and Arabic texts. But Latin readers did have at their disposal other important works such as Macrobius' fourth-century *Commentarii in somnium Scipionis* (Stahl, 1990) in which the basic tenets of the Stoic and Neoplatonic cosmos were laid out, and Boethius' *Consolatio philosophiae* (Walsh, 1999), which would become one of the most popular philosophical texts of the middle ages. And, of course, the west had Calcidius' partial translation of *Timaeus*.

At the heart of the theory lay Plato's conception of the macrocosm as a living creature with intellect and soul. His vision of the universe was thus one that was animated (*anima* = soul) and **organistic**. His description of its creation used anatomical analogies if only to explain the sphericity of the universe and its lack of human form:

> . . . it [the cosmos] would be better self-sufficient than dependent on anything else. He [the **demiurge**] saw no need to give it superfluous hands, which it would require neither for grasping nor for defence, nor yet feet or other support to stand on. For he had assigned it the motion proper to its body . . . which has most to do with understanding and intelligence. Accordingly he spun it uniformly upon itself in the same volume and made it revolve in a circle . . . And since feet were not wanted for this revolution, he begat it without feet or legs.
>
> (Taylor, 1929: 30)

But physical correspondences could be drawn between the globular shape of the human head, the locus for the soul, and the spheroid universe, the seat of the cosmic intellect and soul (Taylor, 1929: 42). Under the influence of

Pythagorean **numerology** other correspondences would also be invoked: the two eyes parallels for the sun and moon, the seven bodily orifices equating to the seven planets, and so on. Together these separate facets, shared physical attributes, including of course the shared elemental composition of the human body and the rest of the cosmos, and their shared possession of a soul, drew Man and the rest of nature together. As the Spanish Jewish Joseph ibn Saddiq (1075–1149) summarised in his *Olam kaṭan* (*Microcosm*): 'that is why man is called a microcosm, for there is in him a likeness to everything there is in the world, his body in respect of the physical world, and his rational soul in respect of the spiritual world' (Haberman, 2003: 54).

European writers would make their greatest contribution to the literature on this subject during the twelfth century. This was the period when **Neoplatonism**, particularly as developed by scholars associated with the so-called 'school of Chartres' (an intellectual grouping rather than a real school), came to dominate medieval scholastic thought. Two works stand out. The first was Bernard Silvester's *Cosmographia* (otherwise *De mundi universitate*), which provided an extended and dramatic account of the creation of the universe divided into two parts that dealt initially with the *megacosmos* and subsequently with the *microcosmos*. Its philosophical borrowings are clear:

> Physis [here a handmaiden to Nature not Nature herself] knew that she would not go astray in creating the lesser universe of man if she took as her example the pattern of the greater universe. In the intricate structure of the world's body, the **firmament** holds the pre-eminent position. The earth is at the lowest point, the air spread between. From the firmament the godhead rules and disposes all things. The powers who have their homes in the ether and the atmosphere carry out its commands, and the affairs of the earth below are governed by them. No less care is taken in the case of man, that the soul should govern in the head, the vital force established in the breast obey its commands, and the lower parts, the loins and those organs placed below them, submit to rule.
>
> (Wetherbee, 1973: 121)

The second was Alain de Lille's *De planctu natura* (*The Complaint of Nature*). His rich description of personified Nature's garments, from the bejewelled diadem representing the fixed stars on her head, to her flowing robes bedecked with a staggering array of birds, fish and land animals, encapsulating the majesty and plenitude of the cosmos, must stand as one of the great literary achievements of the age (Moffat, 1908; Sheridan, 1980). Its emphasis on the perverse actions of Man, working against the universal order – an echo of Boethius' *Consolatio* written eight hundred years earlier (Walsh, 1999) – only serves to demonstrate the longevity and power of the idea of the

Demiurge: The Creator of the universe in Platonic philosophy (see Gnosticism).

Numerology: The study of the hidden (often theological or symbolic) meaning of numbers. Medieval numerology built upon and extended that developed by Pythagoras.

Neoplatonism: Originating in the works of Plotinus in the third century, a philosophical paradigm which combined the ideas of Plato, Aristotle, Pythagoras and the Stoics and which distinguished between the eternal world accessed by thought and the physical world experienced through the senses. Influenced the writings of the early Christian fathers and Islamic scholarship.

Firmament: In Ptolemaic astronomy, the eighth sphere of the heavens on which the stars were fixed.

indivisibility and interconnectedness of the microcosm and macrocosm on western thought. It lay at the heart of Hildegard of Bingen's spiritual vision of the world too (Schipperges, 1997); indeed the wonderful depictions of the microcosm and macrocosm that are found in early manuscripts are thought to have both preceded the text itself and to have been personally supervised by Hildegard (Newman, 2002). By directly connecting the human body to the zodiac and the planetary bodies, microcosm and macrocosm also offered the theoretical underpinning for medieval astrology (see Chapters 3 and 6). And the association of particular celestial signs with particular parts of the body was to be formative in the development of medieval medical practice (French, 1996) giving it one of its greatest artistic icons, the image of the zodiac man (Jones, 1998).

Cosmology: The theoretical science of the universe and the laws which govern and explain its workings.

Bernard Silvester's introduction of the character Physis into his **cosmology** (her name taken from Aristotle's work of the same name) acts as a further reminder of the influence of Aristotelian thought on Neoplatonism. Indeed, when first received through the Arabic translations, Aristotle himself was thought to be a Neoplatonist, a view eventually corrected by Thomas Aquinas. However, Aristotle was dismissive of the idea of microcosm and macrocosm. Consequently, with the translation of his works the concept began to lose its central place in moulding the medieval worldview. However, through a subtle extension of its principles one final grand conceptualisation of the organisation of the universe was produced, one that would become an important intellectual strand in western thinking down to the **Enlightenment** and beyond. This was the Great Chain of Being (Bynum, 1973; Lovejoy, 1976).

Enlightenment: Conventionally covering intellectual developments from the middle decades of the seventeenth century through to the end of the eighteenth, the period of seismic change during which philosophy was freed from its earlier theological constraints and when the foundations for modern western thought were laid down. Spurred by the scientific discoveries in the sixteenth and seventeenth centuries, Enlightenment thinkers emphasised rationalism and reason, empiricism and the scientific method, over the natural philosophies of the Ancients and the doctrines of the Church.

The Chain of Being visualised a hierarchical order within the universe that ran unbroken 'from nothing to the deity'. Contained within it were two important concepts. The first can be traced back once again to Plato. This was the idea of plenitude – that from its very creation everything that could possibly exist was already contained in the universe. A universe that was not constituted upon this basic principle would be imperfect. Since its creator was perfect, such imperfection could not find its place. Any scheme which sought to order the cosmos, therefore and by necessity, was required to encapsulate its totality and omit nothing. The Chain of Being, extending from dust to the prime mover fulfilled this obligation. The second concept derived directly from Aristotle: this was the dual idea of continuity and gradation. Aristotle did not himself subscribe to the notion of plenitude, instead making space for potentiality (things that did not exist might come into being) as well as actuality. The key passage was found in Aristotle's *Historia animalium* (*History of Animals*):

Nature proceeds from the inanimate to the animals by such small steps that, because of continuity, we fail to see to which side the boundary and the middle between them belongs. For first after the inanimate kind of things is the plant kind, and among these one differs from another in seeming to have more share of life; but the whole kind in comparison with the other bodies appears more or less as animate, while in comparison with the animal kind it appears inanimate. The change from them to the animals is continuous, as we said before.

(Balme, 1991: 61–3)

As a universal scheme, the Chain of Being, or *scala naturae*, attracted medieval scholars because of its affinity with the microcosm and macrocosm. The Chain again linked the physical and the metaphysical and demonstrated the co-dependence of all things to each other. Thus Man, who occupied a position in the middle of the Chain, shared aspects in common with those entities to be found above and those below. Whilst gradation ensured that categories of being might blend together, some definition was established through the examination of the different states of existence that particular 'classes' enjoyed and the vital faculties they possessed. Rocks and stones simply existed. Plants existed and had life. Animals existed, had life, but also possessed the power of motion, sensibility (sense of feeling) and appetite. To these people additionally possessed a rational soul and intelligence which they shared in common with the angels but unlike them, since they shared attributes with the lower forms of life, they remained mortal. These ideas formed the basis of medieval taxonomies; they were implicit, for instance, in the division of the natural world into its constituent kingdoms – animal, vegetable, mineral. Within these subcategories further hierarchical orders became established and refined: wild animals, for instance, were privileged over the docile; useful insects occupied a higher place on the chain than those thought only to cause nuisance (e.g. bees against flies); and precious metals were placed above base metals and stones. The Chain of Being thus offered a structure around which medieval discussion of nature might be organised. Whilst never slavishly followed, many of the scientific encyclopaedias (at least those not organised alphabetically), as well as bestiaries and herbals often show the influence of the Chain on the internal arrangement of their contents.

Thus four key models – the elements, the humours, microcosm and macrocosm, and the Chain of Being – underpinned medieval understandings of the natural world. But they were by no means the only theories that circulated. Atomists, for instance, posited a world composed of indivisible atoms and void. It was the existence of this void which stood at odds with other models of the universe and especially that proposed by Aristotle in book four, chapter eight of *Physis* (*Physics*; Wicksteed and Cornford, 1929: 342–61). Those familiar with Aristotle's work, scholars such as Averroes in the Islamic world, were therefore quick to refute the concept. Indeed in the Latin west it appears to have held little of the universal appeal enjoyed by the other models. The resurgence of interest in atomism witnessed in later medieval Europe stemmed from the mathematical implications of the concept, rather than anything more wide-ranging or philosophical. But even then few contemporaries argued that the theory offered an alternative explanation for the structure of the cosmos (Murdoch, 1974). For those who lived in the middle ages, from the monastic scholars to the peasant farmer, their world was elemental not atomistic.

Further reading

Arikha offers a very readable introduction to elemental and humoural theory in *Passions and Tempers*. For masterful evocations of microcosm and macrocosm, readers are directed back to the sources: Walsh's translation of Boethius' *Consolation of Philosophy*, Wetherbee, *The Cosmographia of Bernardus Silvestris*, and Sheridan, *Alan of Lille, The Plaint of Nature*. The definitive discussion of the Great Chain of Being remains Lovejoy, *The Great Chain of Being*.

3

On the Heavens

It is sometimes difficult to draw a clear distinction between what was meant by astronomy and astrology in the middle ages; the terms were often used interchangeably (Burnett, 1996: 369). Even Isidore of Seville could conflate and confuse the two (Barney *et al.*, 2006: 99). In essence they were two facets of the same study: astronomy represented the theoretical science (*pars theoretica*), astrology the practical science (*pars practica*). Fortunately other scholars such as Albertus Magnus were able to provide clearer guidance:

> 'there are two parts to astronomy . . . one is about the locations of superior bodies, their quantities and their individual phenomena; and one arrives at the knowledge of this part through demonstration. The other is about the effects of the stars on inferior things, which effects are impermanently assumed by the mutable things; and therefore one arrives at knowledge of this part only by conjecture.
>
> (Price, 1980: 155)

To compound the confusion for modern students, a number of celestial phenomena, of which the Milky Way, comets and shooting stars feature most prominently, were not considered subjects for medieval astronomy but rather, following Aristotle, belonged to the study of meteorology since they were believed to belong to the lower atmosphere (Lee, 1952: 5).

Both astronomy and astrology were important. This was demonstrated by the inclusion of the former in the school curriculum – the quadrivium [Doc. 16] – while the latter was reflected in the vast number of treatises devoted to the topic, its practical application in many areas of daily life and its entry into popular culture via didactic poetry. In these fields of enquiry Arabic scholars led the way and Latin scholars followed (Hill, 1993: 32–57). In part this is explained by the availability of earlier Greek texts to the Islamic world and the access its scholars had to Indian and Persian literature where celestial observation already enjoyed a long and noble tradition. In part it related to the better atmospheric conditions of the Near East which made viewing of the night sky an easier task. In a telling introduction to his chapter on the movement of celestial bodies, Gauthier of Metz alluded to the problems faced by Europeans: 'Above Saturn which is the last planet and highest from us of all the seven planets is the heaven that men see so full of stars in clear times and weather.' (Prior, 1913: 128) Other factors might also have played a role: the importance of accurate timekeeping for Moslem prayers (although this was not restricted to Islam; Gregory of Tours' sixth-century text *De cursibus ecclesiasticis* (*The Order and Course of Divine Offices*) showed how the stars were used to regulate monastic prayers (LaMonte, 1949)) and the particular requirement to orientate on Mecca; and the utility of the stars for Arabic travellers navigating the featureless desert lands of the Islamic empire.

Together with medical texts, it was works on astronomy and astrology which were among the first to be translated into Latin, a clear sign of their perceived value to western science. By the mid-eleventh century the treatise *De utilitatibus astrolabii* (*On the Use of the Astrolabe*), an instrument permitting the precise measurement and prediction of future movement of celestial bodies, was available in what would later become Germany through a translation by Hermann Contractus (1013–1054). The Englishman Adelard of Bath translated two astrological works including Abu Ma'Shar's *Abbreviation to the Introduction to Astrology* and Al-Khawarizmi's *Astrological Tables* which he must surely have first encountered in Moslem Spain. Here his contemporary John of Seville (*fl.* 1133–1142), probably a Mozarab (a Christian living under Islamic rule) had translated amongst other works of astrological interest, Al-Farhini's *De scientia astrorum* (*The Science of the Stars*) and Abu Ma'Shar's *Great Introduction to Astronomy*. The Slav Hermann the Dalmatian (*fl.* 1138–1143) translated Ptolemy's *Planisphere*, and the Italian Plato of Tivoli (*fl.* 1132–1146) the same author's *Tetrabiblos* (in Latin *Quadripartitum*), Al-Battani's *De motu stellarum* (*The Motion of the Stars*) and other texts. The greatest translator of them all, Gerard of Cremona was responsible for bringing no less than twelve astronomical texts into Latin including Ptolemy's *Almagest* from the Arabic, a work which had been translated 15 years earlier directly from the Greek by Eugene, a Norman administrator in Sicily (Lindberg, 1978). As might be expected, these new translations brought in their wake significant European advances in the fields of both astronomy and astrology.

What these replaced were understandings based on a much narrower range of sources: Calcidius' partial translation of the *Timaeus*, snippets of Greek and Latin learning gathered together in the second book of Pliny the Elder's *Naturalis Historia* (Rackham, 1949: 189–229), Macrobius' *Commentarii in somnium Scipionis* (Stahl, 1990), and the astronomical account in book eight of Martianus Capella's *De nuptiis Philologiae et Mercurii* (Stahl *et al.*, 1977: 314–44). It is surely telling that when Alcuin of York, then travelling without his books, was asked to explain various astrological matters by Charlemagne, he requested that the Emperor send him Pliny before responding and opined that Bede's astronomical account could not be bettered (Allott, 1974: 92). Of course, many of these works were not concerned with mathematical observation but rather with the lessons that could be drawn from the order apparent in the movement of celestial bodies and their creation. But for Christian writers this was the very point of astronomy:

> By this art and science all other sciences of decrees and divinity were made, by which all Christianity is converted to the right faith of our Lord God to love him and to serve the King Almighty from whom everything comes and to whom they return, and who made all astronomy, and heaven and earth, the sun, the moon and the stars.
>
> (Prior, 1913: 40)

However, if the movement of the celestial bodies reflected a divine and perfect order, it was essential that astronomical science explained the observable irregularities in their progress across the sky and three phenomena in particular: **precession**, whereby the stars appeared to drift slowly in a direction contrary to their general motion; **planetary stations**, when planets appeared to occupy a stationary position in the sky over a number of days; and **retrogradation**, when the planets appeared to move in the opposite direction from their normal course.

European astronomy before the twelfth century remained founded on Plato's conception of a **geocentric** universe. Surrounding the earth were a series of concentric spheres carrying the stars and the planets in perpetual circular motion. Later writers used a number of analogies to describe this structure. The tenth-century Arabic geographer Al-Muqaddasī likened the universe to an egg, the earth its yolk surrounded by the albumen and shell – an image familiar to the Hindus (the Brahmānda or 'egg of Brahman' (Sachau, 1910: 211)) and later reused by Hildegard of Bingen (Newman, 2002), William of Conches (Ronca and Curr, 1997) and the rather shadowy thirteenth-century French writer Pierre of Beauvais in his *Mappemonde*; *World Map*; Angremy, 1983: 958–60). Alternatively, Al-Muqaddasī reported:

> [s]ome have made a comparison between the celestial sphere and a turner rotating a hollowed out object having a walnut inside it: when he turns the hollow object the walnut stays in the middle.
>
> (Adapted from Collins, 2001: 53)

Precession: The process, caused by irregularities in the rotation of the earth around its polar axes, which results in the apparent slow retrograde motion of stars.

Planetary station: A planet which appears to remain motionless and fixed in place over a period of time.

Retrogradation: The period during which a planet appears to move contrary to its natural orbit.

Geocentrism: The concept of the universe which revolves around the earth.

For the eleventh-century English monk Aelfric, 'the earth stands in the likeness of a pine cone [*pinnhnyte*] and the sun glides around by God's decree' (Blake, 2009: 87). Whatever simile was used there was general agreement that the stars (thought to be fixed to the outer sphere or firmament and which thus rotated together), as Plato had argued, moved from east to west around the earth on an axis running through the two terrestrial poles; whilst the seven planets – Moon, Sun, Mercury, Venus, Mars, Jupiter and Saturn – rotated in the opposing direction around a second axis set at a diagonal of 23 degrees from the first. Of these two movements the first was the more dominant, taking all the inferior spheres with it. These, however, resisted this movement, offering both the cause of and explanation for astral precession. Around the second axis the planets revolved at different speeds and along different courses.

Plato's structure is clearly described by Isidore of Seville in *De natura rerum* where he dedicated 13 chapters to astronomical and cosmological matters (Fontaine, 1960: 216–63). In addition to the basic framework, he discussed other questions as appropriate for a book whose purpose was to explain and demystify natural phenomena. Did the sun burn – a question arising from its white rather than red appearance? The answer was yes. How big were the sun and moon? The sun, he said, was slightly bigger than the earth, the moon slightly smaller than the sun. Isidore summarised the argument that the stars were fixed to the *firmamentum* (the eighth sphere or firmament), the two moving together. He argued that the course of the sun was independent of the fixed stars, and that the moon and stars did not generate their own light but simply reflected that of the sun. Isidore also discussed the causes of solar and lunar eclipses and the movement of the planets, known as 'errants' since they appeared to 'move according to uncertain rules'. One of the more difficult questions he broached was the possibility of a watery sphere (a ninth sphere) lying above the firmament: could water coexist in such close proximity to fire (celestial bodies occupied the fiery zone) given their natural antipathy or indeed could a body of water physically occupy a convex surface? In contradiction to Plato, Isidore ordered the seven planets by proximity to the earth as Moon, Mercury, Venus, Sun, Mars, Jupiter and Saturn. By this order 'the sun, the most luminous of all the stars finds itself in the middle so that it might give its light to both the inferior and superior planets' (Fontaine, 1960: 216–63).

But a sense of the poor state of astronomical precision also emerges from this discussion. Isidore noted, for example, that the five planets (excluding the sun and moon) appeared to act in contrary ways, at times appearing to be stationary or to move backwards across the sky. Yet these oddities warranted no further explanation. When it came to the timing of planetary and luminary periods (the time taken for a celestial body to return to the same position in the sky) there was also great imprecision. The Moon, Isidore stated, completed its journey across the sky in eight years, Mercury twenty, Venus nine, the Sun nineteen, Mars fifteen, Jupiter twelve and Saturn thirty.

In the hands of Bede a slightly more sophisticated model was presented in *De temporum rationale* (Wallis, 1999). This work of **computus** ('the science of numbering and the division of time') specifically sought to establish a means of calculating the date of Easter through the reconciliation of the 29 or 30 day lunar cycle and the **Julian** (or solar) **calendar**. Because *computus* required careful observation of celestial movements, its contribution to the advancement of Christian astronomy cannot be underestimated. Bede, in fact, was one of the first to entertain the idea of **eccentric** spheres; that is celestial orbits which while still circular were not centred on the earth although they still passed fully around it, an idea he took from Pliny but whose ultimate source was Ptolemy (Toomer, 1984). This helped to explain why the size of the sun would appear to change at different times of the year – on the principle that the closer the object the larger it appeared. Bede also made important contributions to explaining the underlying motions of the sun and moon, and the changing angle observed at their rising and setting, together with establishing the connection between the phases of the moon and tidal heights. But while an advance, the problem of planetary stations and retrogradations remained to be resolved.

In the succeeding centuries, important but largely derivative contributions continued to be written under the influence of the available classical texts such as Rhabanus Maurus' *De universo*, a source book for preachers which drew heavily on Isidore of Seville's *Etymologiae*. These can be contrasted, however, with the ideas mentioned in passing and without further explanation in John Scotus Eriugena's *Periphyseon* or *De divisione nature* written in the 860s (Von Erhardt-Siebold and Von Erhardt, 1940; Sheldon-Williams, 1987) **[Doc. 11]**. Drawing almost certainly from Martianus Capella, who had presented a vision of a geoheliocentric universe in which Mercury and Venus orbited the sun and the other planets the earth, and perhaps influenced by Greek scholarship, for Eriugena was one of the few western scholars of this period who could read this language, he took this a stage further arguing, in a foretaste of what would later develop, that four planets orbited the sun – Jupiter and Mars above it, Mercury and Venus below. In its turn the sun, together with the moon and Saturn, continued to revolve around the earth. The dimensions of the universe he based on multiples of the diameter of the earth: the distance from earth to the centre of the moon was equivalent to one earth diameter, from the centre of the moon to the orbit of the planets another earth diameter, and so on up to Saturn. These six spaces plus the diameter of the earth itself, gave the seven spaces or 'tones' of the musical octave (Betts, 1964: 49). The 'harmony of the spheres', already ancient in

Computus: The science of calculating astronomical phenomena and movable dates in the calendar, particularly Easter.

Julian calendar: A year calculated as 365.25 days achieved by adding a leap year every four years. Because of slight inaccuracies, however, the calendar gained approximately three days every four centuries. This was resolved in 1582 by Pope Gregory XIII.

Eccentric: In Ptolemaic astronomy, a circular orbit which was not centred on the earth, meaning that planets would appear to move faster or slower depending on proximity or distance of their position on their orbit from the earth. In contradistinction to concentric orbits, which all share the same centre.

origin when Eriugena treated them (the idea features in Martianus Capella, Boethius, etc.), would remain a powerful motif in literature and art across the whole of the middle ages (James, 1995). However, Eriugena's view of a geoheliocentric universe had little impact on medieval thought.

Instead the new translations of the twelfth century required scholars to wrestle with two alternative models. These were the mathematical model of Ptolemy – the second-century AD Alexandrian and not one of the Egyptian pharaohs as was commonly thought in the middle ages, even by great minds such as Albertus Magnus – and Aristotle's adaptation of the **kinematic** universe envisaged by the fourth-century BC Greek Eudoxus. Eudoxus had proposed that the movement of each planet resulted from the rotation of not one sphere but a number of interconnected spheres. The outermost for each planet was the sphere of the fixed stars that completed the full rotation of the earth moving from east to west in the course of a single day. Linked to this was a second sphere that moved the planet with constant velocity along the ecliptic or zodiac belt from west to east. A third and fourth sphere moving at different angles and speeds accounted for visible shifts in latitude and longitude. Each planetary set of spheres thus acted independently of all others. Aristotle developed upon this idea in *Metaphysics* (Tredennick, 1947: 153–61), crucially suggesting that each set of rotating spheres, far from being autonomous, was connected to all others. Each sphere was joined to its neighbours by axes set at different angles, accounting for the irregularity of the visible movement of the luminaries and planets alike. In order to allow each planet to move independently from one another Aristotle introduced a compensating sphere rotating at the same speed as the fixed stars as the last sphere in each individual planetary system. It was from this compensating sphere (and not the fixed stars as Eudoxus had previously argued) that the new set of interlocking spheres dictating the movement of the next inferior planet took its movement. Eudoxus's total system required 26 spheres; in the Aristotelian version the movement of the celestial bodies was governed and explained by 47 or 55 spheres plus the sphere of the fixed stars. Medieval opinion remained divided, however, over whether Aristotle's quintessence – from which everything in the supralunary zone was constituted – was found in a fluid state, allowing the celestial bodies to float through each sphere, or crystalline, a translucent solid in which the planet was embedded, the whole sphere itself revolving as Aristotle's model would appear to imply.

At the same time as the Latin scholars were confronted with this extension to the Platonic view of the working of the universe, they also discovered Ptolemy. His *Almagest* (Toomer, 1984: 33–647) forcefully reintroduced the notion that had not entirely been abandoned, as Bede's scientific works show, of the movable eccentric. That is, planets moved around a circle – in accordance with the first principles of Plato – but that crucially the centre of

Kinematics: System of mechanical motion whereby the movement and position of one object affects the movement and position of another.

this circle need not be coincident with the earth itself but could lie some-
where on the line between the earth and the sun. As a result, the distance
between the **deferent**, that is the circle carrying the planet, and the earth was
not constant. Furthermore, Ptolemy proposed that the planets themselves
might also move around a subsidiary point which moved constantly around
and on the deferent itself – what was known as the '**epicycle**'. It was the
rotation of the epicycle that explained retrogradation and planetary stations.
Finally, the observed speeding up of the planetary transit around the deferent as it approached the sun was solved by the addition of an imaginary
point, the **equant**, from which the speed of the planet around its circular
orbit appeared to be constant (Plate 1).

The Ptolemaic system was not without its critics, particularly among those
who sought to rationalise this model with that of Aristotle. Aristotle's worldview required a static solid centre around which circular motion could be
maintained. Eccentrics and epicycles did not fit easily into this model. Thomas
Aquinas, for instance, sought to clarify these problems in his *Summa theologica*
(*Summary of Theology*): there was a difference, he suggested, between a
hypothesis which must necessarily be true (i.e. a physical or metaphysical
hypothesis such as Aristotle's conception of the universe) and one which
merely fitted the facts (i.e. Ptolemy's mathematical calculations):

> . . . in astrology the theory of eccentrics and epicycles is considered as
> established, because thereby the sensible appearances of the heavenly
> movements can be explained; not, however, as if this proof were suffi-
> cient, forasmuch as some other theory might explain them.
>   (Fathers of the English Dominican Province, 2006: 311)

Perhaps he was thinking of Aristarchus of Samos' teachings on the **heliocentric**
universe, which he certainly knew even if the text itself was not available to
him. Ptolemy too had been familiar with this theory, accepting that it might
help to make the mathematical calculations easier and might explain what
was observable. But he rejected the idea on the basis that it did not explain
what could be observed by the naked eye, particularly the idea of a stationary
earth. This would wait for Copernicus in the sixteenth century.

For those interested in cosmology and natural philosophy rather than
pure astronomy, Aristotle's model provided more food for thought and
greater justification – based on his discussion of the role of the prime mover,
primus movens, in giving the system its kinetic energy – for the divinely
created universe. The author of the *Speculum astronomiae* (*Mirror of Astronomy*)
written *c.* 1260 and originally thought to be a work of Albertus Magnus, for
instance, seems to have been particularly drawn to mechanistic explanations.
But he was also attracted to, if a little scathing about, the theory of Al-Bitruji,

Deferent: In Ptolemaic astronomy, the point around which the epicycle rotated. See 'epicycle'.

Epicycle: Astronomical term for the small circle around which planets rotated, which has its centre on a larger circle, and which was used to explain planetary stations and retrogradation.

Equant: A point in space around which a celestial body, travelling along an eccentric orbit, would move at a constant velo-city. See 'eccentric'.

Heliocentrism: The con-cept of a universe which revolves around the sun.

a Spanish Arab of the second half of the twelfth century (Price, 1980: 170–2). In a bold move away from Platonic and Aristotelian principles, Al-Bitruji had suggested that the only movement of stars and planets was a diurnal one east to west; the observed passage of the planets from west to east resulted from their retardation or lagging behind the 24 hour rotation. The driving force of the prime mover over the outermost sphere was total. This power reduced with distance, thus the next closest sphere, the zodiac, already fell behind but only by one degree in every century, giving Ptolemy's precessional figure of 36,000 years. The planetary lags were greater, Saturn losing sufficient to make it appear that it completed its orbit in thirty years, Jupiter twelve, Mars between two-and-a half and three years, the sun one year, Venus slightly less than one, Mercury nine months, and the moon which could be shown to lose 13 degrees each day, completed its west–east circuit in a single month (Goldstein, 1971, I: 78–9; Price, 1980: 170–2).

This was not the end of the astronomical theories which circulated in the middle ages. Writing in the first half of the fourteenth century John Buridan (c. 1300–1358) entertained the thought that it was the *earth* that rotated not the celestial bodies. Some sense of the debate is given in his *The Compatibility of the Earth's Diurnal Rotation with Astronomical Phenomena* (Clagett, 1974: 501):

> Others argue [against the theory of the earth's diurnal rotation] by many appearances. One of these is that the stars appear to us to be moved from the east to the west. But they [proponents of diurnal rotation] solve this [by saying] that it would appear the same if the stars were at rest and the earth were moved from west to east.
>
> Another appearance is this: if anyone were moving very swiftly on horseback, he would feel the air resisting him. Therefore, similarly, with the very swift motion of the earth in motion, we ought to feel the air noticeably resisting us. But these [supporters of diurnal rotation] respond that the earth, the water, and the air in the lower region are moved simultaneously with diurnal motion. Consequently there is not air resisting us.

Medieval opinion on the structure and mechanics of the celestial sky were thus divided. However, it was Ptolemy's mathematical solution and not Aristotle's kinetic model that found widest acceptance in the later middle ages, aided by the adoption of its principles in a popular collection of astronomical texts of the second half of the twelfth century known collectively as the *Theoretica planetarum* (Pedersen, 1981). Its eight chapters explored the sun and moon, how eclipses might be predicted, the movement of the superior planets Mars, Jupiter and Saturn, the inferior planets, Mercury and Venus, solar eclipses and epicyclic phenomena such as stations and retrogradation, latitude theory helping to explain the precession of the equinoxes and fixed stars, finishing with an exploration of the astrological significance of planetary positions (Tredwell, 2005: 474–5). Ptolemaic astronomy was used in other textbooks such as John of Sacrobosco's *Tractatus de sphaera* (*Treatise on the Sphere*) in the thirteenth century. His astronomical explanations were popular because they explained the visible movement of celestial bodies across the sky. But it was the utility of Ptolemy's mathematics in the calculation of accurate astrological tables which probably did more to promote this model over its competitors. As Pedersen (1978: 322) has remarked 'it was astrology . . . which saved the delicate flower of mathematical astronomy from the hot winds of Aristotelian natural philosophy'.

The fundamental premises of later medieval astrology combined Aristotelian natural philosophy with Ptolemaic cosmology. It was founded on the belief that the planets and the fixed stars exerted influence over the terrestrial world; indeed that it was they, and following Aristotle the sun in particular, that were the first cause of all corruption and generation. From Ptolemy's *Tetrabiblos* (Robbins, 1948) was drawn the particular set of qualities each planet possessed. These qualities were further moderated by the signs of the zodiac (the fixed stars). Their power was emitted through straight 'rays' whose potential effect at any given point on earth was directly related to their angle of impact **[Doc. 28]** and to prevailing conjunctions which worked either to compound or to diminish their efficacy.

Astrology in the west had floundered as a science before the translation movement, before the introduction of the astrolabe, and before the appearance of astrological tables (Campion, 2009). Thereafter it flourished becoming part of the university curriculum. More than 70 Arabic texts were translated during the twelfth and thirteenth centuries (Burnett, 1996). Four distinct branches of medieval astrology were distinguished by contemporaries such as Albertus Magnus. 'Revolutions' – noting the recurrent positions of stars in the sky on key dates of the year (often the vernal equinox) – together with conjugations of planets were used to predict the future in three areas: conjugations might be used to foresee plagues and famines; mortality and floods; and great political events. Revolutions of the stars could be used to predict the state of the weather, and could be used to ascertain the humoural temperament of individuals born under certain signs, useful in medicine. 'Nativities', horoscopes based on the constellations at the time of birth could help to predict the future fortune of individuals. 'Interrogations' used the pattern of constellations in the sky at the moment a question was asked to dictate how it should be answered. Finally, there were 'elections', used to predict the best days on which a particular task should be undertaken or journey started. Almanacs, for instance, made it possible to identify good days for medical interventions (Boudet, 2005: 62–3).

Even opponents of astrology recognised that the study of the movement of the celestial bodies was a noble science, and that discussion of the qualities possessed by planetary bodies and their powers rightly belonged to natural science (Coupland, 1974). But other types of astrological prediction, especially those which suggested a form of predestination, potentially threatened the tenet of human free will espoused by the Church. Mystics like Hildegard of Bingen sought to rationalise the two, suggesting that the stars only revealed what people already knew and did so not because of any special powers that they themselves possessed, but through God's permission alone (Berger, 1999). Other clerically trained individuals, however, such as Adelard of Bath clearly embraced the science. He translated key astrological tables, was author of a treatise on the astrolabe – which he dedicated to his student the future Henry II of England – and was probably responsible for ten surviving mid-twelfth-century horoscopes (Burnett, 1987). Towards the end of the same century Daniel of Morley and Roger of Hereford both received episcopal encouragement to write on astrology (Thorndike, 1929, II: 181). Into the 1260s works such as the *Mirror on Astronomy* continued to uphold judicial astrology – the collective term for nativities, interrogations and elections (Price, 1980). And icons of **divination** were clearly deemed appropriate subject matter for the Church since they were incorporated into the rose window at Lausanne designed *c.* 1230 (Figure 3). But by the end of the thirteenth century the Church was taking a much stronger stance against the practice. In 1277 works on geomancy, necromancy and judicial astrology were amongst those condemned by Bishop Tempier of Paris (Wippel, 2003). Despite this, late thirteenth-century clerics were able to tolerate revolutions since these tended to deal with large depersonalised phenomena and indeed their position on nativities remained, in reality, somewhat equivocal. What the Church did not stem was the increasing popularity of astrology, a situation given further impetus by the appearance, almost coterminous with the Paris ban, of what would become one of the most influential of the Latin texts on the subject, Guido Bonatti's *Liber astronomicus* (Thorndike, 1929, II: 825–35).

Astrology did not remain the preserve of scholars. Its practical applications, especially in the fields of agriculture and medicine, ensured that its principles penetrated, and were clearly understood by, the lowest medieval social ranks. The popularity of late medieval poems such as that now known as *The Planets and their Children* demonstrate just how firmly astrology had embedded itself in contemporary culture as does its presence in the prologue to Geoffrey Chaucer's tale of the *Wife of Bath*. It is surely telling that when Nicole Oresme launched his attack on astrology in the fourteenth century, he did so not in Latin, the language of the scholar, but in the vernacular, the language of the people. As he noted: 'I have written this little book in French

Divination: Predicting the future through magical or supernatural means. Includes aeromancy (observation of meteorological phenomena, cloud forms, the flight of birds, etc.); geomancy (signs read from the earth); pyromancy (fire signs); and necromancy (prediction through communication with the dead).

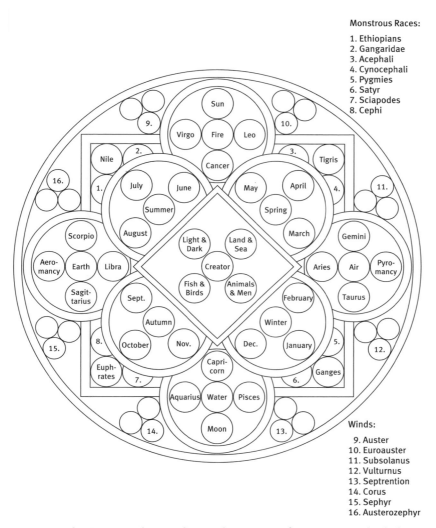

Monstrous Races:

1. Ethiopians
2. Gangaridae
3. Acephali
4. Cynocephali
5. Pygmies
6. Satyr
7. Sciapodes
8. Cephi

Winds:

9. Auster
10. Euroauster
11. Subsolanus
12. Vulturnus
13. Septrention
14. Corus
15. Sephyr
16. Austerozephyr

Figure 3 The Rose window in the south transept of Lausanne Cathedral, Switzerland, thirteenth century. The window provides one of the most eloquent representations of the complexities of medieval cosmology. The centre focuses on the Creation story in Genesis. Surrounding this the seasons and the months are associated with the elements and the signs of zodiac. Beyond these are shown the four rivers thought to flow from the Garden of Eden, a selection of monstrous races (mimicking contemporary *mappa mundi*) and the principal winds. To the extreme left and right are two roundels showing divination – aeromancy and pyromancy.

so that laymen may understand it for I have heard that many of them are overmuch given to such stupidities' (Coupland, 1974: 488). Popular astronomy is difficult to identify, but non-scholastic interest in celestial bodies is occasionally revealed in the alternative names they gave to what they saw. Aelfric noted that 'unlearned people' called Arcton or Septemtri (because of its seven stars) the 'Peasant's Cart' and the Pole star the 'Ship star' (Blake, 2009: 93); Alexander Neckam provides the first medieval reference to the man in the moon, seen as a peasant carrying a bunch of thorns (Wright, 1863: 54), the subject of a late thirteenth- or early fourteenth-century English poem (Davies, 1965: 71–3); and Bartholomew the Englishman calls the Milky Way 'Watling Street' after the great Roman road (Seymour *et al.*, 1975: 497). What is clear, however, is that the idea that the heavens exerted a profound influence on the world permeated every rung of medieval society and profoundly coloured understanding of the natural world.

Further reading

On astronomy, refer to Grant, *Planets, Stars, and Orbs: The Medieval Cosmos, 1200–1687* and McCluskey, *Astronomies and Cultures in Early Medieval Europe*. For a basic introduction to astrology see Page, *Astrology in Medieval Manuscripts* or for a definitive up-to-date survey on astrology Campion, *The History of Western Astrology*.

4

Meteorology

The medieval climate interests historians, for contemporaries it did not matter so much; they were far more concerned with the weather. Exposure to the elements was a daily experience for all those who worked in fields, woods and pastures, who plied their trade on rivers and seas, who marched with the great armies or who undertook pilgrimage. Given the vagaries of the weather it comes as no surprise that the medieval world was full of weather-watchers and forecasters. Military commanders understood its importance: campaigning season began in early summer to make the most of more clement conditions as well as standing crops. As French knights discovered on the field of Agincourt in 1415, the weather might determine the outcome of set piece battles and play an influential part in the great dynastic struggles of the period. Three and a half centuries earlier, unfavourable winds almost came to the rescue of the English as they delayed the Norman fleet from sailing. But it was the medieval peasant who most keenly understood the role that the weather played in guaranteeing a good return from their labours or consigning them to periods of dearth and starvation. So it is to be expected that when the shepherds in the Wakefield mystery plays, performed towards the end of the fifteenth century, complained about frozen feet and watering eyes caused by harsh frosts, many in the audience could empathise with their plight (Sowerby, 2010).

The weather was nowhere more economically important than in temperate north-western Europe where constant shifts in the main weather systems, either warm and wet cyclones/maritime westerlies or cold and dry continental/anticyclones (Kington, 2010), resulted in greater seasonal instability and unpredictability of weather than experienced around the Mediterranean littoral [Doc. 26]. This must explain why the weather was such an omnipresent theme in the historical accounts of the region and why it was Englishmen, such as Roger Bacon [Doc. 30] and later William Merle [Doc. 32] and not southern Europeans, who provided the earliest surviving runs of detailed meteorological records of the middle ages. Well before them, however, annalists and chroniclers had regularly included reports of extraordinary weather conditions and meteorological phenomena among their political and ecclesiastical histories. It is from such sources, for instance, that we learn of the extended winter and spring of 845–6 when seedlings around Troyes in France were destroyed by north-easterly winds, villages and towns were attacked by packs of wolves brought down from their usual habitats by cold and hunger, and the river Seine froze over (Pfister *et al.*, 1998). In comparable vein, the *Anglo-Saxon Chronicle* records the harsh conditions endured in England during 1047:

Candlemas: The feast of the Purification of the Virgin Mary celebrated on 2 February.

> . . . after **Candlemas** . . . came the severe winter, with frost and with snow, and with all bad weather; such that there was no man alive who could remember so severe a winter as that was, both through the mortality of men and mortality of cattle; both birds and fish perished through the great cold and hunger.
>
> (Swanton, 2000: 164)

Contemporary literary sources deriving from the same latitudes show a similarly acute appreciation of the weather. It is difficult not to draw parallels between the discomfort felt by the Wakefield shepherds and that of their Anglo-Saxon forebear, the ploughman's lad in Aelfric's *Colloquy*, whose voice was hoarse from shouting and the cold of a 'bitter winter' (Garmondsway, 1991: 20–1). In the Old English poem *Genesis B* the daily struggles with the elements take on a more apocalyptic tone:

> How will we stay alive, go on living in this land,
> If winds come, from the west or the east
> The south or the north? The world will grow dark,
> Hail will shower down from the sky.
> And the ground will freeze and be horribly cold.
> Sometimes the sun will glare down,
> Blazing hot, and we'll stand here naked,
> With no clothes to protect us. Nothing will shield us,
> Wherever it storms . . .
>
> (Raffel and Olsen, 1998: 93)

Texts such as these clearly demonstrate that by the early middle ages, and over and beyond its economic consequence, the weather was already gaining cultural significance for northern Europeans. But this is not to suggest that other parts of southern and eastern Europe were immune to catastrophic weather events or lacking in eye-witnesses. The winter of 763–4 was one such case, when as a boy the chronicler Theophanes the Confessor witnessed the Black Sea freeze over and watched in astonishment as icebergs, which had broken from this ice sheet, floated south through the Bosporus to strike and damage the walls of Constantinople (Turtledove, 1982: 123–4). This was no exaggerated account; independent sources report in the same winter the destruction of the grain harvest in France and olive and fig trees killed by the cold in Yugoslavia and Thracia (Pfister *et al.*, 1998).

That there were few parts of nature more significant than the weather in the middle ages finds support in travel accounts of the period, where the reporting of local conditions was a common topic. The late tenth-century Arabic geographer Al-Muqaddasī reported, for instance, that in the Haram (Arabia) 'the heat is severe, a killing wind blows . . .' while Hulwān enjoyed an 'equitable climate', before commenting 'but as for Al-Bata'ih heaven help us! Anyone who visits this place in summer has some remarkable experiences to endure' (Collins, 2001: 99). Al-Birunī's description of India is typically more factual and less prone to the embellishment and exaggeration than his contemporaries. He noted, for example, not only when the monsoon season began in different parts of India but also that the further north one travelled, the longer it would last: in Bhātal and Indravēdi four months, in Kashmīr two and a half months (Sachau, 1910: 211). European travellers were particularly struck by the conditions they found in the east. Friar Jordanus, writing around 1330, noted that in southern India 'the heat there is perfectly horrible, and more intolerable to strangers than it is possible to say' (Yule, 1863: 99). Marco Polo was of the same opinion observing that in the kingdom of Coilon on the southern tip of the subcontinent 'the heat of the sun can scarcely be endured; if you put an egg into any river, it will be boiled before you have gone any great distance' (Murray, 1845: 310). These descriptions, of course, tallied well with their readers' expectations. The idea that the world was divided into climatic zones based on their latitude was firmly embedded in both eastern and western medieval culture – within this scheme India lay on the interstices of the temperate habitable zone to the north and the fiery uninhabitable zone running around the equator (see Chapter 5).

Given the havoc it could wreak, people went to great lengths to predict the weather. Some medieval practices such as observing the behaviour of animals already enjoyed a long literary tradition, even if their origins lay ultimately in ancient folkloric custom. Of course few medieval farmers can have been aware when they noted that bees would remain in their hive when wind and rain was forecast, or that ants would not leave their colonies if they sensed an imminent downpour, or that oxen 'when they foresee by natural instinct a change for the better in the sky, they look out carefully and stick their necks from the stall' – all mentioned in bestiaries from the twelfth century (e.g. Barber, 1999: 89–90) – that these behavioural traits had already been commented upon by Pliny the Elder. Even within educated circles, animals might still play their part. The Oxford scholar William Merle, for instance, assessed levels of humidity not only scientifically, noting for example how far the sound of bells carried through the air or the rate at which salt took up moisture, but also experientially by observing the behaviour of fleas and noting how painfully their bites were felt (Kington, 2010: 79).

For Merle and his contemporaries the best source of meteorological information was the sky. In an unbroken tradition transmitted from the Classical world by scholars such as Isidore of Seville and Bede, much weight was placed on the appearance of the rising sun, the colour of the morning and evening sky, the occurrence of thunder and lightning in various quarters, and the colour of the moon during its different phases (Fontaine, 1960; Kendall and Wallis, 2010: 93–4). Signs such as these helped to predict weather in the short term. Minstrels in fifteenth-century Sandwich, for instance, would relay information they had gathered during the previous evening and during the early morning to sailors to inform them of the sea conditions they might expect to encounter (Brimblecombe, 1995).

Long-term weather forecasts, however, were based on the prognostic 'sciences' – astrological revolutions – which flourished during the middle ages producing a vast scholarly and more mundane literature (Chardonnens, 2007). Three forms of **prognostication** dealt specifically with the weather. The most common was the year prognostic or prognostication on the prime based on the day of the week on which either Christmas day or New Year's Day fell. If a Sunday, for instance, people could expect a good winter, windy spring and dry summer. The two other prognostic schemes relied upon registering meteorological events: sunshine prognostics relied on recording on which of the 12 days of Christmas the sun had shone; brontological prognostication was based on noting in which month of the year thunder was first heard. Two of these, the year and thunder prognostication, appear together in an illustrated fourteenth-century girdle book thought to have been the possession of a Worcestershire hayward, an important manorial officer often elected from the ranks of the peasantry and thus suggesting that predictions of these kinds were widely practised on the ground and not simply the preserve of the educated (Friedman, 1995) (Plate 2). A further indication of this is revealed by the scribbled annotations found on the flyleaf of a calendar, probably relating to 1429, where material relevant for future prediction had been noted by its owner:

Prognostication: The act of foretelling a future event.

> Sonday: Crystynmes day laste past was off iij
> Condycions in þe morning rayn at x & xi & xii
> Fayr weddur at aftur none dark and lowryng
> Munday: On sent stevyns day a blake day and a dropping . . .
> Wedōs: On Chyldurmes day a mystie day &
> At ii of þe cloke At aftur none þen yt raynd . . .
>   (Robbins, 1939: 330–1)

If forecasts allowed agrarian communities to plan for future weather eventualities, it was also the case that some sought to influence its course more directly. What evidence there is comes largely from the earlier part of the middle ages, but it must be presumed (since they have survived into the modern era) that superstitious practices and pseudo-magical rites were commonplace throughout the period, particularly amongst subaltern groups (e.g. Frazer, 1993: 645). It is impossible to know how widely followed were the customs reported by Timotheaus of Gaza *c.* 500 of sailors covering ship masts with sealskin to avoid being struck by lightning or using a punctured sealskin to sow seeds to ensure that any hail due to fall on that ground would be diverted to a neighbouring plot (Bodenheimer and Rabinowitz, 1948: 49). Likewise, while Dioscorides' advice that hanging the seeds of the croton oil plant would turn away hail and rough weather was certainly known in Anglo-Saxon England, since the plant was native to south-east Asia and not present in north-western Europe it must be highly unlikely to have been actually practised (Cockayne, 1864: 309). But it would appear that the peculiar ritual, railed against by Burchard of Worms *c.* 1000, of making a naked girl dig up henbane and tie it around the little toe of her right foot to encourage rain may have been based on an actual event (Freitag, 2004: 111). The belief that people could intervene to alter the weather suggests that amongst some sections of medieval society understanding of the actual forces in operation were poorly understood. An extreme example was provided by Agobard, bishop of Lyons, who happened upon a group of people in the environs of the city preparing to stone to death three men and a woman in 815–16. Enquiring as to why this was happening, the bishop was informed that the people believed that cloudships had sailed from a land called Magonia to steal crops damaged by hail and lost to storms. The four to be executed were considered to be captured aerial sailors who had fallen from their vessels. Agobard explained that it was a universally held belief that hail and thunder could be caused by humans, particularly so-called 'storm-makers', capable of targeting hail storms precisely and wreaking untold damage (Dutton, 1995a).

Medieval scholars, of course, held very different views even though there was no real consensus about the precise causes of the eight meteorological phenomena most commonly treated – dew and fog, the formation of clouds, rain, hail and snow, thunder, lightning and rainbows. However each competing thesis ultimately rested upon the common principles of elemental theory and the influence of the celestial bodies upon their formation and movement.

For Bartholomew the Englishman dew was 'little rain and rain much dew'. He stated that it originated in cold and moist vapours which formed droplets upon meeting cold air. Following Aristotle he was of the opinion that dew formed most easily when a naturally moist southerly wind blew. The moon also played its part by making the night air moister and consequently why dew was commonly encountered on grass in the early morning. Dew would be dissipated by both a dry northerly wind and by the heat of the sun (Seymour *et al.*, 1975: 582–3). Clouds began in the same fashion, but as the sun converted the more subtle parts of the watery vapours, so the residue was thickened and gathered together. Under the influence of winds the clouds were sculpted and moved aided by their lightness resulting from the large quantities of air they contained (Seymour *et al.*, 1975: 577–8).

When it came to rain, William of Conches usefully summarised nearly a millennium and a half of theorising in his *Dragmaticon* to offer four possible explanations (Ronco and Curr, 1997: 97–8). First, thick and moist vapours might rise from earth or water containing tiny droplets which would combine to fall as large raindrops. In this scenario the lighter water freed from the earth would naturally rise in order to retake its correct position in the elemental hierarchy. Second, air might be thickened as the result of cold due to its close proximity to earth and water – the cold elements. In this process the air turned to a watery substance forming a cloud. The sun's rays would then dissipate the cloud or pull it apart, the individual parts falling towards earth as rain on account of their weight. Third, the sun might attract moisture for its own nourishment. The liquid particles this moisture contained would be turned into a more fiery substance whilst the heavier particles would form raindrops. This explained why heavy downpours might occur after periods of extreme heat. Finally, wind might lift water directly from rivers, marshes and lakes, the reason why periodically frogs and small fish might fall from the sky.

One aspect of hail particularly vexed scholars. Why should it hail in the summer months and not the winter? This led to rather convoluted argumentation. Gershon ben Shlomah, for instance, explained it thus: the natural aversion of the sun's heat to the cold of the air drove this air to take shelter in clouds, where it froze the water droplets held within it forming hailstones. In the winter cold could expand everywhere in the absence of heat and so did not enter the clouds. The process of freezing, he argued, speeded up when two extremes of temperature were brought together: thus warm water placed in a chilly place would cool more quickly than cold water or the addition of cold water to lime would help to release its hidden heat and encourage its warming, on the principle that each of the actions of the elemental qualities hot and cold were strengthened as they fought against each other (Bodenheimer, 1953: 95). It is interesting to note that Gauthier of Metz also subscribed to the initial part of this thesis, that the sun chased the cold to the clouds (Prior, 1913: 119). More prosaically, William of Conches explained that hail formed as moisture rose to encounter cold and dry wind that froze the water turning it into a 'stony' substance in the upper parts of the atmosphere.

Because water is round – proved, he argued, by the round holes made in stone by continuous dripping – so hailstones were also round. Its seasonal occurrence could be explained because in winter rising moisture was frozen more quickly in the lower atmosphere before the individual droplets coagulated, and thus fell as snow (Ronca and Curr, 1997: 101–2). For Bede, hailstones were 'coagulated in the air from drops of rain, and frozen by the harshness of cold and wind. But they are melted more quickly than snow, and they fall more often during the day than at night' (Kendall and Wallis, 2010: 93).

Isidore of Seville thought that thunder was generated at the moment when powerful winds tore through clouds, likening this to an exploding vessel, and lightning was produced when clouds collided on the analogy of sparks created when stones were smashed together or wheels rubbed against each other. The destructive power of lightning, and its ability to penetrate what it hit, he claimed in the Platonic tradition, stemmed from the fact that it was composed of 'finer elements than our fire' (Barney *et al.*, 2006: 273–4). Adelard of Bath thought that the dissolving power of heat could have the same effect. When this acted on frozen clouds in winter this caused a 'shattering thunder', but in summer a less dramatic 'dissolving thunder'. In violent collisions he argued that what was released first was the lightest of elements (fire), hence the generation of lightning. This did not gain its power from its substance but from the swiftness of its movement. This allowed it to penetrate and break the harder objects it hit (Burnett, 1998: 203). In now familiar fashion William of Conches hedged his bets. Thunder might result from water particles striking each other as they rose though the atmosphere. From the motion of the air the heat generated might become lightning. Alternatively, opposing winds colliding might produce thunder and, if the air which was displaced was forced into the lower atmosphere, lightning too. He was both familiar with the exploding vessel theory, likening it to wind trapped in the bowels and a bursting bladder, and with Aristotle's more technical explanation. Vapour which rose from the earth was both dry and moist. The dry component turned into fire from movement and contact with the sun, becoming a lightning flash if gently diffused, or a lightning bolt if powerful and striking the ground. Finally, William offered the idea that during summer heats (the season for thunder and lightning) moist clouds ascend into the upper atmosphere where the coming together of water and fire creates commotion and sound (analogous to plunging a hot iron into water). The fire produced by the coming together of these two contraries produced the lightning. He concluded his section 'Because they are all possible and verisimilar, I condemn none of them' (Ronca and Curr, 1997: 102–5).

However spectacular thunder and hailstorms might be, and however essential rain was for growth, none of these meteorological phenomena compared in importance to wind. Together with the sun, winds were understood to play a vital role in driving the whole terrestrial system. It was through the power of the wind and sun in combination that the transformation of elements took place. It was these two forces that created the seasonal cycle. There was general consensus that wind was simply a large body of agitated air and that strength of movement helped to differentiate between it and breeze. But beyond that what caused air to become disturbed in the first instance remained moot throughout the period. Now familiar ideas of rising vapours, the compression of air around clouds or escaping from underground caverns were given as possible explanations, but perhaps the most developed idea linked winds with the movement of ocean currents.

A great ocean was envisaged encircling the equator (Figure 4). It was this body of water that tempered the extreme heat caused by the proximity of the sun over this region. Together this warmth and moisture acted as the drivers not only to weather systems but also to the whole process of generation and decay. Currents flowed out of this ocean both to east and west where they met the ocean thought to surround the globe. Here they divided, flowing to north and south around the landmasses in northern and southern hemispheres. As they divided, these waters created great disturbance and this in

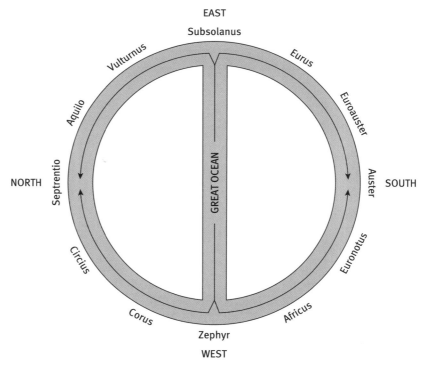

Figure 4 The theory of the winds and ocean currents after William of Conches, *Dragmaticon*. The arrows show the direction of water flow.

turn acted on the air above creating the east and west winds. As the two northerly and southerly flows continued their circuit they eventually met in the region of the poles causing tumultuous seas which generated the north and south winds (Ronca and Curr, 1997: 111–13; Seymour *et al.*, 1975: 570).

Each of the cardinal winds had particular characteristics. The north wind (*Septentio* or *Aparticus*) was cold and dry; the south wind (*Auster* or *Notus*) warm and moist; the east wind (*Subsolanus* or *Apeliotes*) warm and dry; the west wind (*Zephyrus* or *Favonius*) cold and moist. This clearly mapped neatly on to the elemental *rota* but required further rationalisation: why should the north and south winds differ in their qualities when both were formed in the icy regions of the poles? In fact, it was argued that both these winds began as cold and dry. It was only the passage of the southerly wind through the hot equatorial clime and over the Great Ocean where it gathered moisture that ensured that by the time it reached Europe its essential composition had been altered. With the east and west winds things operated in a slightly different fashion. These naturally differed in temperature; the east wind was necessarily hot since it was thought to have been born from literally under the sun (*Subsolanus*), while the west wind was cold from the outset. Both, however, began moist. It was only during the longer passage of the east wind to the west that it lost its humidity meaning that it was dry upon its arrival. Flanking these cardinal winds were their collaterals, either four oriented to the compass diagonals, but more usually eight, producing a *rota* with 12 spokes (Obrist, 1997). Each of the four trios shared common character-istics but differed in their extremes. *Euroauster* at south-south-east was an extremely hot wind; *Euronotus* at south-south-west was only temperately warm. *Vulturnus* at east-north-east dried everything; *Eurus* at east-south-east generated clouds. *Africus* at west-south-west was a stormy wind with the capacity to generate thunder and lightning, *Corus* at west-north-west pro-duced rain clouds. *Circius* at north-north-west was the harbinger of snow and hail; *Aquilo* at north-north-east condensed clouds (Kendall and Wallis, 2010: 90–1). But authorities did not necessarily agree on their effect. Bede reasoned that the north wind generated clouds and rain whereas Bartholomew the Englishman suggested the opposite, stating that this cold and dry wind led to clear weather by chasing them away (Seymour *et al.*, 1975: 572).

Winds did not only exert an influence over the weather. They were held responsible for earthquakes. Wind brought visible and easily appreciated destruction to buildings and crops. The wind's mercurial nature was demon-strated by its power both to kindle flame and to extinguish it. Winds, it was suggested, were created to mop up superfluities of humours, hence why wind might dry up puddles after rain. More invisibly, but no less signific-antly, winds were directly responsible for dictating the gender of babies – a dry north wind for a male, a moist south wind for a female (e.g. Bodenheimer, 1953: 236) and changes of humoural balance. Warm winds might open up the pores on the skin allowing vapours to escape; cold winds would do the opposite, closing the pores trapping potentially dangerous levels of heat or moisture within the body. The popular health book, *Tacuinum Sanitatis*, a synthesis of the medical work of the eleventh-century Arab physician Ibn Butlan, contains individual entries for the winds and their effects:

> Westerly wind (*ventus occidentalis*). Nature: moderately dry in the second degree, at other times in the first. Optimum: coming from the north. Usefulness: it improves the digestion. Dangers: it is bad for trembling and cold. Neutralization of the dangers: with heat and heavy clothing. It is more suitable for temperate complexions, for all ages, in Spring, and in eastern regions.
>
> (Arano, 1976)

Thus in every walk of life wind, and wind direction in particular, mattered. Moralists might even find meaning in the winds as the anonymous author of the Aberdeen Bestiary showed:

> The north wind represents the weight of temptation; the breath of the wind is the first intimation of temptation; its coldness, the numbing effect of moral negligence. The north wind comes, therefore, when serious temptation possesses the mind. It rises when temptation withdraws from the soul.

But for a predominantly agrarian society, it was the changing direction of the wind marking seasonal transition that held greatest significance (Pearsall and Salter, 1973). Soil which had been 'bound and closed' by the cold of winter was opened up by the warmth and moisture of spring in a way analogous to skin pores. What farmers (and physicians) wanted was for the weather to be appropriate to its season:

> If springtime weather and climate is unseasonal this breeds sickness and evil. It is said that if winter is dry and spring and harvest are wet and rainy, then inevitably summer breeds fevers, bleary-eyes and flux, notably amongst those with a wet nature.
>
> (Seymour *et al.*, 1975: 502)

Following Classical models, most medieval commentators on the seasons acknowledged a four-fold division – spring, summer, autumn, winter. There are indications, however, that in parts of Europe that had remained beyond the Roman Empire, other schemes were followed in the early middle ages. The Germanic tradition posited a winter season and another season 'summer', which might be better interpreted as 'not-winter', and there are certainly signs that these two seasons were more linguistically and culturally central to northern European culture than spring and autumn (Anderson, 1996). The four-season partition is used in Old English poems like *The Phoenix*, but in *The Seafarer* and *Beowulf* it is the two-season model that is used (Bradley, 2003: 284–301, 329–35, 408–94). Support for this can be found in the *Anglo-Saxon Chronicle*, where lengths of rule were often defined by the number of winters survived (Swanton, 2000). Indeed, before the entry for 1051 there is no mention of autumn, although it appears thereafter, and spring is never mentioned at all. The replacement of two with four seasons seems to have developed in the wake of renewed interest in Latin learning, the process of *interpretatio romana*. This is most clearly seen in the surviving texts written by the literate and educated. The reconciliation of the two systems appears to be captured in Aelfric's *De temporibus anni* (*On the Seasons of the Year*). Here summer and winter are seasons, spring and autumn shorter periods of the year either associated with the pre-Easter fast or harvesting: 'Four seasons are numbered in one year . . . *Ver* is lententime . . . *Aestas* is summer . . . *Autumnus* is harvest-time . . . *Hiems* is winter' (Blake, 2009). Likewise, in Byrhtferth's *Enchiridion* we find 'the four seasons . . . lenctenis and sumoris and haerfestis and winters' (Crawford, 1929). It is quite possible, however, that the two-season year may have enjoyed greater longevity than the written sources imply within popular folkloric traditions. But irrespective of how they came to be defined it is clear that there were no more structuring forces in the lives of the medieval majority than the weather and the seasons. It was these that lay behind the often depicted Labours of the Months and the annual agricultural cycle.

Further reading

For discussion of the European climate see Alexandre, *Le Climat en Europe au Moyen Age* For the medieval warm period, the pioneering study is Lamb, *Climate, History and the Modern World*. The most up-to-date discussion of climate in the British Isles in the middle ages is provided by Kington, *Climate and Weather*.

5

Image of the World

The hose who wrote about nature in the Latin west did so against the backdrop of three shifting horizons. For scholars, it was the changing intellectual landscape that mattered most as Platonic natural philosophy, unchallenged during the early middle ages, began to be questioned and was ultimately replaced in the wake of the 'rediscovery' of Aristotle. These scholarly works were further influenced by, and had to take account of, new discoveries made well beyond Europe and the Mediterranean basin. Reports from travellers, merchants, missionaries and embassies operating particularly in Asia and the Indian subcontinent helped to expand the geographical range of first-hand knowledge of nature's variety [**Doc. 20**]. For those who remained more closely tied to land and locality, accounts of exotica and descriptions of foreign lands mattered far less than the more immediate environmental changes brought on by the period's social, economic, climatic, technological and demographic dynamism. Together these brought radical reconfiguration of the European landscape between the seventh and fourteenth centuries. It is this changing image of the physical rather than philosophical world which is dealt with here.

The early medieval landscape of Europe owed much to former Roman exploitation: around the Mediterranean economies based on the cultivation of wheat, olives and grapes still dominated; whilst further north more woodland had survived together with its concomitant farming based on animal husbandry, notably dairy cattle and pigs. Of course, this picture is too simplistic. In lowland Britain, the growing of cereals had certainly spread on to less tractable clay lands by the fourth century and likewise the reclamation of fen and marsh through large-scale drainage programmes attests to the Roman capacity for bringing agriculturally marginal land into more intensive usage (Taylor, 2007: 115). Similar colonisation and enterprise could be found across the Empire.

But such gains might be short-lived. Early medieval Italian literature abounds with references to former cultivated land that had reverted to woodland or marsh (Serini, 1997). A similar state emerges from France, where archaeological and palaeoenvironmental evidence points to the conversion of former arable ground to pasture by the seventh century as once market-orientated production made way for mixed subsistence farming activities (Cheyette, 2008; Lewit, 2009). In England, place-names containing Old English words for particular species of trees (e.g. *aesc, ac, bece, elm*), or types of woodland or untended ground (e.g. *braec, grafa, hyrst, thorn, wuda*), or woodland clearing (e.g. *lēah, stocc, rodu*) can be found in areas formerly covered by Roman field systems suggesting woodland regeneration during the immediate post-Roman centuries (Gelling, 1993: 188–230; Rackham, 1993: 39–58).

On balance, what evidence there is suggests that undomesticated nature was in the ascendancy across Europe in the post-Roman periods. Where once the wild had been pushed to the margins, it had begun to reclaim old ground: fields turned to scrub, scrub to woodland. From the tenth century (although there are indications that the process began earlier in some parts of Europe) there are signs that this trend began to be reversed. For the next four hundred years Europe saw agricultural expansion and intensification characterised by the large-scale clearance of woodland, the conversion of grassland to arable cultivation, the draining of wetlands, the irrigation of arid zones and the colonisation of the uplands. The spirit of the age is captured in one of the Old English riddles collected in the tenth-century Exeter Book:

> I keep my snout to the ground; I burrow
> Deep into the earth, and churn it as I go,
> Guided by the grey foe of the forest
> And by my lord, my stooping owner
> Who steps behind me; he drives me
> Over the field, supports and pushes me
> Broadcasts in my wake. Brought from the wood,
> Borne on a wagon, then skilfully bound,
> I travel onward; I have many scars.
> There's green on one flank wherever I go,
> On the other my tracks—black, unmistakable.
> A sharp weapon, rammed through my spine,
> Hangs beneath me; another, on my head,
> Firm and pointing forward, falls on one side
> So I can tear the earth with my teeth
> If my lord, behind me, serves me rightly.
>   (Solution: the plough;
>   Crossley-Holland, 1993: 24)

Driving these changes was the need to bring ever more land into production to support not just a rapidly rising population – it is estimated that the

European population grew six-fold in the period 650–1350 – but one that was increasingly urban in character, meaning that ever greater numbers of agriculturally non-productive consumers required feeding. In northern Europe, at least, the process of intensification was aided by, and perhaps directly correlated with, a climatic upturn which led to longer growing seasons and more temperate rainfall (Lamb, 1995). And it was sustained by important technological advances: the introduction of the heavy plough with coulters and improved horse fittings, such as shoes, meant that heavy ground could be more easily worked; better felling axe designs may have speeded wood-land clearance; whilst windmills helped not only to grind larger quantities of grain but also to pump water around newly created irrigation schemes or away from reclaimed wetlands (Astill and Langdon, 1997). The precise chronology of this expansion and intensification, and the pace at which it was achieved, however, varied greatly across Europe.

In Spain expansion began early and can be directly linked with the estab-lishment after 711 of the Islamic province of Al-Andalus. Arab farmers brought with them new agricultural practices, ultimately derived from Indian models, which enabled the successful exploitation of formerly unproductive land through major irrigation schemes and slope terracing (Glick, 2005). Associated with these changes they introduced new crops – spinach, artichoke and aubergine; citrus varieties, banana and watermelon; rice, cotton and sugar-cane. By the fourteenth century, merino sheep could be found grazing the Spanish upland pastures, introduced to the European mainland by Berber pastoralists from north Africa. Rabbi Chisdai Abu-Yusuf provided an albeit idealised pen sketch of the peninsula's riches in a letter sent to the King of the Khozars *c.* 960:

> The land is rich, abounding in rivers, springs, and aqueducts; a land of corn, oil, and wine, of fruits and all manner of delicacies; it has pleasure-gardens and orchards, fruitful trees of every kind, including the leaves of the tree upon which the silkworm feeds, of which we have great abund-ance. In the mountains and woods of our country cochineal is gathered in great quantity. There are also found among us mountains covered by crocus and with veins of silver, gold, copper, iron, tin, sulphur, porphyry, marbles and crystal.
>
> (Adler, 1987: 26)

Agricultural intensification in some parts of England appears to have gathered momentum in the ninth and tenth centuries. A predominantly arable revolu-tion, its most obvious manifestation was the introduction of open-field agriculture. The precise stimuli for this change remain contentious and unre-solved (Lewis *et al.*, 2001; Williamson, 2003) but it appears to be coincident with the disintegration of large estates and the creation of smaller landholdings. Extensive resources might be marshalled within the former, with different parts dedicated to the production of specialised products as attested by place-names such as Shapwick, 'sheep farm', Butterwick, 'dairy farm', and Barton, 'barley farm'. By contrast, the owners of the new estates and their communities needed to find a means of maximising and diversifying the agricultural return from their more limited land units. A system of two or three open fields provided a solution, increasing the area dedicated to the growing of cereal crops at the expense of pasture and woodland, whilst at the same time through strict rotation providing grazing opportunities for livestock on those fields laid to fallow (Fox, 1981). Over time, the extent of these fields increased often at the expense of woodland. The clearance of woodland (assarting) reached its zenith in the twelfth and thirteenth centuries (Dyer, 2002: 160–2), only slowed down in those areas designated as royal Forest or chase (Jones and Page, 2006), so that by the mid-fourteenth century the fields of some manors might occupy as much as 90 per cent of the total landholding.

Two-course agriculture also seems to have been established in what would become northern France and southern Germany by the end of the eighth century, developing over time into three-course systems. Carolingian polyptyques, inventories of the natural and human resources found on the great royal and ecclesiastical estates, and which enumerated the individual holdings of monastic houses and the obligations of their tenants, provide vivid images not only of prevailing agricultural practices but the landscape itself. On the *villa* of Villeneuve St Georges, for example, tenants were required to plough in advance of both winter and spring sowing. Here most land was given over to arable cultivation, but elsewhere on the estate were vineyards, meadow and woodland used to pannage pigs. By contrast, the estate economy of Nully was founded on large areas of woodland capable of supporting sizeable herds of pigs, supplemented by limited amounts of spring grain grown in a few, small dispersed fields. The estate had no vineyards and managed little meadow (Duby, 1968: 366–70).

From the tenth and eleventh centuries, the expansion of cultivation into forests and wastes, the so-called *grands défrichements*, began in earnest (Bloch, 1966: 5–17). On the rich, heavy clays of the northern plains of France wheat became the principal crop, and as woodland resources became more scarce people turned to sheep rather than pigs as the main source of meat (Berman, 1995). Under monastic influence, systems of transhumance greatly helped to maintain essential animal–crop ratios, and from the twelfth and thirteenth centuries selective breeding led to better stocks of animals. It was the technological prowess of the monks in draining and managing wetlands that also allowed the rich alluvial soils of low-lying areas to be exploited without fear of flooding. In southern France, poorer soils and more mountainous terrain meant that rye remained the main cereal crop and sheep important not just in the diet but as a source of vital manure. But by the end of the medieval period, large-scale irrigation schemes comparable to those found in Spain brought water to previously uncultivated areas of the Midi (Terral and Durand, 2006) and allowed a similarly wide range of crops to be grown.

In the Netherlands, the period 1000–1300 saw the reclamation of coastal salt marshes, the drainage of peat land, and exploitation of sandy soils and heathland where bread cereals could be grown. The extension of the arable zone also impacted on areas of wood pasture; consequently an economy once based on pigs and cattle was replaced by one resting on sheep and corn (Hoppenbrouwers, 1997). The same was true in Denmark, where much land reclaimed from the sea was converted to arable and managed in two- or three-course rotations (Poulsen, 1997). Further north still, across Scandinavia barley remained the dominant cereal crop to the end of the medieval period, although it might be noted that rye began to be introduced into Finland in the eleventh century and would later be grown in parts of eastern Sweden and Denmark, and that oats were also grown in Norway (Myrdal, 1997). As elsewhere, this region saw an expansion of arable, aided by drainage schemes such as those undertaken in eastern Sweden before 1300 and improved plough technology. The result was a reduction in not just deciduous tree cover but also spruce forest. Where these survived, however, as in southern Sweden and northern Scania, and on the heathland of Jutland, mixed live-stock farming of cattle, sheep and pigs continued to dominate. Further east and following a similar trajectory there are clear signs in some parts of Poland of intensification in grain production by the thirteenth century.

From the fourteenth century the developmental trajectory of the European landscape shifted once again. Expansion and intensification were replaced by contraction as people reacted to climatic downturn. The early decades of the century were characterised by poor harvests and outbreaks of animal disease, the resulting famines weakening and even reducing the population. It was against this background that bubonic plague arrived in Europe in 1347, rapidly spreading across the continent, Britain and Scandinavia during 1348 and 1349. Its intermittent return thereafter ensured that there was no rapid recovery in population levels. Labour-intensive agricultural practices such as cereal cultivation were replaced by more reliance on animal husbandry in response to both the lack of manpower and also the collapse of grain prices. Ploughlands were converted to pasture and the need for further clearance of woodland diminished. This reversal, however, was relatively short-lived. By the third decade of the sixteenth century population had returned to its pre-1347 level and the landscape gains made c. 900–1300 were never entirely lost.

The cumulative effect of this expansion was a reduction in woodland, marsh and waste as these made way for ever greater areas of arable cultivation.

By one estimate, *c.* 30–40 per cent of the European landmass was given over to fields at the end of the middle ages, a figure that may have stood at less than 5 per cent in the sixth century (Duby, 1978; Williams, 2000). On the ground these developments showed themselves in the emergence of regional landscape types of sufficiently distinct character to be commented upon by contemporaries. The twelfth-century chronicler Wace, for instance, could differentiate between the open plains and wooded *bocage* of Normandy in much the same way that, four centuries later, the antiquarian William Harrison would divide England into woodland and champion landscapes (Roberts and Wrathmell, 2000). The words of Robertus Anglicus in praise of England (in an echo of Bede's prologue to his *Ecclesiastical History*) provide an evocative sense of the variegated landscape that had developed by the end of the thirteenth century:

> This is a land which ministers whatever is suited to mortal use with unfail-
> ing fertility; for, fecund in every kind of metal, it has fields widely scattered;
> hills, too, in flourishing cultivation, on which varied crops spring in their
> season from the rich glebe. It has forests, too, full of all sorts of game, in
> whose dells and alternate pastures grass grows for the animals and flowers
> of varied colours distribute honey to the roving bees. It has verdant meadows,
> also, pleasantly situated at the foot of its hills, where clear springs, flowing
> with gentle murmur through clean streams, refresh those reclining on the
> fragrant banks.
>
>   (Rothwell, 1975: 998)

But in reality, for those effecting landscape change, and for those affected by it, its ecological impact was invariably more visible and more deeply felt at a local scale. As woodland was cut back to make way for the plough, or as a marsh was drained, so local natural ecosystems were lost or pushed to the margins. As a result, once familiar sets of plants and animals disappeared from par-ticular locales to be replaced by others. Habitual encounters with nature vanished while new encounters would be established. Getting some sense of this reality is not always straightforward, for documentary sources rarely deal with this aspect of rural life. However field and furlong names, coined by the peasantry, can help to throw light on an otherwise obscure world. It is poss-ible to detect, for example, obvious variations in naming conventions used by communities in woodland and open-field landscapes. Field-names recorded before 1500 in the woodland manor of Silverstone in Northamptonshire include references to foxes, badgers, rabbits, cranes, mice, hawks/kites, snails and wolves. This was seemingly a landscape full of wild fauna whilst domestic animals rarely appear. It was a colourful and variegated landscape too, of blacks, whites, reds and greens. By contrast, in the open-field manor of Norwell in Nottinghamshire, the monotone nature of the extensive ploughlands is reflected in the absence of colour names. The main domesticates and crops all get mentioned, but references to wild flora and fauna are conspicuous by their absence. It was, however, a textured landscape where the characteristics of the soils – 'sweet', 'soapy', 'stony' and 'hard' – seemingly offered a way of differentiating different parcels of land. As these examples and others demonstrate, divergent encounters with nature not only helped communities to make sense of their surroundings, but also helped to define their distinctive identities. In this respect the medieval landscape can be seen to have shaped the mental outlook of the people who inhabited it – if people shaped the medieval landscape so these landscapes in turn shaped them. And as the landscape changed, so this helped to shape the outlook that local communities would develop on the natural world that surrounded them, as revealed in the testimony given to inquisitors of the fourteenth-century shepherds of Montaillou in southern France and the sixteenth-century miller of Montereale in Italy (Le Roy Ladurie, 1978: 120–35; Ginzburg, 1992). But what of the wider world?

Early medieval Latin geographies added little to the Classical corpus. Isidore of Seville's brief summaries of countries were largely derived from Pliny the Elder and these, in turn, formed the basis for much that followed in the later encyclopaedias. A parallel tradition, building on Strabo, was followed by the anonymous author of the eighth-century Ravenna *Geographica*, providing a list of world places, a work later revised by Guido of Pisa in 1119. One of the earliest northern European geographical texts belongs to an Irish monk, Dicuil, whose *De mensura orbis terrae* written in 825 was essentially a reworking of a fifth-century manuscript. However its inclusion of a description of an Irish voyage to Iceland made 30 years earlier did add a new dimension to geographical knowledge (Tierney, 1967: 75) [**Doc. 10**]. By the end of the ninth century there are occasional hints of original thinking: when the geographical preface to Orosius' *Historiae adversum paganos* (*History against the Pagans*) was translated into Old English many of the compass directions that it had used to define the spatial relationship between various tribal territories were reoriented (Malone, 1930; Jones, 2012). But this was rare. There was no Latin equivalent to Ibn Hawqal's tenth-century treatise *Sūrat al-'Ard* (*The Face of the Earth*) or al-Bakri's *Kitāb al-Masālik w-al-Mamālik* (*The Book of Roads and Kingdoms*), the earliest geography of a Spanish Moslem written in 1094 which together offered detailed descriptions of Al-Andalus, Sicily and parts of Italy as well as other regions under Islamic control. The early twelfth-century cartographic and geographic contributions to be found in Honorius of Autun's *Imago mundi* (*Image of the World*) and its reworking at the hands of Pierre of Beauvais as *Mappemonde* (*World Map*; Angremy, 1983), or Lambert of St Omer's *Liber floridus* (*Book of Flowers*) all belonged essentially to an earlier age [**Doc. 24; Doc. 25**].

Irrespective of the similes used – whether ball, orb, egg, walnut or pine-cone – Christian, Jewish and Arab scholars of the middle ages knew that the world was not flat but spherical. Those who erred from this position were quickly corrected such as the Hindus (with the exception of their astro-nomers who knew better) encountered by al-Bīrunī in India (Sachau, 1910: 267–8) or in the west those people said by William of Conches to be 'like animals trusting their feelings ahead of their reason' (Ronca and Curr, 1997: 121). However describing and, in particular, illustrating this three-dimensional reality in diagrammatic form presented problems. Early medieval depictions of the known world – Asia, Europe and Africa – tended to be highly stylised and simplified, for didactic reasons rather than out of ignorance of actual geographic irregularities. Commonly they were presented in the form of what have come to be known as T-O maps (Figure 5). Maps such as these belonged to the *rotae* tradition and presented the world as a round disc. Invariably oriented with east at the top, the continent of Asia filled the whole of the upper half of the circle. This was divided from Europe occupying the bottom left quarter of the map and Africa shown bottom right by a horizon line representing the rivers Don (then labelled 'Tanais') and Nile. Separating Europe from Africa was a vertical line (completing the 'T') standing for the Mediterranean Sea. Surrounding all three continents was a circle represent-ing the ocean thought to encompass these landmasses (the 'O'). The precise

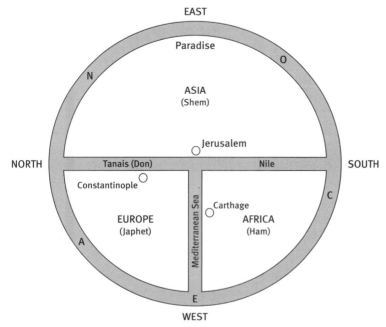

Figure 5   A composite of information regularly included on T-O maps.

origins of this cartographic convention are unknown; it may be Classical, but the occasional association of each continent with Noah's three sons – Shem with Asia, Ham with Africa and Japhet with Europe – might equally point towards a Judaic progenitor (Scafi, 2006: 89).

Despite their circularity, giving the impression that these maps were global in their extent, what was shown on T-O maps and their variants (e.g. Y-O maps) was simply a small portion of the earth – that which was deemed habitable and known to be inhabited. The full sphere was shown in a different way. Drawing on the subdivision of the world by Macrobius presented in his *Commentarii in somnium Scipionis*, himself influenced by the geography of Ptolemy, these maps showed five latitudinal zones. At the poles were two frigid zones, so cold that they were uninhabitable. Around the equator was a torrid or fiery zone, uninhabitable in this instance because of intense heat. Sandwiched between these extremes were two temperate zones, both potentially habitable but of which only the northern one was populated (Figure 6). It was the course of the sun that accounted for these temperature differences;

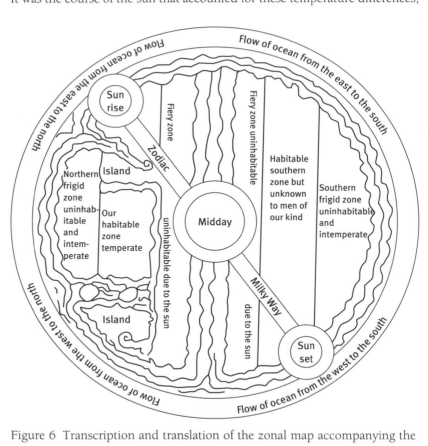

Figure 6 Transcription and translation of the zonal map accompanying the text found in Lambert of St Omer's *Martianus Capella*, Ghent copy, *c.* 1120.

and it was the sun's position at the summer and winter solstices (over the Tropics of Cancer and Capricorn respectively) and at the equinox over the equator that dictated the position and extent of the three central belts, their northern and southern boundaries coincident with the Arctic and Antarctic circles (e.g. Rackham, 1949, I: 311; Fontaine, 1960: 209; Kendall and Wallis, 2010: 78; Ronca and Curr, 1997: 124–6). This partition would enjoy considerable longevity down to the fifteenth century as illustrated in Pierre of Ailly's *Imago mundi* (*Image of the World*) of 1410 (Grant, 1974b: 630–40).

Arab geographers such as al-Muqaddasī and al-Bīrunī further subdivided the inhabited world into seven 'climes' in such a way that the midpoint of each of the strips running parallel to the equator 'differed by half an hour in the length of the longest summer day' (Wright, 1934: 138). Thus the most southerly clime passed through India, Sind, the Sunda archipelago and the east coast of Africa; the second clime through Abyssinia, Aden, Yemen, the Arabian desert and southern Mesopotamia, and so forth. In al-Bīrunī's scheme Byzantium, Andalusia and the land of the Franks belonged to the fifth clime; for al-Muqaddasī the latter to the sixth (Nasr, 1993: 146; Collins, 2001: 53–7).

A further global conceptualisation divided the northern temperate zone into two habitable parts: al-Bīrunī explains it thus:

> The reader is to imagine the inhabitable world, as lying in the northern half of the earth, and more accurately in one-half of this half . . . It is surrounded by a sea, which both in the West and East is called the comprehending one . . . This sea separates the inhabitable world from whatever continents or inhabitable islands there may be beyond it, both towards West and East; for it is not navigable on account of the darkness of the air and the thickness of the water.
>
> (Sachau, 1910: 196)

For William of Conches these other islands were the northern antipodes and this is how they came to be shown on maps on Beatus or quadripartite maps, which combined the T-O scheme with the Macrobian zones. But it was not darkness or the thickness of the water which prevented people from reaching them, rather extreme cold in the north, extreme heat in the south and the strong currents of the surrounding ocean to east and west (Ronca and Curr, 1997: 126). The theoretical existence of the southern temperate zone was equally subdivided.

By the early eleventh century medieval world maps such as the Cotton Tiberius map of *c*. 1025 (Plate 3) if still recognisably based on their more stylised predecessors, were starting to become more sophisticated showing, for instance, individual islands, serrated coastlines and major rivers. But it would be a mistake to read these maps as true geographical records. As the European map-making tradition matured through the twelfth century, reaching its apogee in the thirteenth with the great maps of the age – the Ebstorf world map and the Hereford *mappa mundi* – so the purpose of these maps changed (Harvey, 1996). In their most developed form, these maps were encyclopaedic in their scope, filled with figures and text that presented world history as much as world geography. Such maps were interested in time as much as space; they were more cosmological than realistic, symbolic rather than cartographic (Munkler, 2002: 196; Woodward, 1985: 511), visual equivalents for near contemporary textual descriptions such as Honorius of Autun's *Imago mundi* or its French translation, Pierre of Beauvais' *Mappemonde* (Angremy, 1983).

The principal source for the Hereford mapmaker, Richard of Holdingham, was Solinus' *Collectenea rerum memorabilium* (Mommsen, 1958). From this, with its focus on the fabulous and marvellous, Richard drew the information that accompanied the many **cryptozoological** creatures such as the bonnacon, dragon, griffin, manticore, minotaur and tigolopes which he placed in Asia. Fascination with the East stemming from Classical reports of its many natural wonders and abominations, unsubstantiated yet believable in the absence of firsthand witnesses, ensured that works dealing with subjects of this kind enjoyed popularity across the middle ages. It was from Solinus too that the Hereford mapmaker took his accounts of the people of Asia and the **monstrous races** which were often depicted on the edge of the known world. Of the Scythians, we read:

> A race of Scythians dwelling in the interior; unduly harsh customs; cave dwellers; making cups, not like the Essendones out of the skulls of friends but of their enemies; they love war; they drink blood of enemies from their actual wounds; their reputation increases with the number of the foes slaughtered, and to be devoid of experience of slaughtering is a disgrace.

Of the Turks:

> The island of Terraconta where the Turks dwell, descendants of Gog and Magog; a barbarous and unclean race, devouring the flesh of youths and abortions.

And of monstrous people:

> The monocoli in India are one-legged and swift, when they want to be protected from the heat of the sun they are shaded by the size of the foot.

Cryptozoological: Creatures now considered by modern science to be legendary, or mythical. They include: the bonnacon (probably based on the European Bison); the griffin (a lion-like animal with the head and wings of an eagle); and the manticore (a lion-like animal with a human face, occasionally horned or winged).

Monstrous Races: Otherwise known as the 'fabulous tribes', sub-human creatures thought to inhabit the edge or the opposite side of the inhabited world. These include the Antipodes (opposite-footed people), a term which eventually came to stand for the region as well as the people; the one-eyed Cyclopes; Cynocephali or Dogheads (human figures with canine faces); Essedones (a cannibalistic tribe found in Scythia); Androgyni or Hermaphrodites; Pygmies; Sciapodes (possessing a single large foot used as a sun-shade); and Tigolopes (semi-human creatures with webbed feet and tails).

The wonders of the East not only enthralled Europeans but Arabic writers too. The Islamic caliphate enjoyed extensive trading links in the area of the South China Sea and the Indian Ocean from a relatively early date and sailors brought back tales of what they had seen. One compilation of 136 stories was made by Buzurg ibn Shahriyar, a sailor of Khuzistan, in the second half of the tenth century (Freeman-Grenville, 1981). These told of encounters with mermaids, monstrous snakes, exotic birds and cannibals as well as reporting on natural riches such as precious stones and spices. Buzurg, however, was far from credulous when it came to the truth of these yarns [**Doc. 12**]. But perhaps the greatest work of geography (better described as an anthropology) of the early middle ages to treat a part of the world lying beyond the Christian and Islam polities was al-Bīrunī's *Ta'rikh al-Hind*, a magisterial study of the customs, religion, culture and science of the Hindus and the geography of India (Sachau, 1910).

As Christian missionaries went further afield, they too reported back on their discoveries. In the mid-ninth century the missionary Rimbert wrote to Ratramnus, a monk of Corbie, concerning a community of dogheads that he had met in Scandinavia (Bartlett, 2008: 97–101). But as the missions made inroads in Asia in later centuries it began to become clear that the existence of monstrous people had to be doubted in the absence of direct contacts. William of Rubruck, for example, a Franciscan who spent some time with the Monguls in Karakorum in 1253 commented:

> I asked about the monsters or monstrous humans that Isidore and Solinus tell about. They [the Monguls] said to me that they had never seen such beings, wherefore we wonder very much whether it were true.
>
> (Barlett, 2008: 102–3)

From 1260, Venetian merchants such as Maffeo and Nicolò Polo began to make journeys to Asia. Whether Marco Polo got as far as China as he would claim has been questioned (Wood, 1998). However, his return to Europe in 1295 and the appearance of his travel account three years later, should also have helped to demystify the east through his more sober descriptions of the lands of Prester John, Gog and Magog and elsewhere [**Doc. 31**]. But the text continued to be embellished by illustrators with images of wonders and monstrous races presumably pandering to readers' expectations (Plate 4) (Friedman, 1981: 154–8). More faithful representations of distant lands also characterised Odoric of Pordenone's *Description of the East* recounting his travels in Persia, India, Sumatra, Java, Borneo and China a generation later, but this work never enjoyed the popularity of Polo's *Travels* and thus exerted little influence on the public imagination (Chiesa, 2002). The Christian Church was also active in India and it is from here that Friar Jordanus, bishop of Columbum, wrote his account of the subcontinent in *c.* 1330 (Yule, 1863). The work is revealing. Jordanus' familiarity with the flora and fauna of India ensured that he was able to provide some of the first detailed descriptions of many animals and plants that still remained largely unknown in the west. The elephant for example:

> The animal has a big head; small eyes, smaller than a horse's; ears like the wings of owls or bats; a nose reaching quite to the ground, extending right down from the top of his head; and two tusks standing out of remarkable magnitude [both in] bulk and length, which are [in fact] teeth, with six hoofs like those of an ox, or rather a camel.
>
> (Yule, 1863: 26)

But he also included stories of the east coast of Africa ('India Tertia'), a land he had not visited and as a result his accounts revert to fable:

> Of India Tertia I will say this, that I have not indeed seen its many marvels, not having been there, but have heard them from trustworthy persons. For example, there be dragons in the greatest abundance, which carry on their heads the lustrous stones which be called carbuncles. These animals have their lying place upon golden sand, and grow exceedingly big, and cast forth from the mouth a most fetid and infectious breath, like the thickest smoke rising from fire.
>
> (Yule, 1863: 41–2)

In the medieval mind the existence of monstrous creatures and races was hardly dented by more extensive knowledge of world geography; it was simply the case that these now had to be accommodated in places where contacts still remained relatively rare or impossible. First Africa rather than south-east Asia became that locus and by the fifteenth century, as Africa too opened up, the monstrous races were consigned deep into the southern hemisphere (Friedman, 1981: 53). The western appetite for stories of this kind continued unabated and were fed by fictional travel accounts, perhaps the most popular of which were the tales of Sir John Mandeville written in the 1360s (Letts, 1953) [**Doc. 33**]. As for the significance of the unusual for understanding nature, this was captured by Ranulf Higden in his *Polychronicon* ('Universal History') written a generation before Mandeville: 'Note that at the farthest reaches of the world often occur new marvels and wonders, as though Nature plays with greater freedom secretly at the edges of the world than she does openly and nearer to us in the middle of it' (Friedman, 1981: 43). By the end of the middle ages, then, the image of the world had changed, it was better understood and mapped, but wonderment at its marvels remained undiminished.

Further reading

The classic discussion of changes in the rural economy of Europe, containing translated source material, is Duby, *Rural Economy and Country Life in the Medieval West.* This should now be read against more recent regional studies. For medieval cartographic traditions refer to Kline, *Maps of Medieval Thought* and Scafi, *Mapping Paradise.* For the monstrous races see Friedman, *The Monstrous Races in Medieval Art and Thought.*

6

Man and Nature

In medieval thought Man may have enjoyed a special place within the cosmic scheme, for the account of Creation found in Genesis clearly placed humankind in charge of nature (see Chapter 10), but this did not equate to the distinction that is now often drawn between the human/cultural sphere on the one hand and the natural world on the other. Notions such as these simply did not exist, because it was universally accepted that people belonged to the totality of nature, divinely created together with the birds and the trees and from which they could not be separated. Not only did they share space with the rest of Creation, mankind shared its material composition. And just as people shaped the natural environment they found around them, so that same environment played a formative role in shaping who they were.

Philosophical discussion of the medieval period was much concerned with defining what it meant to be human. To this end, human nature was explored in terms of the nature of the soul, intellect, emotion, free will and the senses (Pasnau, 2003). For those working in the Platonic tradition the most powerful paradigm was that of Man as microcosm; for later scholars influenced by Aristotle it was the *scala naturae* that provided them with their structuring device. But while the place of humankind in the Great Chain of Being (and thus the wider natural world) was fixed, the principle of gradation ensured this was not without its complications. Distinguishing between humans and superior beings – the angelic host – was relatively simple: a clear line could be drawn between the corporeal and mortal on the one hand and the ethereal and immortal on the other. But the line of demarcation separating humans from animals was less clear. Each possessed life and movement. Both were subject to the cycle of generation and decay. Both were considered to possess intellect and souls. Nevertheless, differences could be found. Humans had the capacity to reason; their soul was rational not irrational like brute creatures. It was this trait, more than any other, which helped to establish people's superiority over the animals and their claim to a higher place on the Chain. And the more elevated their position the greater their powers since they enjoyed closer proximity to God from whom everything ultimately derived its strength. In an original contribution to his monumental commentary on Aristotle's *De animalibus* (*On Animals*) Albertus Magnus explained it thus:

> . . . whatever an inferior power can do, a superior, more excellent, and more eminent power can do. It is clear, then, . . . that the human is the most perfect animal not only by virtue of the addition of reason but also in terms of all the powers and the manner of the carrying out of the powers, both sensible and rational.
>
> (Kitchell and Resnik, 1999: 1411)

If rationality could be used as a defining marker of humanity there remained a number of grey areas. Were infants (up to 7 years of age) who were capable of sensation but who exhibited no signs of reason or intellect to be classified as human (Ronca and Curr, 1997)? And how might evidence for apparent rational behaviour in animals be equated or accommodated into this polarised separation? Animals, for instance, could be shown to possess judgement particularly when it came to avoiding things that might do them harm or they might discern between two scents; some animals could obey oral commands proving that they possessed the capacity to understand (Burnett, 1998: 111–17). Whilst these might approach rationality Latin scholars tended to believe that they fell short of full reason. In contrast, writers such as the Byzantine Timotheus of Gaza (Bodenheimer and Rabinowitz, 1948: 46) and others in the Arab world appear to have been more comfortable in accepting the rationality of animals than their Christian counterparts. And interestingly, as thought developed through the medieval centuries, the clear distinction that had been drawn between Man and beasts by early Christian authorities would become ever more blurred as Latin scholars assimilated Graeco-Roman learning into their writings developing the idea of Man as animal (Salisbury, 1996) **[Doc. 35]**.

A second expectation was that human beings would conform to an accepted physiological norm. This issue was particularly pertinent when it came to the status of the physically abnormal monstrous races, a question that especially exercised medieval theologians (Friedman, 1981: 178–96) (Plate 4). The subject was treated at some length by St Augustine in *De civitate dei* where rationality was again invoked in his argument. After listing many of the more commonly accepted races – Cyclopes, Pygmies, Hermaphrodites, Sciapodes, Antipodes – he opined that any mortal animal, irrespective of body shape, colour of skin, the way they walked or the sound of their voice, must be descended from Adam if they exhibited rational thought. Only the Cynocephalae failed this test 'whose dog-heads and barking voices prove they are more like animals than men. There is no reason to believe that species like this are human even through they are called men' (Walsh, 1963: 502). This concerned men of the Church, of course, because only those with rational souls were capable of salvation. Thus it is noteworthy that by the ninth century the status of the dog-heads had changed. Despite their appearance and speech, the fact that they lived in communities, practised agriculture and covered their genitalia (respectively signs of lawfulness, reason and modesty) proved that they must be rational beings and ripe for conversion (Bartlett, 2008: 98–9; Friedman, 1981: 188).

The cause scholars proposed to explain the physical anomalies of the monstrous races – the environment – also served to explain physiological and anatomical differences among ordinary men. Temperate conditions would breed well-formed individuals with balanced complexions; excesses of heat and cold led to aberrations and abominations (hence why the monstrous races were invariably assigned to places with extreme climates). Necessarily for Latin writers the perfect archetype was European society and its peoples' physique. For Albertus Magnus, the inclement conditions of the north spawned white, fleshy, stupid people; the people of India and Ethiopia by contrast were dark-skinned, thin and sharp-witted as a result of the heat (Park, 1997: 141). The middle climes produced handsome, brave, noble and peace-loving individuals (Tilmann, 1971: 101–5).

Following Hippocratic principles (as noted in Chapter 2) the wider environment also played its role in defining the character of particular individuals at different times of the year: seasonal change, for instance, would lead to temporal shifts in humoural balance (e.g. Wallis, 1999: 102). More fundamentally, individuals who naturally leant towards a particular complexion – sanguinity, phlegmatism, melancholy or choler – also helped to account for behavioural traits and bodily characteristics. Thinking of this kind is laid out in the early twelfth-century anonymous *Tractatus de quarternario* (*Treatise on the Number Four*):

> Melancholy renders men blackish, or pale and ashen, with black and brittle hair, and like beard, with black and sluggish blood, dull leaden colour, pointed and longish faces, long fingers and hands, and black beady eyes. It makes them slow, serious, and short of breath; it also makes them greedy, stingy, looking to the future, elongated in their entire bodies, severely angry for a long time, full of suspicion, and cowardly, and susceptible to the quartan fever.
>
> (Dutton, 1995b: 151)

It was the celestial bodies more than any other factor which medieval scholars viewed as formative of human temperament. It was believed that people's physical and mental make-up corresponded in a dependent and sympathetic relationship to the celestial spheres, in particular the power of the planets over the body and the general disposition of those born under particular zodiacal signs. It was stated in the *Secretum secretorum* (Manzalaoui, 1977), for example, that Saturn, the highest planet was cold and dry, melancholic in complexion, an enemy to mankind, masculine, of the day rather than night, evil disposed and the harbinger of great misfortune. Slow to make its orbit, Saturn governed in a man's body the right ear, the milt (spleen) and the bladder. Its planetary influence brought many potential illnesses and ailments: phthisic (any illness of the lungs or throat), catarrh, palsy (muscle paralysis), dropsy (accumulations of watery fluids), quartan ague (a recurring hot fever), consumption, gout, leprosy, morphew (scurfy eruption), cancer, flux (discharges of blood or fluids) and griefs of the spleen. Those born under Saturn and its two principal houses – Capricorn and Aquarius – would be proud, sad, prone to remain angry, upright in counsel, disagreeable with their wives and malicious. Physically Saturn's children would be lean, pale, slender, thick lips, wide in the nostrils and cold in nature (Best and Brightman, 2000: 65).

In Leopold of Austria's thirteenth-century astrological textbook *Compilatio de astrorum scientia* (*Compilation of Astrological Science*) one finds general agreement if not exact parallels. Saturn, he suggested, was responsible for 'long illness and particularly those occurring because of melancholy humours . . . such as leprosy, gout, fistula, cancer, frosts, quartan fevers, black and white morphew, fetid odours, and bad breath from the mouth and nostril' (Page, 2002: 54). Likewise for Bartholomew the Englishman, Saturn was evil-willed, cold and dry, causing harm to the terrestrial realm particularly when in retrogradation (Seymour *et al.*, 1975: 479–80). Following Ptolemaic ideas he suggested that children born under the influence of Saturn would be brown and foul, misdoing, slow and heavy, unpleasant and sorry, and seldom glad. He also indicated problems with the feet and deformities of the body. And such ideas were clearly understood beyond scholarly circles since they were freely transmitted in non-scholarly works such as the late medieval poem known as *The Planets and their Children* (Blume, 2004).

Hildegard of Bingen provided greater precision based on the timing of birth and links to the various phases of the moon. Those conceived at the new moon when the air was temperate would be healthy but greedy (Berger, 1999: 75). Someone conceived on the fifth day after the new moon:

> . . . if it is a male, will be virtuous and loyal, courageous and steadfast. He will be physically health and live long. But if it is a female, she will be virile, quarrelsome and vindictive, but honest nevertheless. At times, though not very often, she suffers from some mild infirmity. She too can live quite long.
>
> (Berger, 1999: 123)

And from the *Secretum Secretorum* came advice about taking laxatives. Care should be taken that the moon was in Scorpio, Libra or Pisces. At all costs the moon should not be under the influence of Saturn for this planet would congeal the humours and the medicine in the body (Manzalaoui, 1977: 63–4).

Planets, then, were considered to have certain basic characteristics: Jupiter was viewed as warm and moist, Mars warm and dry, the Sun hot and dry, Venus cold and moist, Mercury variously hot, dry, cold and moist, and the Moon cold and moist. These did much to dictate the nature of people and in so doing might have both deleterious and restorative medical faculties. Astrological medicine held, for example, that the outermost belt of the zodiac governed the external anatomy; while the inner circles of the planets dominated the viscera or inner organs. Of all the planets, the moon, closest to the centre of this anthropocentric scheme, enjoyed a preponderant influence on all terrestrial fluids such as the tides, and in people was the cause of increases and decreases in the four humoural fluids. Moreover each zodiacal sign was held to govern a particular part of the body. Whilst never entirely consistent, a commonly encountered system in medical manuals (such as the late fourteenth-century English medical almanacs BL MS Sloane 2250 and Cambridge MS K26) had Aries ruling the head, Taurus the neck, throat and ears, Gemini the arms and fingers, Cancer the chest, Leo the heart, Virgo the abdomen, Libra the hips, Scorpio the genitals, Sagittarius the thighs, Capricorn the knees, Aquarius the ankles and Pisces the feet. Physicians were warned to avoid incisions in those parts of the body during periods of the year when the relevant zodiac sign ruled (Talbot, 1967: 129–30). Establishing when the celestial bodies exerted most power was critical for successful treatments such as blood-letting (Carey, 2004). Hildegard of Bingen counselled that:

> One should bleed when the moon is on the wane, that means on the first day the moon begins to wane, or on the second, third, fourth, fifth or sixth day. Then one should stop, because any earlier or later bloodletting will not be effective.
>
> (Berger, 1999: 89)

How the human body functioned not just day to day but across an individual's life cycle also intrigued medieval scholars who devised a range of theoretical schema to describe the passage from birth to death. These aimed to explain physiological change and – in their most developed form at least – sought to offer explanations for shifts in deportment, temperament and mental faculties over the course of a lifetime; they also served to unite human life with God, nature, and the divinely ordered cosmos (Youngs, 2006: 20–1). The lack of unity of thought exhibited is a reflection of the wide range of models from which medieval commentators were able to draw and demonstrates how emphasis could shift from one to another over time. Scholars of the late middle ages were often drawn to the idea of three ages – growth, stability and decline – in line with the Aristotelian concept of generation and decay. But, by this period there were already three other well-established traditions (Burrow, 1986). The first was the numerical/physiological four-age scheme, Pythagorean and Hippocratic in origin, which stressed the association of childhood, youth, maturity and old age with the four elements and their four qualities, the four humours, and the four seasons. The undoubted popularity and universal appeal of this scheme is reflected in the many diagrammatic depictions of these synergies which accompanied medieval texts dealing with the subject. The second model identified six ages. This was set out by Isidore of Seville – infancy from birth to 7, childhood from 7 to 14, adolescence from 14 to 28; youth from 28 to 50; maturity 50 to 70, and old age from 70 to death (Barney et al., 2006: 241). Its base was essentially theological, draw-ing in particular upon St Augustine's division of the biblical history of the world into six ages. It would be depicted in stained glass at Canterbury Cathedral (Typological Window n. XIV) in c. 1180 and would reappear in a variety of places such as the thirteenth-century Aberdeen Bestiary. The third model proposed seven ages of Man, and would come to prominence during the twelfth century in the wake of the translation of Ptolemy's astrological treatise Tetrabiblos (Quadriparititum). This scheme associated the stages of life with the planets – the Moon with infancy through to Saturn in old age. Theologians on the other hand looked to parallels with the Christian idea of the seven vices and virtues. Moral literature of the period, for example, equated youth with lustfulness and old age with avarice. The sum of four (the earthly number – e.g. the elements) and three (the divine number – e.g. the Trinity), seven also stood for perfection and completeness (Man made in the image of God) and the universe (microcosm and macrocosm). Thus one finds in Bartholomew the Englishman's encyclopaedia the seven age system: infancy from birth to 7; childhood ending at 14; adolescence to 21; youth to either 28 or 35 depending on authorities; adulthood terminating around 50; old age stretching to 70; and finally decrepitude (Seymour et al., 1975: 291–3). At the beginning of the fourteenth century these stages were por-trayed amongst the murals of Longthorpe Tower near Peterborough in Northamptonshire.

There were other schemes too such as the 12 ages of Hildegard of Bingen, associating the life cycle with the 12 months of the year, or the 10-age scheme representing the 10 great 'weeks' of seven years adding up to the biblical three score and ten, illustrated in the fourteenth-century Psalter of Robert de Lisle, but these were less common. In de Lisle's sumptuous depiction of this model two images portrayed infancy: first a baby in his mother's arms in front of a fire; and then a young boy with a set of scales. Adolescence was represented by a youth looking narcissistically into a mirror and a young male out hunting and hawking on horseback. A king on his throne represented maturity, while the slow process of ageing was shown sequentially by a man leaning on his staff, being led by a child, in bed with a physician studying his urine, his funeral and finally his tomb (Sandler, 1999: 43).

When it came to explaining the functioning of the human body great advances were made during the middle ages although it might be questioned just how far beyond the medical schools this knowledge permeated medieval society. Dissection, such as the examination of a pig carried out at Salerno during the first half of the twelfth century (Corner, 1974a) and, in the late thirteenth century, human dissection (Singer, 1974) together with improvements in surgical techniques as presented, for instance, in Roger of Salerno's *Practica chirugia* (1170), the *Anatomia magistri Nicholai Physici* (*Anatomy of Master Nicolas the Physician*, c. 1200; Corner, 1974b), Maurus of Salerno's *Anatomia* (a. 1214), William of Saliceto's *Chirugia* (1275), Mondino de'Luzzi's *Anatomia* (1316), and Guy of Chauliac's *Chirugia magna* (*Great Surgery*, 1363), led to major advances in anatomical knowledge (Ogden, 1971). Consequently by the end of the middle ages this field of inquiry enjoyed solid scientific and empirical foundations. However, and despite its invariable inclusion within encyclopaedic literature, the structure and workings of the internal organs clearly remained rather vaguely understood. Bartholomew the Englishman, for example, relied largely upon Constantine the African and thus Galen for his discussion of the stomach. This he described as round to protect it from vaporous superfluities which might have harmed any protruding parts, hollow to accommodate what had been consumed and fleshy to aid digestion, and connected to the liver. A healthy stomach would be hot and moist in order better to break down the food that it received (Seymour *et al.*, 1975: 243–5). A similar lack of detail surrounds his description of the anatomy (structure) and **physiology** (functioning) of the limbs and other bodily parts. Of the fingers, he described their three bones 'chained and bound' together and attaching to the palm of the hand. Their lack of flesh enabled the digits to move easily and enabled them to sense quickly what they were touching, whilst their articulation was driven by sinews that pulled against the outermost parts of the fingers (Seymour *et al.*, 1975: 225–6).

Physiology: The functioning of a living body.

Scholars such as Bartholomew were far more likely, however, to opine on the relationship between the body as servant and the soul its master. Each limb or organ performed one or a number of functions. These were classified as 'animal', 'natural' and 'spiritual'. The animal function allowed the body to feel, move and sense. The natural function was performed by organs such as the heart and lungs which maintained the vital spirit, and the stomach and liver which ensured that the body was able to absorb nourishment, and those organs which encouraged growth. Arteries served the heart and veins, the liver carrying the vital spirit around the body in the blood. Other structures and organs such as the nostrils, gall, spleen and kidneys helped to purge the body of unwanted matter; others still such as the skull, breastbone and ribs acted to protect the brain, heart and liver respectively. The body's spiritual function was performed by the heart, but it was the head as the locus for the wits which was deemed the superior part of the body. This was expected to be well proportioned, neither too large nor too small, and its inner disposition was revealed by outward signs such as hair growth – a good head of hair resulted from a warm and moist complexion, slow growth or hair loss a sign of internal coldness or dryness. As for the brain itself, this was thought to comprise three parts: the foremost part housed the imaginative faculty where feeling was registered; the mid section accommodated reason where external information was ordered; and it was in the back of the brain where this was stored as memory. It was through this process, via the senses, that the outside world and nature in all its variety was intimately encountered.

The senses turned the natural world into human experience (Nichols *et al.*, 2008; Woolgar, 2006). In the hands of poets this mediation was fully celebrated no more eloquently than in Matthieu de Vendôme's twelfth-century *Ars versificatoria* (*The Art of the Versemaker*):

> The flowers give fragrance, the grass grows, the trees bear,
> Fruit overflows, the birds chatter, the river murmurs, the air is cool.
> Birds please by voice, the grove by shade, the air by coolness
> The fountain by drinking-water, by its murmur the stream,
>   by its flowers the ground.
> The murmur of water is charming, the voices of birds are harmonious
> The smell of flowers fragrant, the stream cool, the shade warm.
> The beauty of the mentioned place feeds the five senses,
> Were you to note all the marked points together
> The water delights the touch, flavour the taste, the bird is
> The friend to the ear, and grace to sight, scent to the nose.
> The elements are not absent: the earth conceives, the air
> Caresses, heat awakens, moisture nourishes.
>   (Zonk, 2008: 99)

The senses were also a common theme for artists of the age irrespective of the medium in which they worked. In the ninth century an accomplished silversmith produced the Fuller Brooch conveying the five senses through carefully crafted gestures and actions (Plate 5). The early fourteenth-century muralist of Longthorpe depicted the senses as animals – a monkey representing taste, an eagle or vulture sight, a spider touch, a boar smell, and a cock hearing – set around a spoked wheel. And in the fifteenth century the senses

were the articulating theme of the sumptuous tapestry series now known as
The Lady and the Unicorn.

How the senses operated was of no less interest to the natural philosophers and scientists not just because the functions they performed were so
vital to being human, but because their precise workings were so difficult to
pinpoint. In a succinct passage Avicenna summed up the state of early eleventh-
century scholastic understanding (Achena and Massé, 1986: 56–7) [**Doc. 13**].
To the five senses, those who wrote under the influence of Aristotle added a
sixth – common sense. As Avicenna elsewhere stated:

> Know further that the sense organs – as the eye, the ear, the nose, the
> mouth, the hand, and the foot – are all like avenues by way of which
> entrance can be found into the city that is the sensible faculty itself, until
> the *sensus communis* itself is reached. And these five senses are like the
> men-at-arms who take prisoner whoever passes near them – in other
> words, 'apprehend' him. The *sensus communis* is their chief, and it is
> through his intermediation that the captives come to the other faculties.
>
> (Corbin, 1960: 351–2)

The sensation of touch was perhaps most easily explained. This faculty
resided in the skin and muscles whose ability to perceive changes in their
state resulting from contact with external bodies was provided by the nerves.
Fundamentally, sensation arose when the natural complexion of the recipient
was altered by an external source. Thus Adelard of Bath explained:

> Since the palm of the hand has heat and cold and the other related effects
> in a temperate state, when something more hot than cold meets the hand,
> its heat, which before was balanced, now becomes unbalanced. One can
> give similar examples concerning the other senses. The ever-watchful
> soul, thus perceiving the imbalance of her instrument, and guessing from
> one similar thing that another has been increased, proposes that what has
> been touched is hot. By a similar reasoning occur the sensible effects of
> smell and taste.
>
> (Burnett, 1998: 155–7)

Despite this assertion, however, the question of smell was more elusive to
resolve and throughout the middle ages a number of theories competed (Kemp,
1997). Platonists held that odiferous particles were themselves physically
moved through the air. Aristotelian thought posited that objects could transfer
their scent to a surrounding vapour which in turn transfused the smell.
Avicenna appears to hedge his bets: scents he concluded were transmitted
through an intermediary very fine airy or watery body that either carried

odours or mixed with odiferous vapours, which were able to pass via the nostrils to two teat-like protuberances, which directed the smell to the brain. In the Latin west the rediscovery of Aristotle did not wholly remove earlier ideas. Thus while William of Conches would follow Aristotle in the mid-twelfth century [**Doc. 18**], one hundred years later Bartholomew the Englishman remained an adherent of the idea that physical scented particles were transported through the air to the brain. Like Avicenna before him, Albertus Magnus also entertained the fact that smell might be both a medium and a body (Kemp, 1997: 213–15).

Hearing functioned in much the same way that the sound of thunder was explained: ripples of air resulting from a sudden shock or collision would spread through the air, and reaching the ear would create turbulence in the ear cavity which would stimulate the auditory nerve. Taste resulted from an impregnation, via the intercession of humidity, of the tongue which excited its nerves (Achena and Massé, 1986: 56–7). Of all the senses, however, that which attracted most attention was sight. Arabic scientists made great leaps forward in terms of optics, so too did Latin scholars such as Robert Grosseteste and Roger Bacon (Grant, 1974a: 376–441). Beyond this small group, however, sight was considered in more general terms. Some held that the soul saw through the eyes, nothing coming from the soul, nothing from the object perceived. Those who sought to counter such views argued that if the eye simply acted as a window then only things directly opposite the eye would be visible; moreover, since the eye was solid, this would act as a barrier rather than vector for sight, whereas a perforated organ such as the nostrils or mouth would be more appropriate. Then there were those who suggested (in terms common to hearing) that the forms of objects informed and shaped what was around them, such moulding stretching right to the observing eye which captured and interpreted these. Opponents questioned that if this was so, then one would not be able to see through a glass vessel. Third, there was the idea that the soul emitted a visual spirit which hit the object, recorded its form, and returned to the eye. But what would happen if there were two equidistant objects, both bouncing their forms back and which would cancel themselves out or interfere with each other's shape so as to make them incomprehensible? Finally there were those, approved of by the likes of Adelard of Bath, who posited that the visual spirit passed down the optic nerves to the eyes; here it left the eye and was impressed like a wax mould by the object. It retained this form, returning to the eyes where it was sent to the brain for interpretation. The problem of reflected images was resolved by suggesting that the visual spirit bounced away from the mirror surface to find the original object where the form was impressed (Burnett, 1998: 153).

However body and soul and their functions were understood, for most medieval people Man and nature were indivisible. Nowhere was the concept more elegantly expressed than in the work of the Brethren of Purity. Here the complex nexus of interconnections forming the very fabric of the natural world, of which everything represented the whole and each whole was just a part, was made manifest in all its poetic and philosophical glory:

> The body itself is like the earth, the bones like mountains, the brain like mines, the belly like the sea, the intestine like rivers, the nerves like brooks, the flesh like dust and mud. The hair on the body is like plants, the places where hair grows like fertile land and where there is no growth like saline soil. From its face to its feet, the body is like a populated state, its back like desolate regions, its front like the east, back the west, right the south, left the north. Its breath is like the wind, words like thunder, sounds like thunderbolts. Its laughter is like the light of noon, its tears like rain, its sadness like the darkness of night, and its sleep is like death as its awakening is like life. The days of its childhood are like spring, youth like summer, maturity like autumn, and old age like winter. Its motions and acts are like motions of stars and their rotation. Its birth and presence are like the rising of the stars and its death and absence like their setting.
>
> (Nasr, 1993: 101–2)

Further reading

Burrow, *Ages of Man*, is a useful point of departure for discussion of the human life cycle along with Sears, *The Ages of Man*. Readers should refer to the relevant sections of medieval encyclopaedias for insights into the workings of the human body. Matters anatomical and gynaecological are treated in detail in Kitchell and Resnik, *Albertus Magnus, On Animals*. On the senses, the best introduction and contextualisation available is Woolgar, *The Senses in Late Medieval England*.

7

On Animals

Animals have been described as the 'ubiquitous other' of the middle ages (Cohen, 1994; Hassig, 1999). Certainly their social, economic and cultural importance should not be underestimated for their omnipresence in the historical and archaeological records must surely reflect how they came to dominate all aspects of life and thought across the period (Resl, 2007; Salisbury, 2010). It was animals, after all, that provided the European populace with its meat, fat and dairy products. It was their pelts and wool that were turned into clothing, their leather which was made into gloves and footwear, and their bones which became knife handles, combs and ice-skates. Sheep and calves' hides furnished medieval scriptoria with parchment, birds provided scribes with their quills and shellfish their various dyes and colourings. Monks copied and illuminated to the light of tallow processed from cattle or sheep suet or beeswax candles, and built their vast fortunes on sheep flocks. Feathers were as essential to the fletcher's craft as the warhorse was to the knight. Animal dung and urine fertilised the soil and helped the tanner to strip his hides. It was the ox, the mule and later the horse that provided traction for the plough, and that pulled the carts loaded with produce destined for the manorial granary or market, giving Europeans a motor power estimated to be five times that of their Chinese counterparts by the fifteenth century (Thomas, 1984: 25). Horses carried the king and his household on their peripatetic journeys and manorial messengers on their errands. Wild animals provided the elite with their sport and others the opportunity to poach. Cock-fighting (first recorded in England by William Fitzstephen in the twelfth century (Anon., 1772: 45)), bull- and bear-baiting were all popular amusements even for schoolboys (Nelson, 1956; Reeves, 1995: 100–3); and by the end of the middle ages angling had become an established pastime (Hoffmann, 1997). In their turn, cats such as the famous monastic feline Pangur Bán memorialised in a ninth-century Irish poem (Green, 1998: vi) and dogs (together with parrots, monkeys, squirrels and the like) offered companionship, distraction and solace.

The impression that animals were everywhere is only reinforced when one turns to their representation in the medieval artistic and literary repertoire (Benton, 1992; Hicks, 1993; Klingender, 1971). Europe's monasteries, cathedrals and parish churches were richly decorated with animals, as craftsmen adorned capitals, fonts, doorways, stained glass, pew ends, roof bosses and misericords with zoological subjects. Recurring motifs etched themselves into the popular imagination – *agnus dei* the lamb of God, the self-mutilating pelican feeding her offspring, Reynard the Fox and associated characters (Varty, 1967), or the three interlocked hares known as the Hunt of Venus. Animals also inhabited the illuminated folios of liturgical texts such as the Lindisfarne Gospels. Of all the animals these featured it was the ox, lion and eagle – symbols of three of the four evangelists – that are most striking (Backhouse, 1981). Private psalters of the later medieval period were often richly adorned with animals too, such as the late thirteenth-century Bird Psalter (Hutchinson, 1974) with its highly detailed and naturalistic depictions of 27 bird species; the Luttrell Psalter where commonplace animals shared space with cryptozoological grotesques (Camille, 1998); or the fourteenth-century Queen Mary Psalter (Warner, 1912). As personifications of the zodiac, animals found a place in Books of Hours (private devotional texts often richly illuminated containing religious calendars and the liturgical offices) owned by the medieval European social elites (e.g. Backhouse, 1991; Dufournet, 1995). Few saints' *Vitae* or *Lives* fail to mention animals and in many these played central roles (Alexander, 2008). The story of St Cuthbert and the seals and puffins of Lindisfarne Island is well known, less so St Richard of Chichester's miraculous catch of mullet in a Sussex river (Salzman, 1925: 71–2), but both are representative of a much larger corpus. It was after seeing a vision of Christ between the antlers of a stag whilst out hunting that the Roman commander Placidus converted to Christianity (Skeat, 1900, II: 193), changed his name to Eustace and was later canonised, a scene portrayed in the fifteenth century by Pisanello in his *The Vision of St Eustace* (Plate 6). At around the same time, a similar story came to be appropriated by another saint, Hubert of Liège, patron of hunting, dogs, woodcutting and many other forest activities. But it is St Francis of Assisi who became most associated with the animal kingdom through the stories told in the *Fioretti* or 'Little Flowers' written shortly after his death in 1226 where such episodes as his intercession on the part of the community of Gubbio who were being terrorised by a wolf and his preaching to the birds were first recorded (Sorrell, 1988).

It is clear that animals were particularly central to elite culture from an early date. When the tomb of the Merovingian King Childeric was opened in the seventeenth century, he was found to be buried with 30 gold-and-garnet bees or cicadas and a golden ox head (perhaps horse harness adornments). The richly furnished 'royal' burial at Sutton Hoo contained a plethora of objects including *cloisonné* shoulder clasps and other jewellery together with the famous helmet that carried zoomorphic designs of boars, serpents and raptorial birds, all animals which held a special place in pre-Christian Germanic mythology. Animals commonly featured on later royal insignia: the leopard of the Dukes of Normandy; Edward III's griffin and falcon; the white hart associated with Richard II; the swan of Henry IV and the princes of Wales. They appear also on livery badges and coats of arms of magnates such as the bear and ragged staff of the Beauchamp earls of Warwick, now the county emblem, or the Percy lions displayed on the walls of the keep at Warkworth castle in Northumberland. As lesser aristocratic families adopted their own heraldic devices during the age of chivalry so the number of animals found on coats of arms increased, amongst which are the hedgehogs of the Harris family, a word play based on the Old French name for this creature, *hérisson* (Cannan, 2003). Animals were common motifs on seal matrices and it is clear from surviving decorated medieval interiors that they were a common subject in aristocratic chambers. One might think of the pastoral scenes painted on the walls of the Eagle Tower, Trentino, Italy, the ornate murals in the papal palace in Avignon, France or the water fowl in the fourteenth-century murals of Longthorpe Tower near Peterborough in England. Tapestries and embroideries too often featured animals in their design, such as menagerie in the upper and lower panels of the Bayeux Tapestry or the six famous tapestries known as the Lady and the Unicorn associated with the French courtly family of le Viste. Even in death animals continued to be associated with high-status individuals, featuring as foot rests on stone effigies and monumental brasses, including it would seem pets such as the dog named Terri on the brass of Lady Cassy at Deerhurst, Gloucestershire (*c.* 1400) and Sir Bryan Stapleton's dog Jakke at Ingham, Norfolk, England.

Animals also held an important place in peasant society. While the lower orders may have owned far fewer animals than their social superiors, their livestock often represented significant and valuable assets. Manorial surveys list their possessions. In 1307 Richard Est, a villein on the manor of Cuxham in Oxfordshire, was recorded with one draught horse, a cow, a yearling calf, two piglets, eight ewes, four two-year-old sheep and three chickens, together valued at 15s 9d. His other possessions including cereals, an ale cauldron, three sides of bacon and household goods only amounted to 15s 7d. Thus, including the bacon worth 20d, Est's animals represented well over half of his total assets. Belonging to the demesne in the same year were two cart-horses, two draught horses, six oxen, four cows, four calves, six pigs, three geese and eight capons totalling £4 12s 5d (Harvey, 1976). No small wonder then that provision was made for the care of animals and their treatment carefully monitored by estate managers [**Doc. 27**]. On the peasant holding itself, it would appear that women took a leading role in looking after the animals if the duties outlined in the late medieval satirical poem that has come to be known as *The Ballad of the Tyrannical Husband* are taken at face value. Here the wife's unacknowledged domestic tasks included the early morning milking of the cow and feeding the chickens, ducks and geese (Salisbury, 2002: 85–9).

But utility, economic value and companionship only partially account for the medieval obsession with animals. Significant also, certainly in elite and educated circles, was the symbolism that became attached to them. Such animal 'lore' was transmitted to its willing audience in a new type of manuscript which emerged in the twelfth and thirteenth centuries, the bestiary or Book of Beasts (Clark, 2006; Payne, 1990). Containing descriptions of exotic and domestic mammals, birds, fish, amphibians, reptiles and insects, these were not zoological treatises but allegorical and moralising texts designed to remind readers of the divine origins of nature and the theological guidance it offered to the Christian observer [Doc. 17; Doc. 21]. The bestiarists who compiled these texts drew principally upon four earlier sources: the Bible, Isidore of Seville's *Etymologiae*, Pliny the Elder's *Naturalis historia* and *Physiologus*. Of these the last was the most significant [Doc. 4]. The date of the composition of *Physiologus* remains uncertain, some placing it as early as the mid-second century AD, others as late as the fourth century. Its authorship is also unknown. What can be said, however, is that this Greek work probably composed in Alexandria and utilising Indian, Egyptian and Hebrew animal legends that were filtered through classical scholarship, would become one of the most influential and widely read works of the middle ages (Curley, 1979: xvi–xxxiii). It was translated early into both Latin and Arabic and by the ninth century was already known in England in a vernacular version attributed to Cynewulf of which only a fragment survives (Cook and Pitman, 1821). Several versions of *Physiologus* circulated, the longest of which provided descriptions and allegorical meanings for around 40 animals together with a few plants and minerals. But the most popular medieval version was the *Theobaldus-Physiologus* attributed to the eleventh-century abbot of Monte Cassino, Theobald (Rendall, 1928) [Doc. 15]. Written in metrical form it contained descriptions of 12, and on occasion, 13 animals.

By the twelfth century, this small menagerie had grown to the one hundred or so animals described in the medieval bestiaries (e.g. Barber, 1999; White, 1954). Typical of the shorter entries is that of the hare. It began with an Isidorean explanation of its name *lepus* derived from *levipes* 'light-footed'. Its propensity for flight, speed and timidity was noted. Then the bestiarist moved to his principal purpose of allegorising: the hare stood for those who feared God, a notion supported with quotations from the Old Testament (Barber, 1999: 66–7). Longer entries were provided for animals such as the panther, whose mild manner, sweet fragrance and habit of sleeping in its lair for three days before awakening provided a clear analogy for Christ's resurrection; and the elephant, a creature which intrigued medieval society more than any other with perhaps the exception of the Nile crocodile (Druce, 1919; Flores, 1993). More extended treatments were also provided for what might be described as the more privileged species associated with the medieval elite – horses, dogs and beasts of the chase – and insects such as the bee and ant which provided models for industry and social order.

Physiologus and those early bestiaries which descended from this tradition treated their zoological subjects in a fairly arbitrary order. But by the twelfth century a common structure began to appear even if individual texts exhibited important variations. Following an account of Adam naming the animals, the lion was invariably the first creature to be treated often followed by other exotic and cyptozoological species such as the griffin (part lion, part eagle) and the bonnacon (part bull, part horse) who escaped from its pursuers by drenching everything behind it with its odious excrement. Wild animals tended to be given precedence over their domesticated relations, while economically productive and useful animals such as dogs and sheep were placed before the unproductive (e.g. the badger) or those that caused nuisance (e.g. mice and moles). Typically mammals and quadrupeds were discussed before turning to birds, amphibious and reptilian animals, sea creatures and fish. Of course, such an internal arrangement reflected, if only imperfectly, the hierarchy of the *scala naturae*, but it was far from universally followed: later encyclopaedists, for instance, tended for ease of consultation to favour a strict alphabetical arrangement which undermined this structure.

If bestiaries were not principally works of reference, they were certainly designed to instruct. That they were used for this purpose is indicated by the tell-tale pattern of finger marks found on folio 34r of the Aberdeen Bestiary that can only have been produced by an instructor turning the page towards his students and holding it in position so that they could examine the image that accompanied its text (www.abdn.ac.uk/bestiary/history.hti). In fact the famed images of the medieval bestiary, whilst certainly adding to their aesthetic value and thus their popular appeal, must be seen first and foremost as didactic devices. Images were explicitly used in this manner in Hugh of Fouilloy's *Avarium* (*Book of Birds*) where he stated in his preface that he was determined 'by a picture to instruct the minds of simple folk, so that what [the intellect] could scarcely comprehend with the mind's eye, it might at least discern with the physical eye' (Clark, 1992: 117) **[Doc. 22]**. With the exception of the occasional illustrated *Physiologus*, such as the early ninth-century Bern exemplar, most early versions of this text did not carry images (Clark, 2006: 51). In contrast, it was rare for medieval bestiaries not to be sumptuously illustrated, a phenomenon that some have associated with the instruction of largely illiterate communities of lay brothers associated with monastic houses (Clark, 1992: 23). Bestiaries were certainly commonplace within monastic libraries of the period (Baxter, 1998). The depictions themselves remained rather stylised, borrowing from archetypes that were long established by the twelfth and thirteenth centuries (Plate 7). This was particularly the case for exotic creatures; but even with more familiar animals it is only rarely that naturalistic poses or behavioural traits were portrayed. In contrast to the forward-looking realism of botanical illustrations found in contemporary herbals (see Chapter 8), zoological depiction in the bestiaries tended to perpetuate conventions of an earlier era. Accurate animal art, faithful to life, would only be fully realised during the course of the fourteenth and fifteenth centuries (Plate 8). But before turning to this transition, it is worth setting the changing nature of medieval encounters with, and attitudes to, animals in their broader context.

The effect of increasingly exploitative land management policies on the ecosystems of medieval Europe has already been sketched (see Chapter 5). But adding a further layer of complexity to peoples' relationship with animals were direct human interventions with wild nature and exotica motivated by more than simple economic productivity. Of these activities, the medieval obsession with hunting had the greatest impact not just on the landscape itself but on the fauna that it supported. As early as the Carolingian period, large areas of woodland had become the hunting reserves of the ruling elite. Royal ownership and legislation served to protect these spaces against the tide of tree clearance and helped to preserve the otherwise dwindling habitats of the beasts of the forest – the bear, the wolf, the wild boar, the red deer, the roe deer, the fox and the marten – at the heart of Europe. Borrowing from this Carolingian model, the early dukes of Normandy had established similar hunting grounds in the duchy, albeit on a smaller scale, by the tenth century (Marvin, 2006). Royal protection over the hunting of animals may also have already existed in some form in Anglo-Saxon England, and professional huntsmen were certainly employed in the royal court of King Alfred. It is not surprising, therefore, to find that the distribution of place-names incorporating the Old English word *deor*, originally a generic term for 'wild animal' and later specifically 'deer', was restricted to those areas where other indicators suggest extensive stands of trees. In the aftermath of the Norman Conquest rights over hunting in England became more formalised, as William I established royal **Forests** and imposed new laws. Such institutions, of course, were part of his ducal heritage, but it is also plain that William's love of hunting was second to none. His famous epitaph, recorded in the Peterborough version of the *Anglo-Saxon Chronicle*, could state without fear of refutation that 'He loved the high game so mightily as though it was their father . . .' (Swanton, 2000: 221). In England areas subject to Forest Law, the legal machinery which restricted the exploitation of venison (a range of forest

Forests: A legal term for an area under Forest Law, in which royal monopoly over the hunting of animals (venison) and use of timber and underwood (vert) was protected. A medieval Forest is not necessarily heavily wooded.

animals not just deer) and vert (timber and underwood) in the Forests for the king's sole use, covered nearly a third of the country by the early thirteenth century. This extensive and exclusive coverage became a subject of considerable contention to the king's barons, their dissatisfaction reflected in several clauses of Magna Carta which sought to curb this royal monopoly and which led directly to the reissuing of a new Forest Charter by Henry III two years later (1217).

Unquestionably, giving over land to hunting helped to preserve biodiversity. Indeed it might even add to it. The growing fashion for emparkment, almost certainly a European borrowing from the Arabic world led to the reintroduction, after an absence of several centuries, of species such as fallow deer to England by the twelfth century, probably through Norman contacts with Sicily, and from here back onto the continental mainland (Sykes, 2007; O'Connor and Sykes, 2010). The impact on other animals was more mixed. Charlemagne's *Capitulare de Villis* written *c*. 800 required that stewards of estates:

> . . . shall at all times keep us informed about wolves, how many each of them has caught, and shall have the skins delivered to us. And in the month of May they are to seek out the wolf cubs and catch them, with poison and hooks as well as with pits and dogs.

Yet despite such efforts to exterminate these animals they, together with bears, would survive in the European forests to the end of the middle ages. By contrast, in Britain bears appear to have become extinct by the sixth century, and the last recorded wolf in England appears in a document dated 1304–5 (Yalden, 1999). Where the Frenchman Gaston Phoebus was able to write in his fourteenth-century hunting manual, *Livre de Chasse* 'A wolf is a common beast enough and therefore I need not tell of his make, for there are few men that have not seen some of them', Edward, duke of Norwich's early fifteenth-century English translation of this text tellingly inserted the words 'beyond the sea' after 'few men' (Baillie-Grohman and Baillie-Grohman, 2005: 54). By the end of the middle ages, then, it is clear that encounters with wild animals had become regionally distinctive: just as there was no one European landscape but many, so there was no one European fauna.

It is indisputable that medieval advances in the field of zoology owed much to the elite's fascination with the hunt. Huntsmen needed to understand their quarry; they needed to be able to predict where animals might be found, to know something of their daily movements and seasonal habits, and to know how they would respond when raised from their cover. The otter, for instance, was known to live in rivers and ponds and travel considerable distance in order to hunt for fish. They were also observed grazing in meadows and chewing at the roots of trees, bearing their whelps in holes dug under trees near the river bank in April and May (Baillie-Grohman and Baillie-Grohman, 2005: 72–3). All this required careful monitoring of their behaviour undertaken within their preferred habitats, taking hunters from the comfort of their great halls and personal chambers into the very heart of the natural world, an experiential immediacy exquisitely captured in the prologue to the *Parlement of the Thre Ages* (Offord, 1959). In similar fashion, how animals might be efficiently despatched and the highly ritualised procedures which were followed to butcher animals at kill sites – in particular the unmaking of deer – required an intimate knowledge of animal anatomy. Medieval hunting was far more than a leisurely pursuit: it was an art, its 'scientific' principles laid out in an extensive corpus of **cynegetic literature** (Cummins, 1988; Almond, 2003). Many hunting manuals enjoyed considerable popularity foremost amongst which were Gaston Phoebus' *Livre de Chasse* and its English translation *The Master of Game* already mentioned. These followed earlier texts including the thirteenth-century *La Chace dou Cerf* (*The Hunt of the Red Deer*; Tilander, 1960) and Frederick II's *De arte venandi cum avibus* (Wood and Fyfe, 1943) and in the fourteenth century William Twiti's *L'Art de Venerie* (*The Art of the Hunt*; Tilander, 1956; Danielsson, 1977) and Henri of Ferrières' *Les Livres du Roy Modus et de la Royne Ratio* (*The Books of King Modus and Queen Ratio*; Tilander, 1932). These belonged to a much longer tradition stretching unbroken back to Xenophon in the Hellenistic period (Phillips and Willcock, 1999) and transmitted via Roman poets such as Oppian (Mair, 1928), Grattius, and Nemesianus (Duff and Duff, 1935). This was an inheritance that could also be drawn upon by medieval Arab writers such as al-Mansur and al-Kafi (Clark and Derhalli, 2001).

Such manuals and other treatises dealt not only with those wild animals to be hunted, but also with those animals used for hunting – horses, dogs and birds of prey. As valuable commodities their breeding, selection, diet and health were of considerable import to their owners [**Doc. 34**]. Improvements in veterinary science owed much to the treatment and care given to these three elite animals. It is no coincidence that one of the earliest western veterinary treatises, Adelard of Bath's *De avibus tractatus* (*Treatise on Birds*), should focus almost exclusively on the treatment of sick hawks; those suffering from watery discharges from the eyes, nose and mouth, fungal growths, vomiting, lice, worms, and many other maladies (Burnett, 1998: 237–67). Nor is it perhaps coincidence that Adelard had had contacts with Islamic scholarship. For in the Arabic world, where veterinary science was more advanced than in contemporary Europe, their early texts similarly and invariably tended to deal with horses – such as al-Asma'ī's ninth-century *Kitāb al-Khail* (*On the Horse*) – and hunting birds (Van den Abeele, 1994). Where these two parallel cultures came together new translations brought in their wake new texts on the subject. Most notable of all were the scholastic achievements of Frederick II's Sicilian court. It was in Palermo that Michael Scotus provided the west with the first translation of Aristotle's *De animalibus* (*On Animals*) *c.* 1204. It was Frederick's keeper of animals, Jordanus Ruffus, who wrote the most important European treatise on the horse, *De medicina equorum* (*On Equine Medicine*) *c.* 1250–1254. And to this growing body of knowledge, Frederick himself contributed. The veterinary sections of his treatise on falconry applied Aristotelian principles with Arabic learning tested against close first-hand observation. Arabic veterinary works continued to be translated into the late thirteenth century – such as Moses of Palermo's *De curationibus infirmatatum aequorum* (*The Treatment of Sick Horses*) commissioned by Charles of Anjou, King of Naples and Sicily – and written, for example Ibn al-Mundhir al-Baitār's *Kitāb al-Nāsirī*, a treatise on horse diseases.

On the few occasions that it can be glimpsed, veterinary science beyond scholarly circles appears to have remained firmly embedded in a triad of long-lived traditions – Classical knowledge, herbal medicine and folklore. One Old English charm counselled that cattle with lung complaints should be given ashes on the day after midsummer whilst psalms and the creed were recited over them; and that sick sheep should be given a drop of new ale. In the Old English translation of the *Medicina de quadrupedibus* (*Medicine for Quadrupeds*) of Sextus Placitus, the author recommended that a mixture of badger's blood and salt, given through a horn into the mouth of an animal over the course of three nights, would ensure that they would not fall victim to murrain or cattle plague (Cockayne, 1864, I: 389, 329; see also Pettit, 2001). Further remedies were provided by Hildegard of Bingen (Throop, 1998). Ailing sheep should be made to drink a concoction of fennel and dill; asses suffering from pains in their stomach should be given prickly lettuce with their bran; nettles and lovage would help to cure horses of rheum; and cows and sheep that ate something to cause them to swell up or who suffered from coughs should be given the juice of *calendula* (marigold).

The new zoological works of the thirteenth century, informed by Aristotle and Arab scholarship, did much to debunk ideas that had for a long time never been questioned. For, far from accepting what had gone before (even what Aristotle himself had written), writers such as Frederick set out:

> to correct the many errors made by our predecessors who, when writing on the subject, degraded the noble art of falconry by slavish copying the misleading and often insufficient statements to be found in the works of certain hackneyed authors.
>
> (Wood and Fyfe, 1943: 3; Oggins, 1993: 54)

Others like him were capable of considerable originality in their close examination of nature and in their writings. A case in point was the barnacle goose. The traditional account of their hatching is provided by Gerald of Wales (O'Meara, 1982: 41–3). Acting against nature – no eggs were laid, no physical mating took place – barnacle geese were said to hatch from shells attached to the underside of floating logs. Gerald claimed to have seen many thousand birds emerging from their shells in this fashion with his own eyes. Frederick's investigations led him to conclude differently:

> There is, also, a small species known as the barnacle goose, arrayed in motley plumage (it has in certain parts white and in others black, circular markings), of whose nesting haunts we have no certain knowledge. There is, however, a curious popular tradition that they spring from dead trees. It is said that in the far north old ships are to be found in whose rotting hulls a worm is born that develops into the barnacle goose. This goose hangs from the dead wood by its beak until it is old and strong enough to fly. We have made prolonged research into the origin and truth of this legend and even sent special envoys to the North with orders to bring back specimens of those mythical timbers for our inspection. When we examined them we did observe shell-like formations clinging to the rotten wood, but these bore no resemblance to any avian body. We therefore doubt the truth of this legend in the absence of corroborating evidence. In our opinion this superstition arose from the fact that barnacle geese breed in such remote latitudes that men, in ignorance of their real nesting place, invented this explanation.
>
> (Wood and Fyfe, 1943: 51–2)

Albertus Magnus was equally sceptical about certain received ideas. He offered empirical proof that the long-held notion that beavers castrated themselves to relieve themselves of those parts of the body most sought after by hunters, and by so doing saving themselves from being killed, could be shown to be incorrect (Kitchell and Resnik, 1999: 1467). His failure to engage with the Aristotelian view that weasels gave birth through either their mouth or ear, a zoological phenomenon perpetuated in *Physiologus* (Curley, 1979: 50) and repeated by later bestiarists (e.g. Barber, 1999: 110), also appears to imply that Albertus had rejected this fable in favour of observable fact. Amongst the European scholarly community, then, by the end of the thirteenth century the behavioural ecology of familiar animals, whether migratory birds such as the barnacle goose or mammals such as the beaver and weasel, had, through first-hand observation of nature, experimentation and scientific enquiry, been set on much firmer foundations. In the Islamic world such attention to detail and close study of animals in their natural environment was already well established [Doc. 23].

But direct contact with animals in the Latin west was not restricted to indigenous species found on the European mainland or its Atlantic and

Mediterranean islands. From the early medieval period, kings and emperors had maintained menageries of exotic animals. Indeed such collections quickly became essential symbols of monarchy, the mastery over beasts acting as a metaphor for mastery of men. The gifting of rare species formed a key part of royal patronage and alliance building. Charlemagne's menageries at Aachen, Nijmegen and Ingelheim, which included lions, bears, camels, monkeys and exotic birds, were built up from gifts, such as the Asian elephant presented to him by Harun al-Rashid, caliph of Baghdad in 797 (Hoage and Deiss, 1996: 13). William of Malmesbury recorded Henry I's fondness for 'the wonders of distant countries, begging with great delight, as I have observed, from foreign kings, lions, leopards, lynxes, or camels – animals which England does not produce' (Giles, 1904). These he kept in his park at Woodstock in Oxfordshire (Thomas, 1996).

Frederick II was a great collector of exotica too. He possessed, at various times, lions, cheetahs, leopards, hyenas, elephants, a giraffe, camels and monkeys. So attached was he to these animals that he took some of this menagerie on his travels. In 1231, elephants, camels and dromedaries, panthers and a whole host of other big cats and birds of prey accompanied him to Ravenna. Animals were even taken to Worms in 1235 on the occasion of his marriage to his third wife, Isabella, sister of Henry III (Hoage and Deiss, 1996: 13), to whom he later presented the three leopards which would form, together with the animals at Woodstock, the beginnings of the menagerie maintained thereafter in the Tower of London (Thomas, 1996; Clark, 2006: 18–20). This royal menagerie benefited from other gifts, a white bear (presumably a polar bear) from Norway, and in 1255 the elephant given by Louis IX of France to Henry III and immortalised by the chronicler Matthew Paris in two miniatures (Lewis, 1987). Matthew himself visited the beast, accompanying his chronicle entries with a detailed illustration of the animal that he had evidently drawn from direct observation. By so doing, Matthew provided one of the earliest naturalistic depictions of any fauna – indigenous or introduced – to be found in the medieval artistic corpus, and in the process ensured that the fame this singular elephant enjoyed during its own lifetime would endure for nearly eight further centuries. These were socially exclusive animals, seen by the few rather than the many. However, as Paris himself reported, amongst comments that are clearly mistaken:

> We believe that this was the only elephant ever seen in England, or even in the countries on this side the Alps; wherefore the people flocked together to see the novel sight.
>
> (Giles, 1854: 115)

Exotic beasts evidently attracted public attention and curiosity. For the most part medieval lives were spent surrounded by more mundane creatures.

Many gave pleasure, others relieved the burden of work. But others might cause nuisance and infuriation in ways that modern students of nature and devotees of the great outdoors might recognise with empathy such as the flies so vividly described by al-Jāhiz [**Doc. 9**].

Further reading

There is an extensive literature on medieval animals. Their cultural significance is treated in Salisbury, *The Beast Within* and Resl, *A Cultural History of Animals in the Medieval Age*. Artistic representations are dealt with by Klingender, *Animals in Art and Thought* and Hassig, *The Mark of the Beast*. Those seeking wider context for the bestiary tradition might look at the introductions to Clark, *The Medieval Book of Birds* and *A Medieval Book of Beasts*, and Baxter, *Bestiaries and their Users*. The best account of medieval hunting remains Cummins, *The Hound and the Hawk*. For hunting treatises see Wood and Fyfe, *The Art of Falconry* and Baillie-Grohman and Baillie-Grohman, *Edward of Norwich, The Master of Game* which also contain much information regarding veterinary science.

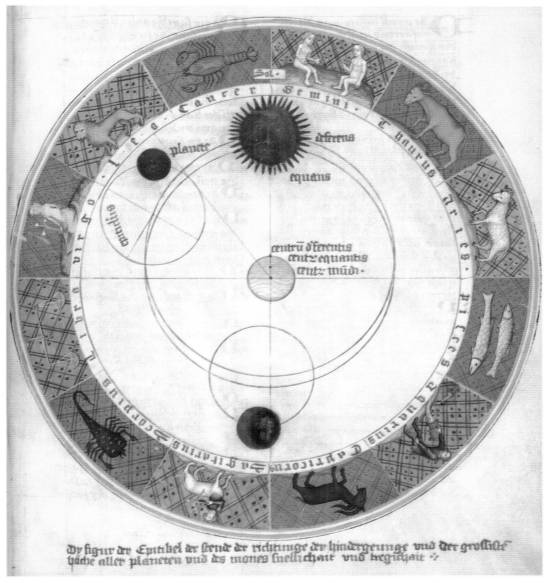

Plate 1 The zodiac from Konrad of Megenberg's German translation of John of Sacrobosco, *Sphaera Mundi*, showing the three centres – the centre of the world, the equant and the deferent, producing concentric and eccentric orbits, together with the planetary epicycles. Austria, *c.* 1425.

Source: The Pierpoint Morgan Library, New York. MS M.722. Purchased in 1927

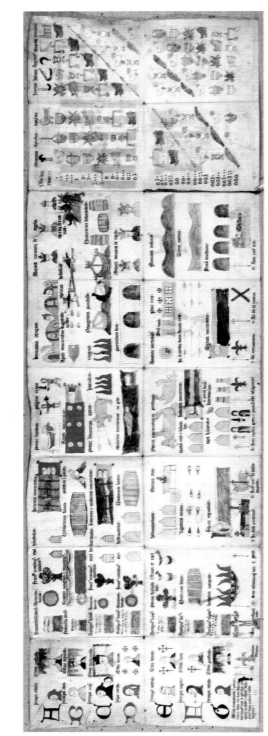

Plate 2 The seven-year cycle of weather prognostication and other annual predictions relating to agricultural activity based on the prime (the first day of the week on which New Year falls) found in a girdlebook associated a Worcestershire Hayward. Symbols enable this scheme to be readily understood by both the lettered and unlettered. c. 1350–1400.

Source: The Bodleian Library, University of Oxford, MS. Rawl d. 939, fol. 4v

Plate 3 The earliest surviving English *Mappa Mundi*. The map shows representations of Roman provinces, evidence that this was based on an earlier Classical exemplar. *c.* 1025–1050.

Source: Copyright © The British Library Board. Cotton Tiberius B.V. f56v

Plate 4 Monstrous races, showing a Blemmyae, Sciapod and
Cyclopes, from an illustrated page from Jean san Peur's copy
of Marco Polo's *Wonders of the World*, 1410–1413.

Source: Bibliothèque nationale de France, MS FRANCAIS 2810

Plate 5 The Fuller Brooch showing the five senses. Sight is
shown in the central panel surrounded (clockwise from
top-right) by smell, touch, hearing and taste. Ninth century.
114mm diameter.

Source: © The Trustees of the British Museum

Plate 6 Pisanello, *The Vision of St Eustace*, showing Christ crucified on the antlers of a stag, together with other beasts of the forest and warren, wild animals and fowl, and a number of different breeds of dog. *c.* 1438–1442.

Source: National Gallery / Bridgeman Art Library

Plate 7 Hugh de Folieto, *Avarium and Bestiary*, showing conventional elephants, a dragon (bottom left) and mandrake (bottom right). Northern France/Southern Netherlands, *c.* 1225–1275.

Source: Copyright © The British Library Board. Sloane MS278, fol 48v

Plate 8 The achievement of realism: water fowl in Gaston Phoebus, *Livre de Chasse*, French 1405–1410.

Source: Bibliothèque nationale de France, MS FRANCAIS 616

Plate 9 The Labours of the Months from Pietro di Crescenzi's, *Opus ruralium commodorum*,
mid-fifteenth-century copy.

Source: Musée Condé / Bridgeman Art Library

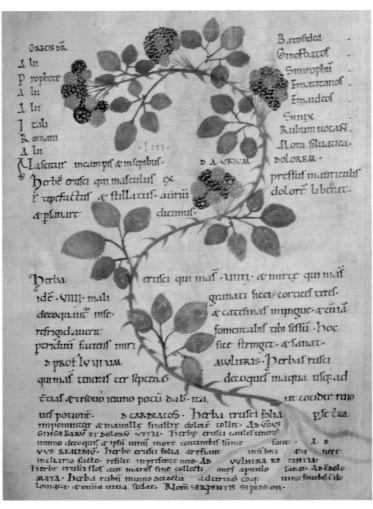

Plate 10 Brambles and blackberries shown in Psuedo-Apuleius, Dioscorides, *Herbals*; *De virtutibus bestium in arte medicinae*, English, late eleventh century.

Source: The Bodleian Library, University of Oxford, MS. Bodl. 130, fol. 26r

8

On Plants

For medieval society, the economic and cultural importance of its animals was easily matched by its plants. This broad category encompassing trees, cereal crops, vegetables, fruits, herbs, grasses and flowers supplied the period with the majority of its food and drink, medicines, fuels and building materials, and made further contributions in areas of life as diverse as clothing and aesthetics. As with animals, the treatment of this subject in the surviving literature takes a number of different forms. It is possible to contrast, for instance, the pragmatic reports of crop yields in manorial accounts with the symbolic values ascribed to various plants by the poets and astrologers (Voigts, 2008), or discussion of flora among the natural philosophers and theologians and those found in scientific treatises or folklore such as the Anglo-Saxon charm used to ensure bounty from unfruitful land (Rodrigues, 1993: 131–5). Ironically, for a natural scientific study that was initially influenced more by popular tradition than the received wisdom of the philosophers, it was in the field of botany that the scholars of the middle ages made their greater strides towards modern classification and definition.

For those whose livelihood and well-being depended on plants, and these were the majority, nothing was of greater import than how these might be successfully grown (see below for the importance of their identification also). Agronomic texts often dealt at great length with the subject, providing practical advice regarding the preparation of seed-beds, the timing of planting, and aftercare. The Latin west inherited its basic agricultural principles from a small number of Roman writers, among whom Cato, Varro and Columella were pre-eminent. Their thoughts together with others were collected, synthesised and ultimately transmitted to the middle ages in three key works: Pliny's first-century *Naturalis historia*; the fourth-century treatise of Palladius (Owen, 1807) the basis for Pietro di Crescenti's early fourteenth-century *Opus ruralium commodorum* (Plate 9); and a tenth-century Byzantine compilation, occasionally ascribed to Cassianus Bassus but in fact only incorporating the work of this seventh-century Greek writer, known as *Geoponika* (Dalby,

2011). Islamic agriculturalists made use of the same authorities but additionally they took much from a parallel and contemporary compilation, Ibn Wahshiyya's *Nabatean Agriculture*, a work which reported on the ancient practices of Mesopotamia.

Successful agriculture revolved around managing the elements and their qualities. When *Geoponika* counselled that lemon trees required plenty of moisture, that they enjoyed a southerly aspect, were harmed by the north wind, and that these trees should be covered with mats in winter, readers would have immediately understood how each of these practical steps was designed to ensure how an appropriate balance between hot and cold, wet and dry, might be maintained for the benefit of vigorous growth. In the hands of the later encyclopaedists this interplay between the elements and their properties was explicitly stated. On the process of germination, Bartholomew the Englishman wrote:

> . . . the grain that is put in the earth must first be provided with the moisture of water and air, which is spread and enlarged by the natural heat that [the grain] encloses. And by the last workings of the heat, the moisture is eliminated, leading the more crude and earthy parts [of the grain] downwards to the earth: these parts the earth takes within itself, and renews and curdles them by its own heat, turning them into a kind of root by mixing the moist and the dry: and that moisture working within the root, draws to itself [wet] humour because of its likeness as well as by the virtue of heat that it also contains.
>
> (Seymour *et al.*, 1975: 140–1)

People would have appreciated too why *Geoponika* insisted that lemon trees should be planted between the autumn and vernal equinoxes. Conceptually nature was unable to do two incompatible things at once. Since it was manifestly clear that from spring through to summer nature nourished the upper parts of plants – hence leaves, buds, flowers and fruits – so it followed that it could not also be working on the roots during this half of the year. Consequently, the visible dormancy of the same trees during autumn and winter proved that it was then that nature concentrated its efforts on encouraging root growth. To give a sapling tree the best chance of establishing itself, then, it should be planted at the moment when its root system would be given most opportunity.

Standing alongside these two concepts was the need to harness, or at least work with and not contrary to, the power of the moon. When the eleventh-century Spanish Moslem Ibn al-'Awwām, deferring to earlier sources in his highly influential *Kitāb al-Filāha*, insisted that garlic should only be sown during a waning moon, the literate (and almost certainly the non-literate) medieval farmer would have appreciated that this was because during this lunar phase water was being drawn deeper down into the soil and would thus provide sustenance for root crops and bulbs (Clément-Mullet, 2000: 663). A waning moon was also good for those plants whose edible seeds grew within the fruit itself, again because of the centripetal forces that it set in motion. Contrariwise, at the new moon and during its waxing, water was instead drawn up and out of the soil making this a prime time to plant crops whose seeds grew outside the fruit or crops that grew above ground. The longevity of these ideas is reflected in a fifteenth-century Spanish planting scheme, the *Capitols singulars deles llauors que deuras sembrar* (*Individual Chapters on what Seeds to Sow*), based on the months and phases of the moon:

> March: Melons, cucumber, gourds, oats, sorghum, onions, and green beans can be sown in the waning moon. Cabbage seed and radishes in the old moon. Green beans and sorghum and spelt can be sown in the new moon. Graft fig trees and other trees in waning moon [because sap was forced back into the core of the tree at this period] . . .
>
> November: Trees that lose their foliage can and should be transplanted in this month. Rose bushes, sage, rue, walnuts and almonds can now be transplanted in waning moon. Barley, beans and rye in new moon. Trees that keep their foliage, orange trees, lemon trees, bay-laurel, olive and similar trees transplant in waxing moon close to full. Garlic and lettuce in waning moon.
>
> (Capuano, 1998: 31)

Based on what was visible and easily proven empirically, these three simple tenets of farming – consideration for the actions of the elements, the sun, and the moon – must surely have been widely accepted across all the medieval social orders. Aspects of Walter of Henley's later thirteenth-century agricultural treatise *Husbandry* would have been incomprehensible otherwise. This was written for reeves, estate managers who were often members of the local peasantry elected to the office at the manorial court by their peers, men who may only have had a limited education. When Walter advised them that animal dung should be mixed with soil if it was to be spread in summer on gravelly ground because '[t]he time of summer is hot, and the gravel is hot also, and the dung is hot. And when these three heat do meet together, by their great heat they vex and burn', he was able to do so only because these farmers must already have understood just how unhealthy such a union of these elemental qualities would have been (Oschinsky, 1971: 327). Walter also identified that if incorrectly applied, the benefits of manure might also be lost and in so doing he again drew on ideas similar to Bartholomew the Englishman surrounding the movement of elements through the soil. He stated that if manure was ploughed in too deeply its value would be lost, 'for dung wastes downwards', presumably because its major components were earthy and watery in nature. Consistent with this view was a second observation, 'Know you for sure that marl lasts longer than dung, because dung wastes downwards and marl expends itself upwards'; thus when ploughed under the heat of the marl was thought to rise through the soil horizons.

Agronomists wrote practical guides not theoretical textbooks. What mattered to them was how a plant might be grown, not how it grew. On the question of plant growth, they were clearly influenced in what they wrote by the prevailing views of natural philosophy; but in their hands rather complex concepts were greatly reduced and simplified, leaving only those elements which farmers might themselves modify through particular interventions. For once, those who tackled the inner workings of plants could not fall back on a work of Aristotle even if they thought they could. The main text the west possessed was *De plantis*, translated from the Arabic into Latin by Alfred of Sareshel *c.* 1180–1190 (Otte, 1972, 1976). While thought to have been written by the great philosopher himself, in reality it was probably the work of the first-century BC Greek writer Nicolas of Damascus. It was this text which Albertus Magnus would paraphrase and expand in the late thirteenth century as *De vegetabilibus* (*On Vegetables*; Reeds, 1980; Stannard, 1980).

De plantis comprised two books. The first dealt with the life of plants, their various attributes, and their diversity. Naturally for a book written in the Aristotelian mould, it focused on distinguishing plants from minerals and animals in the *scala naturae*. They differed from the latter in their lack of voluntary movement, their particular behaviours – plants unlike animals did not sleep for instance – and their physical forms. But the most important defining feature was that they possessed a vegetative soul – which gave them their nutritive, augmentative and generative functions which minerals did not have – but had no sensible soul of the kind possessed by animals. The second book dealt with plant anatomy and physiology covering the role of the four elements in constituting the material substance of plants, how particular environments helped to determine the shape and form of plants, the growing process itself, the form and function of certain parts of particular plants, and natural processes such as defoliation and the ripening of fruits.

Because he found the work to be rather inadequate for accounting for the observable diversity of plants, Albertus Magnus rearranged *De plantis* adding a further three explanatory books before concluding with a descriptive list of plants. The first two of these books dealt with plant **morphology** (form and shape). Here Albertus treated sequentially the various parts of plants which they had in common – roots, stems, pith, bark, etc. – before discussing leaves and flowers. The second focused on seeds and fruit. In what would become book five of *De vegetabilibus*, Albertus turned to plant physiology (functioning)

Morphology: The form and shape of an object or living thing.

and in particular how plants grew and regenerated, from what they were made, before finally turning to why they should exhibit such variety in terms of their substance, powers and effects. For Albertus, plants required a life-giving heat emanating from the celestial bodies to grow, together with an ambient heat deriving from the particular location in which the plant grew, and the innate heat found within the seed. Additionally plants required three moistures, the first found within the seed itself, the second deriving from the earth in which the seed was planted, and the third the nutritious moisture from dew and rain. All these heats and moistures were then tempered by the cooling and drying effects of the air which surrounded the plant.

The material substance of plants depended on the appropriate mix of elements, the presence of the vegetative soul, the necessary quantity of matter, and the adoption of an appropriate form. A simple obovate leaf like that of privet, for example, was formed when watery vapour acted on the emerging leaf as it left the stem. This initially allowed the leaf to spread out, giving it its wide base. But an insufficient quantity of matter in the leaf meant that it was quickly constricted in its growth. It continued to be pushed out from the stem through the action of heat and thus narrowed to a sharp point. The poor combination of watery vapour with dry earthy matter produced the veins of the leaf. Variations of leaf shape could then be explained by the interaction of the matter and the elemental qualities they contained. For instance, wherever a vein met the edge of a leaf, the heat in the fluid it carried would be forced back towards the centre, producing serrated leaf shapes. Smooth, circular leaves such as those of the water lily resulted either from an abundance of watery vapour which allowed them to expand in all directions equally, or wherever the leaf contained an appropriate mix of earth and water that might cancel out any drying effect that would allow a sharp tip to protrude (Reeds, 1980).

For Arabic scholarship, from whence they transferred into Judaic natural philosophy, it was the non-Aristotelian ideas of the Brethren of Purity which did more to shape botanical understanding than any other natural philosophy (Zonta, 1996). The Brethren recognised seven creative forces operating in plants. An attractive force absorbed moisture and fine earthy particles into the roots of the plant. From here a fermenting force converted this mix of earth and water into a sap allowing its absorption into the root. Then a nutritive force moved this sap to those parts of the plant where it was needed allowing it to establish its core skeleton. Sap not used in this process was then sucked into buds and sprouts by an attractive force and held there under the power of a retaining force. A fermenting force boiled this sap for a second time, changing its composition and allowing it further to assimilate in all parts of the plant. The process repeated itself once more, until after a third fermentation the now refined sap was able to produce flowers, seeds and fruits. Completing the life cycle the plant was able to reproduce through the action of a reproductive force, and able to reject unwanted matter (such as resin) through the work of the expelling force (Bodenheimer, 1953: 43–4).

Particular characteristics of plants were in large part explained by environmental factors by the philosophers. According to Gershon ben Shlomah, exposure to warm and dry southerly winds would remove moisture from plants making them lean. Furthermore, whatever natural warmth they contained was superseded by the external heat making these plants cold and weak, dry and hard. Similarly, warm wet easterlies resulted in very moist fruits but generally thin and smooth plants as the moisture was driven off and dried from the outside (Bodenheimer, 1953: 134). Ambient temperatures in different regions also affected the kinds of plants that might grow. Hot and dry spices such as pepper and cinnamon only grew in the second clime (see Chapter 5) because it was perennially hot and dry. Sugar-cane whose sweetness signalled that it was neither hot nor cold grew in the more temperate fourth clime:

> In France which is close to the sixth climate, no southern ('warm') fruits, such as figs, olives or pomegranates will grow. This district is too cold to develop these fruits, while grapes grow there, as they possess a natural warmth which the cold of the district cannot overcome.
>
> But in England, which belongs to the seventh climate, the cold is so strong that even grapes cannot grow there, not to speak of figs, olives or mulberries.
>
> (Bodenheimer, 1953: 136)

These were grand overarching schemes with global connotations but scholars were faced with explaining very localised differences too. How could two plants, for instance, growing next to each other vary in their complexions when they drew their material substance from the same ground? For Adelard of Bath, following Plato, this was because it was not from the earth *per se* but from its earthiness (that composite mix of the elements in which earth predominated but where water, air and fire were also present) that they took their nature. Thus hot plants were able to extract more of the hotter parts they required while those that were cold did the opposite (Burnett, 1998: 95–7). For Albertus Magnus, even miniscule offsets in location ensured that the angle of the rays emitted by the celestial bodies from which all things gained their virtues differed from plant to plant giving them their unique properties [**Doc. 28**]. The complexion of plants mattered, of course, because it was from these that they derived their medicinal uses and it was from the pharmaceutical tradition that the botanical treatises known as herbals developed.

Herbals, together with bestiaries and lapidaries, comprised the trinity of medieval natural science literature and like their animal and mineral equivalents they owed much to Classical precedents. They took several forms, either stand-alone manuscripts or substantial sections in encyclopaedias and medical texts, and might be presented in both prose and verse. Of the archetypes the most heavily used, by Christian, Jew and Moslem alike, was Dioscorides' mid-first-century text *De materia medica*. Presenting the medical qualities of around five hundred plants, almost all writers dealing with matters medical and botanical from the beginning of the eleventh century down to the end of the fourteenth century borrowed something from this source. Available in Latin from the sixth century Dioscorides ordered his discussion according to a basic **taxonomy** – aromatics, trees, cereals, vegetables, roots, herbs, vines, etc. From around 1100, however, this was superseded by what became known as *Dioscorides' alphabeticus* (*Alphabetical Dioscorides*), an arrangement which lent itself to the preferred treatment of the later encyclopaedists (Hunt, 1989). What information that Dioscorides' entries provide regarding plant attributes had to be gleaned through passing reference. Thus the fronds of fennel are mentioned only in relation to a decoction good for inflamed kidneys and disorders of the bladder that could be made from them. Its roots were found to be helpful in dealing with dog bites; the juice from its bruised stalks and leaves aided ailments of the eye; and its green seeds and the gum which it released during flowering could also be used to restore sight (Osbaldeston, 2000: 456–9). But essentially the text lacked the kinds of description that would allow field identification.

Taxonomy: Systematic classification of animals, plants, etc.

Alongside Dioscorides, medieval writers could refer to Pliny's botanical books in his *Naturalis historia*. Pliny's importance was two-fold: first, it was through his work that the middle ages accessed the precocious botanical investigations of Aristotle's student, Theophrastus, whose *De historia plantarum* and *De causis plantarum* were only finally translated into Latin in the fifteenth century; second, and unlike other areas covered in his great compendium of knowledge, in the field of botany Pliny made a number of original contributions. His description of the Madonna Lily or Great White Convolvulus, for example, is the first to mention a plant stamen (Rackham, 1951: 177) and the very precise details regarding the formation and coloration of its leaves appear to suggest that he took his observations directly from nature (Stannard, 1965). Not all entries contained such a level of precision but most offered additional information not found in Dioscorides. His entry for fennel (which we shall use as our exemplar) distinguishes between the cultivated and wild varieties, the latter having a larger leaf and more acrid taste than its domestic counterpart as well as a thicker stem and white root, and a variant with a narrower leaf and seeds like coriander (Rackham, 1951: 149–53). Further medicinal uses were enumerated: in various preparations fennel would alleviate the feeling of nausea, eradicate 'worms' found in the ears, could be used to cure tumours, purge the kidneys, rectify irregularities with menstrual flow, and remove stones (bladder, kidney?); it was furthermore a diuretic, an aphrodisiac, and a cure for impotence, diarrhoea, dropsy (accumulations of watery fluids) and venomous bites. It was Pliny who was also the source of what would become a common motif in later treatments of this plant, linking its abilities to cure problems with human eyesight with the belief that snakes perennially sought out this herb after hibernation to help them shed their skins and sharpen their vision.

The third foundational text for later herbalists was the fourth-century *Herbarius Apulei Platonici* or Pseudo-Apuleius. This medical text – ostensibly derived from Pliny and Dioscorides – provided etymologies of plant names and specific preparations for certain ailments. Although it did not treat as many plants as its antecedents, nor in so much detail, its brevity ensured its popularity amongst later generations just as Solinus' epitome of Pliny's *Naturalis historia* had done. Psuedo-Apuleius would be translated into Old English by the mid-eleventh century, the text by this stage accompanied by detailed illustrations of individual plants making up for the obvious descriptive lacunae in the accompanying text (Plate 10). These naturalistic illustrations, easily allowing precise identification of particular plant species, stand in great contrast to the rather stylised way that animals continued to be shown at the same period (see Chapter 7) and reflect how those interested in botany were quicker to turn to more scientific practices of observation and presentation. This should come as no surprise, of course, since distinguishing between edible and poisonous plants was literally a matter of life or death.

Following in this tradition were two important verse herbals, the earliest composed by the Benedictine monk Walahfrid Strabo and known as *Hortulus* or 'Little Garden'. Walahfrid's poem lacks botanical detail: fennel is praised for its sweet smell and flavour and singled out for its utility to improve poor vision, to deal with boils in the stomach, to loosen the bowels, and for asthma and croup (Dutton, 1999: 380). Its charm instead lies in its descriptions of the travails of the gardener with which many of his contemporaries must have empathised. It stands out for its realism and honest earthiness, best expressed in the monk's personal battle with nettles that had grown over the winter:

> Then the little courtyard that adjoins my front door
> And eastward extends its diminutive floor,
> Became covered with nettles that spread and grew high,
> And reared up their venomous stings to the sky.
> What was I to do? Their roots formed a thick mat
> Just like what the plow-boys so cleverly plait

For their stables of osiers twined in a knot
To protect horses' hooves from the damp and the rot.
Well, away with delay! Armed with mattock and rake,
I attack the caked earth. From each dull clot I break
The wild nettles, expose many worms to the day
And scatter the molehills that get in my way.

(Dutton, 1999: 376)

The second verse herbal enjoyed more fame and was drawn upon more freely by those that followed than Walahfrid's elegy to the garden plot. It, and not Walahfrid, was still being cited by Vincent of Beauvais in the mid-thirteenth century. This was the anonymous *Macer floridus* or *De viribus herbarum* (*On the Power of Herbs*), thought to have been composed by a French layman Odo of Meung living in the region of the Loire in the first part of the eleventh century (Grant, 1974a: 779–80). Dealing with 77 plants it added new medicinal applications to those detailed by earlier sources – fennel, for instance, could work if it was simply placed over the chest as well as being taken by a decoction – and importantly specifies the complexion of each plant. Dioscorides, Pliny and Pseudo-Apuleius had been silent on this matter. Thus Macer states that fennel was hot and dry in the second degree. Such elemental qualities would become the major obsession for medieval herbalists.

The framework for plant complexion was established by Galen. The influence of his *Pantegni*, available in the Islamic world through Israeli ben Solomon's early tenth-century translation, is visible in the early Arabic treatments of plants [Doc. 14]. For Galen, fennel was one of the four hot herbs – the others celery, parsley and asparagus – and was said to be hot in the second degree and dry in the first. The tenth-century philosopher, physician and alchemist al-Razi, under the influence of Galenic texts, simply stated that fennel was hot. While a few generations later, Avicenna distinguished between wild fennel, hot and dry in the third degree, and the cultivated variety only in the second. European writers only began to include such details in the wake of the translation movement. Thereafter commentators remained in agreement that fennel was more hot than cold, more dry than moist, but did not necessarily agree precisely in terms of their strength: in Mattheaus Platearius' *De medicines simplicibus*, known by its opening line as *Circa instans*, written under the influence of the medical school at Salerno in the mid-twelfth century, fennel was hot and dry in the second degree; for the encyclopaedist Bartholomew the Englishman it was the same; such was the case too in the great mid-thirteenth-century medical handbook *Tacuinum Sanitatis*, a Latin translation of an earlier Islamic text attributed to Ibn Butlan, although here it was further noted that it might be warm in the third degree and dry in the second.

A second principle followed by herbalists was the doctrine of 'signatures' stating that a plant's resemblance to either an afflicted part of the body or to that thing which had caused an ailment might signal its use as an antidote. Thus the snake-like shape of the petals of Dragon Arum marked it out as a cure for venomous bites (Stannard, 1980: 373). But the most celebrated example was the anthropomorphic root of the mandrake (Plate 7):

> Whoever suffers some infirmity in their head should eat from the top of this plant, in whatever way he wishes. If he suffers in the neck, he should eat from its neck; if in the back, from its back; if in the arm, from its arm; if in the hand, from its hand; if in the knee, from its knee; if in the foot, he should eat from its foot. In whatever part he is ailing, he should eat from the similar part of this image, and he will be better. The male form of this plant is stronger medicine than the female, since a man is stronger than a woman.
>
> (Throop, 1998: 34)

Occasionally included in bestiaries as well as herbals (e.g. Meyer, 1872; Wright, 1841), the elaborate rituals designed to extract the mandrake safely without hearing its deathly shrieks when pulled from the ground were repeated down through the medieval centuries.

What is apparent is that the transmission of botanical information was in general remarkably consistent and stable throughout the period. One exception was the treatment of plants in Hildegard of Bingen's *Physica*. For her fennel had a mild heat but was neither hot nor cold (Throop, 1998: 39–41) in contradistinction with other authorities. And where they had deemed it difficult to stomach, she claimed that it would aid digestion. It would help those who could not sleep, those with runny noses, and women in childbirth, and on the principles of opposites and humoural balance would be particularly useful in fighting melancholy. Such ideas, however, leave her somewhat out on a limb. Another person not to follow precedent slavishly – but in ways quite different to Hildegard – was Albertus Magnus, whose herbal, containing entries for around four hundred plants and forming books six and seven of *De vegetabilibus*, provided much richer descriptions of the plants themselves than anything that had gone before:

> Fennel is a seed having very spread leaves, as if they were threads, and the stem and major branches are hollow like lovage, and it has a yellow flower, and its crown disperses seeds like dill and elder. And there are many types, namely wild and cultivated: and some have seeds like coriander, some others have broad oblong seeds and not round.

In the vanguard of a wider movement taken forward by Italian scholars like Rufinus, who completed his herbal based on direct observation of plants in their natural habitat soon after 1287, and his contemporary Bathelemy Mini of Siena, who used the same methodology in his *Tractatus de herbis* (*Treatise on Herbs*), Albertus and these herbalists had begun, by the end of the thirteenth century, to establish the format of the modern scientific *flora*.

Culturally, plants left their mark too. They were essential components for those writing in the Classical tradition of the *locus amoenus* ('pleasant place'). Idealised descriptions of monastic landscapes which sought to depict these as earthy paradises invariably contained evidence of their natural fertility and botanical riches as, for instance, Glastonbury:

> The island of apples [Avalon], which is called fortunate, is truly named, for it brings forth all things of its own accord. It needs no farmers to till the fields, and there is no cultivation save that which nature provides. It freely brings forth fertile stalks and grapes, and apples born of precious seed in its forests. The earth nourishes all things, as bounteous as tended land; one lives there a hundred years or more. This was the new Jerusalem, the faith's refinement, a holy hill, celebrated as the ladder of heaven. He scarcely pays the penalties of hell who lies buried there.
>
> (Clarke, 2006: 72–3)

For writers of the medieval romances, gardens offered a range of powerful topoi – of nature tamed; backdrops for lovers' trysts with all their incumbent (and dangerous) sensual pleasures – and plants an encyclopaedia of symbolism. If it is doubted that plants shaped medieval society, then the starring role of one special flower in one of the age's most popular secular tales, the thirteenth-century *Roman de la Rose* (Kay, 1995), and the recurrent images of the tree of life and the vine as religious motifs, must surely put paid to such ideas.

Further reading

An easy and beautifully illustrated introduction is provided by Fisher, *The Medieval Flower Book*. The medicinal uses of plants are treated in Van Ardsall, *Medieval Herbal Remedies: The Old English Herbarium and Anglo-Saxon Medicine* and contributions to Dendle and Touwaide, *Health and Healing from the Medieval Garden*. Albertus Magnus' botanical studies are covered in Weisheipl, *Albertus Magnus and the Sciences*. Useful information is also included in Hunt, *Plant Names of Medieval England*; Reeds, *Botany in Medieval and Renaissance Universities*; and Biggam, *From Earth to Art*.

9

On Minerals

T he mineral and metal resources of Europe were known and celebrated from an early date. Bede's description of Britain lists copper, iron, lead and silver among its metals and amber and jet among its semi-precious stones (Colgrave and Mynors, 1992). Rabbi Chisdai Abu-Yusuf made much of the silver, gold, copper, iron, tin, sulphur, porphyry, marbles and crystal of Al-Andalus (Adler, 1987: 26). Arab geographers also reported on the resources in other parts of the Islamic world too. Al-Muqaddasī's description of Syria noted iron mines around Beirut and red sandstones near Aleppo; in Palestine quarries of white stone and marble; in the region of Ghawr sulphur mines; and the recovery of salt from the Dead Sea (Collins, 2001: 154). Such accounts appear to imply relatively large-scale exploitation by the late tenth century. Exploitation of mineral and metal resources in Europe at this period tended to be more local in extent and restricted to the working of shallow or exposed deposits. The discovery of rich silver-bearing ores, first at Goslar in the Harz mountains of Lower Saxony in the mid-tenth century, and more importantly those at Frieberg in the eastern Erzgebirge during the twelfth century, however, prompted a boom in mining and prospection. By the end of the medieval period, mineral and metal extraction was being undertaken on an industrial scale often from deep mines. Gold was found and extracted from veins in the Alps and the Balkans. Further discoveries of silver were made in the Carpathian mountains, in Alsace, the Spanish Meseta, and south-west England. Important deposits of lead and zinc were found in the Ardennes, and iron in the Low Countries and northern Italy, and the long tradition of tin production in England was revitalised (Riddle and Mulholland, 1980; Long, 1999; Radkau, 2002).

Explanations for the physical formation of stones, minerals and metals are almost entirely absent among European writings before the thirteenth century. One slightly tangential exception was salt. Why sea water should be salty intrigued those interested in natural phenomena. Both Isidore and Bede posited, following Pliny the Elder, that under the evaporating action of the sun, water became denser and more bitter (Fontaine, 1960: 308; Kendall and Wallis, 2010: 96). Adelard of Bath extended this idea. Using the analogy of extracting salt from a pan of brine over a fire, he explained that it was during the passage of the oceans through the torrid equatorial zone that most of this evaporation occurred, whilst seasonal differences in the salinity of seawaters resulted from the subsequent localised effects of the sun in different parts of the world (Burnett, 1998: 185–7). Rarely was the origin of this salt sought, but this critical issue was dealt with by William of Conches who stated that as water penetrated through soils and rocks it picked up certain of their qualities. Thus water passing through sandy and stony ground would become sweet, water passing through sulphurous, chalky or metallic soils would become bitter, and that which percolated through salty ground, saline (Ronca and Curr, 1997: 113–14).

When it came to metals, one of the very few to offer a theoretical explanation was Hildegard of Bingen. Writing in Germany only a generation after the discoveries at Frieberg, it is difficult to ignore the probability that it was the mining activities themselves which had rekindled interest in formation processes. A product of its time, Hildegard's explanation found in *Physica* drew heavily on the workings of the elements:

> . . . where the fiery power that flows in water penetrated the earth, the fire of the water transformed the earth into gold. Where the purity of the flooding water penetrated the earth, that purity transformed itself and the earth which it suffused into silver. Where the fluctuation of the water penetrated the earth, moved by the wind, it and the earth it transfused were changed into steel and iron . . .
>
> (Throop, 1998: 237)

Hildegard's account of the creation of precious stones, however, appears to have more in common with fable than natural philosophy [Doc. 19]. These, she stated, all originated in the east. Here mountain streams were boiled by the heat of the sun. When these occasionally burst their banks the waters were turned to sticky froth on contact with the surrounding rocks. Over the course of a few days this foam would harden and eventually dry. Variations in the length of daylight and temperature during this process gave each stone its particular colour and properties. Eventually these gems would fall from these rocks and embed themselves in the surrounding sands. When the rivers next flooded, these precious stones were washed out and carried around the world to the various locations where people were known to find them (Throop, 1998, 137–8).

The space left by the absence of empirical evidence, particularly with reference to gemstones, was more than filled by the medieval creative imagination.

These were variously said to originate in the four rivers emanating from Paradise so often shown on *mappae mundi*, in the streams of the mythical land of Cockaigne or in the gravelly sea of the land of Prester John (Lee, 1952). One of the more enduring stories concerned the challenges facing those looking to recover diamonds. In a tradition stretching back to the *Arabian Nights*, the sailors' tales compiled by Captain Buzurg spoke of a burning and inaccessible valley protected by snakes in Kashmir where they could be found. Unable to descend because of its many imminent dangers, men of low caste instead elicited the aid of vultures to retrieve the precious stones by throwing the butchered parts of lean sheep into this chasm. Occasionally diamonds would adhere to these joints. Carried off by the vultures, these men would follow the bird in the hope that diamonds would fall out during its flight (Freeman-Grenville, 1981: 75). The essential elements of this story would be repeated by Marco Polo nearly three centuries later although here it was said that the men would chase the birds away from their prize to recover the diamonds, or, if the meat had been consumed, they would follow the birds to their nests and recover the stones from their excreta (Komroff, 1982: 297–8). An alternative was provided by Sir John Mandeville, who claimed that diamonds grew in what appears to be an organic way on outcrops of crystal: 'They grow together, male and female, and feed on the dew of heaven and continue and breed, and they make children beneath them, which multiply and grow each year' (Tzanaki, 2003: 105).

Such stories entertained their medieval audience but for some at least they stretched credulity. Al-Birunī was one such doubter. In discussing rain stones in his major work on minerals he brought into question not just earlier authorities such as al-Razi and Ibn Zakariyya but also highlighted the gullibility as well as ingenuity of ordinary people. He described the powers of this stone to cause rain as 'imaginary'; he admonished other scholars for not checking their facts; he embarrassed individuals who had tried but failed to use the stone in his presence; and even suggested that one community had exaggerated the stone's properties in order to encourage others to remove them from their fields in order to improve their agricultural potential (Said, 1989: 188–90). What is certain is that the scholarly texts emanating from northern Europe during the first half of the middle ages, whilst easily differentiated from the literary tradition, nevertheless contained much that was exotic and magical too.

Most early medieval mineral and metal lore in the west derived from a narrow but eclectic set of Classical sources. One such was a first-century Greek text on the magical qualities of stones by an otherwise unknown, Damigero, adapted into Latin by the fifth century. But the most important was undoubtedly Pliny the Elder's treatment of the subject in books 33 to 37 of his *Naturalis historia* transmitted either directly or through either Solinus or book 16 of Isidore of Seville's *Etymologiae* (Barney *et al.*, 2006: 317–36). Typically each individual entry provided details of shape, colour, geographic occurrence, indications of their physical properties (hardness, flammability, etc.) and potential uses for apotropaic and medical purposes. The latter were dealt with in more depth in the last section of Dioscorides' *De materia medica*. Here brief descriptions were provided of colour variations, brittleness and malleability, and again where they could be found. But Dioscorides' main concern remained how earths, minerals and other chemical compounds should be prepared and against what ailments they proved most efficacious (Osbaldeston, 2000: 781–830). In combination these works spawned one branch of one of the most popular literary genres of the middle ages – the lapidary.

The most influential of lapidaries that drew upon these authorities was that compiled by Marbode, bishop of Rennes in the early twelfth century. Written in metrical form it was immediately popular and would become the basis for an enduring lapidary tradition in France and elsewhere down to the end of the medieval period. Entries for jasper and beryl are typical of the content and scope of the *Liber lapidum seu de gemmis* – what mattered was the stone's virtues and powers:

[Jasper] There are, they say, seventeen types of jasper. They say that there are many colours and they confirm that it is made in many places in the world. The best is that which is green and translucent: everyone agrees that this is the one which possesses the greatest virtues. Piously worn, it drives away fevers and water retention; placed next to a sleeping woman it protects her and helps during pregnancy. If blessed, it gives grace and power and it is believed chases away dangerous spirits. Its force is greater than that of silver.

... [Beryl] What gives beryl its sparkle is its hexagonal shape: were it not for this its shine would be dulled. Some maintain that the most eye-catching of these resemble oil that floats on water. This stone comes to us from the Indies. It is said that it promotes conjugal love and that it strengthens those who wear it. It burns, they say, the hand of those who hide it in the palm. Put in water this helps to cure eye disease and if one drinks it, it prevents burping and hiccups. It also soothes all ailments of the liver. Experts are of the opinion that there are nine types of this stone.

(Translated from Monat, 1996: 23, 31)

Other lapidarists took their cue not from Classical sources but from two lists of precious stones found in the Bible. Both were a regular subject for early biblical exegeses such as Augustine and Jerome. The first related to the description of Aaron's breastplate, the so-called 12 stones of the pectoral, found in Exodus 28:17–20:

> And you shall set in it four rows of stone. In the first row will be a sardius stone, and a topaz and an emerald; in the second a carbuncle, a sapphire and a jasper; in the third a ligurius, an agate and an amethyst; in the fourth a chrysolite, an onyx and a beryl.

It was more common, however, for lapidaries to use as their basis the 12 stones of the apocalypse or heavenly Jerusalem found in Revelation 21: 19–21:

> And the building of the wall thereof was of jasper stone: but the city itself pure gold like to clear glass. And the foundations of the wall were adorned with all manner of precious stones. The first foundation was of jasper; the second, sapphire; the third, a chalcedony; the fourth an emerald; the fifth, sardonyx; the sixth, sard; the seventh, chrysolite; the eighth, beryl; the ninth, a topaz; the tenth, a chrysoprase; the eleventh, a hyacinth; the twelfth, an amethyst.

Their allegorical meaning was treated in works such as Bede's *Explanatio apocalypsis* (*Explanation of the Apocalypse*). The green of jasper stood for the 'unfading verdure of faith' and was capable of putting 'to flight vain fears', the pale light of chalcedony was symbolic of those who practised their faith modestly, and sard's ruddiness was emblematic of the glory of the martyrs (Marshall, 1878; Kitson, 1983). Using such images in this way, the Apocalyptic Lapidaries complemented the treatment of animals to be found in *Physiologus*. Indeed this work too had included certain stones among its beasts – the agate stone, pearl, adamant, Indian stone and magnet (Curley, 1979).

Just as bestiaries expanded upon *Physiologus*, so lapidaries quickly became enlarged. Marbode's work contained descriptions of 60 precious stones, and the earliest surviving Old English lapidary written around the same time appended brief entries for 10 stones to those of the Apocryphal dozen (Evans and Serjeantson, 1933: 13–15). In the hands of later encyclopaedists these numbers grew ever greater as they combined the two parallel traditions. Bartholomew the Englishman included descriptions of 103 stones and metals arranged alphabetically in the tenth book of his *magnum opus* (Seymour *et al.*, 1975: 825–81). The wealth of sources that mid-thirteenth-century compilers could draw upon is graphically illustrated in book eight of Vincent of Beauvais' *Speculum naturale*. Here the three great Roman works – Pliny's natural history, Solinus' wonders and Dioscorides' medical manual – shared space with Arnold of Saxony's *De finibus rerum* (*The Purposes of Things*), Bartholomew the Englishman's *De proprietatibus rerum*, Thomas of Cantimpré's *De natura rerum* and an unspecified lapidary. Tellingly, Vincent also included references to the works of Aristotle and Avicenna (Vincent of Beauvais, 1494: 82–91). It was through these two authorities, and a third work by Theophrastus entitled *De lapidibus* (*On Stones*; Eichholz, 1965), that crucial advances came to be made by European scholars regarding the origins of stones and metals.

Aristotle, of course, had long been available in the Arabic world and his influence can be detected in almost everything that was written on stones and metals in this cultural and religious milieu. Aristotle's theory on the formation of stones and metals was laid out in books three and four of his *Meteorologia* (*Meteorology*; Lee, 1952: 287–9; 318–25). Two principles applied. The first was the action of two 'exhalations' or vapours, one wet and one dry, generated by the energy of the sun. Underground and through interaction with the earth these became compressed to produce either stone from dry vapour or metals from wet. The second centred on the dual processes of liquefaction and solidification driven by exposure to heat or cold. Compounds of earth and water were particularly susceptible to these forces. When heat drew out the moisture these would become more densely packed. Cold might equally create something more solid by driving off heat and with it evaporated moisture. Aristotle differentiated between a material cause – proportions of water and earth present in a particular body – and an efficient cause, the application of heat and cold. The ratio of earth to water in combination with full or partial removal of moisture by heat and cold accounted for the great variety of stones and metals. In the latter water continued to predominate, in the former earth.

The earliest extant Islamic systematisation of the creation of metals and stones is found in epistle 19 of the Brethren of Purity dating to the tenth century (Levey, 1967). Elements of Aristotelian thought can be clearly identified. But the thoughts of the Brethren were more influenced by the idea, first developed by the eighth-century alchemist Jaber ben Hayyān (known in the west as Geber to whom many hundreds of alchemical texts were later ascribed), that all metals were made from compounds of mercury and sulphur. Thus, various moistures in earth buried in caverns, they argued, were dissolved by vapours caused by heat. The moistures evaporated, rising to the top of caves where they cooled and coagulated, became viscous and ran down the sides of the cave where they mixed with dust and clay. This liquid amalgam then collected at the bottom of the cave where it was simmered by heat to become purified, heavy and thick. This produced mercury. Where additionally oily and airy particles became incorporated into the mix, the result was sulphur.

What subsequently happened was dependent on a number of external and internal factors. Where sulphur dried out the mercury through the action of heat so that no further cold or dryness was gathered, this produced gold. If affected by cold after they had united this gave silver or by dryness then red copper. Fluctuations in temperature and initial composition before union produced other things. Cold resulted in hardening to tin-lead. If they met cold before they were refined and dust was present in large quantities this produced black iron. If there was more mercury than sulphur and less heat this would create black lead, but if heat was excessive the result was antimony. Marrying Aristotle and ben Hayyān, they concluded:

> . . . the mineral obtained depends on the relative quantities and the varied conditions, whether sulphur or mercury is in excess or is light, or the heat is too strong or weak, or the minerals become cold before maturation, or they lose their proper weights. This is true of all minerals [i.e. metals] which may be melted.
>
> (Levey, 1967: 15–19)

The origins of stony materials such as crystal, hyacinth, chrysolite and carnelian were thought to be different. These the Brethren considered to derive from rainwater and sediment (although no dust and clay in these instances) that could not escape from the cave due to its relative purity, weight and viscosity and which under heat was hardened into stone. Earthy minerals also began as mixes of water and earth that were subsequently fused by heat. If the earth contained saltpetre or salt it produced natron (a kind of soda ash) and alum (probably a kind of iron sulphate); if acidic, it produced green and yellow glass and calcite, and if the water passed through pebbles and sand it would create gypsum. Environmental conditions thus played an important part in what would be created as did the time it took for the process to reach full maturity. Sulphurs, salts, alums and vitriols (metal sulphates) were produced in those places where dust, clay or salt predominated and were produced quickly in less than a year. In contrast gold, silver, copper and iron were usually formed within cavities in mountains and inside other rocks and took many years to complete. Hyacinth, chrysolite, opal, onyx, ruby, turquoise and diamond, produced under the same conditions, took many decades or even centuries to be created. Differences of colour stemmed from the influence of the planets: golds and yellows were solar in origin, whites lunar. This spectrum would later be extended: blacks ascribed to Saturn, reds to Mars, greens to Jupiter, and blues to Venus.

Writing a century later Avicenna's position on the formation of stones was very broadly Aristotelian in conception (Holmyard and Mandeville, 1974). Stones, he stated, were created either through the hardening of clays under the influence of the sun (clays that were naturally sticky were more likely to undergo conversion to solid stone than those that were dry which would simply crumble) or through the congelation of water in interaction with a mineralising or earthy force. Aqueous stone either formed from water droplets (here Avicenna was presumably thinking of the formation of stalagmites and stalactites or something similar) or through the petrifaction of deposits adhering to river beds. Both of these metamorphoses from liquid to solid were prompted by the earthy drying force found in the ground into which the water came into contact or again through the influence of heat. Just as heating and drying lay behind the formation of stones, cold and moisture were potential corrosive powers that could lead to their disintegration and erosion.

Towards the end of his life, al-Birunī provided the Islamic world with its most extensive treatment of stones, minerals and metals, *The Sum of Knowledge about Precious Stones*. He too followed the theory of the vapours and advocated the union of mercury and sulphur as the cause of metals. Together Aristotle, often through the filter of Averroes, ben-Hayyān, the Brethren of Purity, Avicenna, and al-Birunī provided the middle ages with its most coherent account for the natural process implicated in the formation of stones and metals. Their impact on thinking beyond the Arabic world is reflected in the total reliance that Gershon ben Shlomah placed upon their works in his encyclopaedia. And they were also heavily drawn upon when the first original work on mineralogy in the Latin west, Albertus Magnus' *De mineralibus* (*On Minerals*) was written some time before 1280 (Wyckoff, 1967). On stones Albertus followed the usual authorities, but in the field of metallurgy his contribution was more original because of his methodology. In the first instance, Albertus visited the mines in the Erzgebirge and examined the metal-bearing veins at close quarters [**Doc. 29**]. By using miners' testimony alongside what by the later thirteenth century was a vast corpus of alchemical literature, he produced a work that went beyond natural philosophy and anticipated the scientific method (Riddle and Mulholland, 1980).

But it was an earlier work that was truly remarkable for its precocity and which stands out as one of the greatest contributions to the advancement of the natural sciences made during this middle ages. If Avicenna had followed Aristotle on the formation of stones, what he said about large-scale geological processes belonged to him alone. His theory of superimposition and sedimentation, when linked to explanations for uplift – the two processes which he rightly identified as responsible for why fossils should be found in strata high up mountains – pre-empts the final acceptance of these principles in the west by approximately eight hundred years:

> It is possible that each time the land was exposed by the ebbing of the sea a layer was left, since we see that some mountains appear to have been piled up layer by layer, and it is therefore likely that the clay from which they were formed was itself at one time arranged in layers. One layer was formed first, then, at a different period, a further layer was formed and piled [upon the first, and so on]. Over each layer there spread a substance of different material, which formed a partition between it and the next

layer; but when petrification took place something occurred to the partition which caused it to break up and disintegrate between the layers.

As to the bottom of the sea, its clay is either sedimentary or primaeval, the latter not being sedimentary. It is probable that the sedimentary clay was formed by the disintegration of the strata of mountains.'

(Holmyard and Mandeville, 1974: 620)

Pedology: The science of soils.

In the area of **pedology** other real and substantive advances were made during the middle ages. Agronomists of antiquity had used a very restricted range of criteria to characterise soils. In essence they were interested in their elemental qualities – whether a particular soil was hot or cold, wet or dry. Agricultural activities such as fallowing, manuring and crop rotation were all designed to balance levels of temperature and humidity. Those soils that were naturally or through intervention in equilibrium were deemed good, those that remained in a state of imbalance were poor. Consequently soils were often described in terms of very simple oppositions: a soil might be heavy or light, smooth or lumpy, wet or dry. Medieval farming methods certainly continued to use this framework and it is the case that when medieval agronomists such as Walter of Henley or Pietro di Crescenti in the Latin west or Ibn Al-Awwam in Moslem Spain wrote about soils they did so under the influence of elemental theory (Oschinsky, 1971; Clément-Mullet, 2000). But more generally, the medieval sources also reveal a growing descriptive vocabulary. Over and above the classical criteria, additional emphasis was placed on new aspects of the soil – their colour, texture, taste, smell – determined through the use of all the human sensory powers. Thus soils were described as sandy, clayey, muddy, ashy and burnt; malleable, limp, greasy and slippy; fat, thick, compact, dense and porous; honest, sweet, fresh, sour and bitter (Bolens, 1975). These terms were born in the fields not in the folios of learned texts. They came from experience of the soil rather than the thoughts of earlier agronomists. Nor was it confined to a particular cultural context. It might be expected that farmers operating in more northern latitudes would find the Graeco-Roman agricultural corpus, transmitted to the middle ages through compilations such as *Geoponika*, wanting since this tended to deal exclusively with Mediterranean climes. But even in Moslem Spain this descriptive revolution was also played out.

All of this may seem rather inconsequential, a shift in terminological preference and nothing more. In fact what it reveals is deeply significant. It shows that those who were not bound to the conventions of the Classical canon were much freer to develop alternative methods of classification that had no precedent. If medieval scholarship was conventionally derivative, the same charge could not be ranged against the unread. It was beyond the written word that brand new ways of thinking about and conceptualising nature were developing during the middle ages. Farmers not scholars were the real innovative thinkers of the age. It was the anonymous masses who were as much responsible for ushering in the scientific age as the celebrated names whose works have been trawled for evidence of its beginnings. For it was out of this seemingly disorganised mass of distinguishing soil markers, as much as the work of Avicenna, that the detailed disaggregating scientific classifications of later ages would evolve.

Further reading

Accessible texts of English lapidaries can be found in Evans and Serjeantson, *English Mediaeval Lapidaries*. See also Riddle 'Marbode of Rennes' (1035–1123) 'De lapidibus'. On medieval geology Riddle and Mulholland, 'Albert on stones and minerals' provides an excellent way in to the subject; so too the introduction to Wyckoff, *Albertus Magnus, De Minerabilibus*. Said, *Al-Beruni's Book of Minerology* provides an Arabic perspective.

10

The Book of Nature

Whether real or imaginary, forensically dissected or just accepted for what it was, the natural world remained a source of wonderment and inspiration throughout the middle ages. It has been the purpose of this short text simply to begin to introduce how what was seen and experienced came to be rationalised, explained and understood. Inevitably many aspects of the natural world that worried or intrigued medieval observers (to judge by the regularity that they were discussed in texts) have either been passed over in silence or mentioned only fleetingly – comets and rainbows, for instance, or the existence of the Antipodes, human embryology, plague, the Nile crocodile, marine life, the mandrake, or the loadstone to name but a few. Questions with profound implications for how nature was thought to operate, posed by medieval scholars and for which they found answers, have simply been left unasked. If a hole were to be dug straight through the centre of the earth, what would happen to a stone that was dropped into this void, would it emerge on the other side? Why were humans not born with horns? Why do some animals chew cud whilst others do not? Why, when one can see from the dark into the light cannot one see from the light into the dark? What do stars eat if they are animate?

The medieval response to such questions will delight those that seek them out for their sophistication, ingenuity and apparent otherworldliness. They reveal just how different the medieval concept of nature and its workings was when set against modern benchmarks. Furthermore, they reveal how a small set of fundamental ideas, at times boiled down to the four elements – earth, water, air and fire – and their qualities – hot, cold, dry and moist – was able to provide the foundation for a coherent, all-encompassing and ultimately rational explanation for all physical and sensible phenomena. While this way of thinking serves to divide the modern world from the medieval, a disjuncture essentially established by the seventeenth century, critically it connected the middle ages to the culture and learning of Antiquity. Much has been made in this text of the debt that the medieval world owed to Graeco-Roman scholarship and natural philosophy. The influence of its major figures – Plato and Aristotle, Hippocrates and Galen, Pliny and Dioscorides – can be found on almost every page. Yet it is important to stress that medieval understandings of the natural world were neither borrowed unthinkingly nor accepted uncritically from the great authorities of the past. The middle ages was a far less credulous age than some might wish to suggest. Its scholars were prepared to question their authorities wherever these were found wanting, whether it concerned the structure of the cosmos or how weasels gave birth. Some, indeed, were explicit in their intention to correct the errors of previous ages. Medieval natural philosophy, then, and for all its outward appearances, was not simply a watered down version of Platonic and Aristotelian ideas – Antiquity-lite so to speak. It had its own identity, its own paradigms and its own stars as the Who's Who found at the start of this text reveals. The contributions of just some of those listed there have been covered in this text. Other important figures of the age, such as St Francis of Assisi or St Thomas Aquinas, really deserved to have been given much fuller treatment (e.g. Sorrell, 1998). But readers, it is to be hoped, will fill these gaps.

Giving the middle ages its new points of reference were the three great religions of the period – Judaism, Christianity and Islam. It was under their influence that medieval writings on nature gained their originality and their independence from slavish adherence to earlier ideas. For those who specifically studied the natural world, this demanded that its origins, essential qualities and operative forces needed to be rethought so that they might be aligned to and made consistent with theological teaching. One unintended consequence of these reconfigurations was that towards the end of the middle ages Jewish, Christian and Moslem scholars had begun to establish the technologies and precepts (direct observation, experimentation and hypothesis testing) that would ultimately form the basis of modern scientific methods in the seventeenth century.

Giving coherence to medieval natural science and philosophy was a powerful metaphor: nature as divine Creation and text, a book not just to be read but one that was required reading. All three religions could draw inspiration from their sacred writings. For Jews, the Old Testament books of Wisdom and Job provided their inspiration:

> For he has given me true knowledge of the things that exist: to know the structure of the world and the virtues of the elements; the beginning and ending and midst of times, the alternations of the solstices and the changes of the seasons, the revolutions of the year and the positions of the stars, the natures of living creatures and the rage of wild animals, the force of winds and the reasonings of men, the diversity of plants and the virtues of roots; all such things as are hidden, and not foreseen, I have learned.
>
> (Wisdom 7:17–21)

> But ask now the beasts, and they shall teach you; and the fowls of the air, and they shall tell you: Or speak to the earth, and it shall teach you: and the fishes of the sea shall declare to you. Who knows not in all these that the hand of the Lord has wrought this?
>
> (Job 12:7–9)

To these writings early Christian writers could also turn to the New Testament where they found in Paul's letter to the Romans:

> For since the creation of the world, God's invisible qualities – his eternal power and divine nature – have been clearly seen, being understood from what has been made, so that men are without excuse.
>
> (Romans 1:20)

For Moslems, the *Qur'an* was equally unequivocal [**Doc. 7**]; indeed so infused with natural imagery were the divine revelations received by Mohammed that it might be said that the *Qur'an* was in and of itself a Book of Nature.

The idea that the visible world held clues to the invisible, and that the latter if understood would reveal the essence of the formative force behind its creation was one that linked Platonist thought with Judeo-Christian and Islamic worldviews. The Book of Nature thus offered a means of partially resolving one of the greatest challenges that late antique and medieval theologically oriented thinkers faced: how to square the natural philosophies of Antiquity with their religious ideas. One of the first to take on this task was Philo (20 BC–AD 50) whose *De opficio mundi* (*On the Creation*) sought to fuse Platonic and Stoic philosophy together with Pythagorean numerology with Judaic worldviews (Marcus, 1987). The issue was also addressed head on by early Christian writers such as Origen (185–c. 254). In *Contra celsum* he tested the veracity of Christian positions by ranging pagan arguments against them and, by so doing, not only demonstrated the superior of the former over the latter, but also showed how hidden meanings might be extracted from the visible and physical forms of creation (Chadwick, 1980). Origen's work set the foundations for a Christian Book of Nature, an idea he expressed with more clarity in his commentaries on the Song of Songs (Lawson, 1957: 220). For the long-lived desert father St Anthony (c. 250?–c. 356–357?) the idea was all encompassing: 'My book, O Philosopher, is the nature of created things, and anytime I want to read the words of God, the book is before me' (Merton, 1961: 62).

The *Hexaemeron* of St Basil (c. 331–379), a collection of homilies on Creation prepared for an uneducated audience, was perhaps the most influential of all early writing on this subject. Essentially Basil's writings sought to reframe Graeco-Roman natural science around Christian principles. For him, therefore, the world could not be eternal in contradiction to Greek philosophy, it had a definite beginning and would have an equally clear end. As for the natural world more generally, Basil saw the earth as a school:

> . . . where reasonable souls exercise themselves, the training ground where they learn to know God: since by the sight of visible and sensible things, the mind is led, by a hand to the contemplation of invisible things.
>
> (Jackson, 1894: 218)

Despite this, however, Basil tended to reject allegorical readings of nature, instead insisting that when the Scriptures mentioned grass they really mean grass and not the hidden message to be read from it (Flores, 1993: 13). For those who worked the fields, this uncomplicated stance must have appealed: after all, for many both then and now, there is something integrally honest in calling a spade a spade. Basil's appeal was also broadened by his notion of Creation as unfinished business, one that Man was required to perfect through the cultivation of crops and the close management of meadows, pastures and woods, a task that involved the medieval peasant just as much the scholar or theologian (Jackson, 1894: 228). In this Basil was followed by St Ambrose (c. 337–397), who stressed that while the Creation had taken six days to complete in order that people would be in no doubt that it had been created, it nevertheless required finishing and adorning. The image Ambrose used was that of an embroidery which only followed weaving (Glacken, 1967: 195).

But it was the 'book' which became the medieval world's preferred metaphor. In the twelfth century Hugh of St Victor would write in *De tribus diebus* (*On the Three Days*) that 'the whole sensible world is like a kind of book written by the finger of God' (Coolman, 2010: 86); a century later and in similar vein St Bonaventure likened the universe to a book, and in the sermons of the German mystic Meister Eckhart (1260–1327), 'Someone who knew nothing but creatures never need to attend to any sermons for every creature is full of God and is a book' (Walshe, 1981: 115). It was not lost on the **Church Fathers** or later writers that nature had the potential to speak of God to more people than the Scriptures themselves. John Chrysostom laid out their common position (Glacken, 1967: 203–4). If God exclusively instructed through books then only the literate and the wealthy – those who could afford to own a Bible – might learn. The Book of Nature, the visible and material world of forms and signs, thus acted as an essential instruction manual for the poor and illiterate. Moreover there was the question of language. Those that did not understand the language of the Bible were excluded from its teachings, while nature, 'our best teacher' offered a universal unspoken and unwritten language accessible to all (Migne, 1862: 127–35). Time and again the sermons

Church Fathers: The most influential writers of non-canonical texts during the first few centuries of Christianity, whose works helped to define theological doctrine. They divide into three time-frames relative to the adoption of the Nicene Creed at the Council of Nicaea in 325: ante-Nicene writers such as Origen; Nicene writers such as St Augustine; and post-Nicene fathers such as St Jerome, St Basil and St Ambrose.

of the Church Fathers return to natural imagery, the universal language, in order to explore and expose deeper truths.

Not only did the Book of Nature link the middle ages to the past, as an overarching device able to supersede the cultural, social and religious boundaries in the present, it also provided a model for the future. The appearance, in 1351, of Konrad of Megenberg's *Das buch der natur* marked in many ways a new departure for medieval pronunciations on nature and heralded, in part at least, the kinds of approaches that would be taken to the subject in the early modern period (Pfeiffer, 1861). For in this encyclopaedic work natural philosophy can clearly be seen to be making way for the kinds of natural history that would follow. The model for the book was Thomas of Cantimpré's *De natura rerum*, the last in the long line of medieval speculations on 'the nature of things' with which this text began (see Chapter 1). But far from being bound by his chosen template, Konrad's organisation of his material was novel. Stripped away were extended discussions of the elements and the soul. Reoriented too was the purpose of the book: where Cantimpré had written with religious intent, to produce a book synthesising the natural sciences so that they could be marshalled by preachers, Konrad's book was written in the vernacular for a wide intellectual readership, secular as much as ecclesiastic. He dealt with all that was visible, tangible and sensible, what we would now call today the 'natural world'. His seven books covered in turn, human anatomy, the stars and the planets, animals (mammals, birds, marine animals, fish, snakes and small creatures), common trees and exotic spice bushes, vegetables, stones and metals. By so doing, this work stood at the threshold of the study of nature as an entity in its own right and predicted how natural histories would manifest themselves in subsequent centuries.

While it is clear that a level of unity can be found in the treatment of the natural world during the middle ages, this should not be exaggerated. Important intellectual fracture lines also existed, ensuring that there was no single view of the natural world but many. Much has been made, for instance, of how medieval scholars wrestled with the alternative views of nature provided by Plato (and later Neoplatonists) and Aristotle, and how Aristotelian ideas came to dominate later medieval thought where once Platonic ideas had prevailed. Important differences have been noted between Christian and Hebraic-Islamic writings on nature, and the contrast between the realism of the Arab descriptions of nature and the conventional/allegorical readings of nature in the Latin west has been drawn. Irrespective of cultural and religious context, it has been suggested that understandings of nature during the middle ages developed against the backdrop of three shifting horizons: first, scholarly advances relating to the growing availability of earlier texts; second, increasing knowledge of the natural phenomena of the wider world;

and third, more localised changes to the medieval environment affecting its flora and fauna.

Socially contingent readings of nature added further complexity to interpretations of, and attitudes expressed towards, the medieval natural world. It might be argued, for instance, that elite attitudes to nature in Christian Europe (the *bellatores* of the three orders of medieval society) became ever more exploitative and domineering across the period: they fiercely guarded their rights to economically valuable resources such as woodland and mineral deposits; their parks and gardens became symbols of their ability to tame the wild, a subjugation of nature that mirrored the control they were able to exert over their social inferiors. Yet paradoxically, as they consumed nature, so they also appear to have distanced themselves from it even as they sought to gain its mastery. For the *laboratores*, the massed ranks who tilled the soils and oversaw the livestock, their relationship with nature (seen through a glass darkly) emerges as more intimate, embedded and necessarily more symbiotic and sympathetic. These men and women could not stand back and admire; they appear not to have ascribed aesthetic values to the natural world they encountered if the conventions that they used to name the landscape can be used as a guide. Rather their outlook was driven by pragmatism; they had to work with and not against nature, to understand its rhythms and cycles, and to be prepared for its caprices if they were to make a return from the land. Nature dictated their lives, dirtying their hands, tanning their skins, and straining their muscles. Those that prayed, the *oratores*, sought to understand nature too, but in different ways. Nature, as the Book of Nature so clearly demonstrates, was to be contemplated and examined for the divine revelations that it might reveal. But it might also be brought inside and presented on the walls of their religious buildings and on the richly illuminated folios of their liturgical books.

Of course, such characterisations offer little more than bland caricatures of a more complex reality. Monastic attitudes to nature could be as exploitative as their secular peers as the vast wealth accumulated by the Holy Orders through their great agricultural estates attests; and the elites might be no less contemplative of nature than monks or clerics as reflected in its presentation and representation in their books of hours, bestiaries, poetry, literature or the decorative designs of their private chambers. Peasants might be as interventionist as their lords in manipulating their soils and clearing trees, and just as alive and often more willing to celebrate nature's symbolism than any other social group. All three orders showed interest in the well-being of animals in their care, all exhibited knowledge of plants and minerals, all at one time or another looked up at the night sky or had cause to celebrate or curse the weather. Thus in reading the evidence one must expect the narrative that emerges to be messy rather than straightforward. Medieval attitudes towards nature varied across time and space, from community to community, and individual to individual. Relationships that were forged with nature developed along different lines depending on status, context and outlook. But ultimately people could not escape the natural world. Nature, personified or otherwise, provided a common set of experiences and lessons that transcended all cultural, social, religious, intellectual and geographic boundaries. Quite simply the natural world gave articulation to the whole of medieval society.

On many levels encounters with nature in the middle ages differed little from those enjoyed or endured today. Our attention is still drawn to the night sky; media outlets continue to feature daily horoscopes based on planetary conjunctions among their output; lunar and solar eclipses remain newsworthy with reporters sent around the world to beam back pictures of these special events. The visual impact of volcanic eruptions remains undiminished as a source of awe; floods continue to bring destruction to crops and livestock. The cycle of the seasons continues to mark the passing of the year often in more significant ways than the calendar – the now rare sound of the first cuckoo, the return of migratory birds, the first frost, seasonal vegetables. Flies still pester and infuriate and flea bites remain painful. And despite the indoor lives now led by the majority, and the protection of the car when going about our daily business, weather remains an obsession for the English at least. These are reminders that interactions with the natural world continue to shape our lives.

So what should we make of how nature was understood in the middle ages? An idiosyncratic and now outmoded episode in the development of human thought, or a period which produced ideas which still hold relevance in the age of science and technology? As we become increasingly aware of the potential damage caused by solar flares to our telecommunications systems and power supplies, it is clear that the potential of celestial bodies to exert influence over the terrestrial world is as real now as it was then, and in some cases as little understood. As we search for alternative sources of clean energy through harnessing the power of the sun, wind and tides, we are essentially returning to medieval technologies and the notion that we must work in harmony with the natural world just as our medieval ancestors did. The rejection of agricultural practices reliant on chemical fertilisers in favour of organic farming methods sees us returning to the idea of natural balance so well understood by the medieval peasant. And as the growing number of biodynamic farms prove – on which plants are sown and harvested according to the phases of the moon, and where planetary and astral forces are recognised to play a crucial role in the cycle of growth and decay – twenty-first century farmers are still finding useful those very principles which were acknowledged to govern the workings of the natural world in the middle ages. The medieval book of nature, then, remains essential reading.

Further reading

A useful collection of writings – ancient, medieval and modern – with emphasis on Islamic interpretations of the Book of Nature, is provided by Helminski, *The Book of Nature*. For anyone interested in the medieval natural world, however, there are no better places to begin than the Bible and the *Qur'an*.

Part 2

DOCUMENTS

The source material presented here is arranged in chronological order of writing. Relevant cross-references are provided where two or more of the documents deal with the same theme.

Document 1 PSALM 104 (VULGATE PSALM 103) (*c.* 1000–300 BC)

The two biblical accounts of Creation (Genesis 1:1–23 and Genesis 2:4–25) provided a common framework for thinking about the natural world for Jews, Christians and Moslems alike. It is a theme returned to by the psalmists, a book also shared by these three religions. Psalm 104 bears a strong resemblance to Akh-en-Aton's hymn to the sun-god Aten composed in Egypt c. 1360 BC.

1. For David himself. Bless the Lord, O my soul: O Lord my God, you are exceedingly great. You have put on praise and beauty.
2. And are clothed with light as with a garment. Who stretches out the heaven like a pavilion.
3. Who covers the higher rooms thereof with water. Who makes the clouds your chariot: who walks upon the wings of the winds.
4. Who makes your angels spirits: and your ministers a burning fire.
5. Who has founded the earth upon its own bases: it shall not be moved for ever and ever.
6. The deep like a garment is its clothing: above the mountains shall the waters stand.
7. At your rebuke they shall flee: at the voice of your thunder they shall fear.
8. The mountains ascend, and the plains descend into the place which you have founded for them.
9. You have set a bound which they shall not pass over; neither shall they return to cover the earth.
10. You send forth springs in the vales: between the midst of the hills the waters shall pass.
11. All the beasts of the field shall drink: the wild asses shall expect in their thirst.
12. Over them the birds of the air shall dwell: from the midst of the rocks they shall give forth their voices.
13. You water the hills from your upper rooms: the earth shall be filled with the fruit of thy works.
14. Bringing forth grass for cattle, and herb for the service of men. That you may bring bread out of the earth.
15. And that wine may cheer the heart of man. That he may make the face cheerful with oil: and that bread may strengthen man's heart.

16. The trees of the field shall be filled, and the cedars of Lebanon which he has planted.
17. There the sparrows shall make their nests. The highest of them is the house of the heron.
18. The high hills are a refuge for the harts, the rock for the ibex.
19. He has made the moon for seasons: the sun knows his going down.
20. You have appointed darkness, and it is night: in it shall all the beasts of the woods go about.
21. The young lions roaring after their prey, and seeking their meat from God.
22. The sun arises, and they are gathered together: and they shall lie down in their dens.
23. Man shall go forth to his work, and to his labour until the evening.
24. How great are thy works, O Lord? You have made all things in wisdom: the earth is filled with thy riches.
25. So is this great sea, which stretches wide its arms: there are creeping things without number: creatures little and great.
26. There the ships shall go. This sea dragon which you have formed to play therein.
27. All expect of you that you give them food in season.
28. What you give to them they shall gather up: when you open your hand, they shall all be filled with good.
29. But if you turn away your face, they shall be troubled: you shall take away their breath, and they shall fail, and shall return to their dust.
30. You shall send forth your spirit, and they shall be created: and you shall renew the face of the earth.
31. May the glory of the Lord endure for ever: the Lord shall rejoice in his works.
32. He looks upon the earth, and makes it tremble: he troubles the mountains, and they smoke.
33. I will sing to the Lord as long as I live: I will sing praise to my God while I have my being.
34. Let my speech be acceptable to him: but I will take delight in the Lord.
35. Let sinners be consumed out of the earth, and the unjust, so that they be no more: O my soul, bless thou the Lord.

EXTRACTS FROM PLATO'S *TIMAEUS*, 30a–b, 31b–32b and 49b–d (*c.* 360 BC)   **Document 2**

Plato's natural philosophy provided the early middle ages with its principal model for how the visible and tangible universe worked. The text, known in the Latin west through the partial translation of Calcidius, exerted an unparalleled influence over all later thinkers until its cosmological vision was first challenged by Arabic scholars who had access to the works of Plato's own *student Aristotle. In the short extracts reproduced here will be found Plato's conception of an animate universe (**anima** = soul), the necessity for four elements and their interrelationship, and discussion of their essential qualities.*

[30a–b] God's desire was that all things should be good, nothing, so far as might be, bad; so he took in hand all that was visible – he found it not at rest, but in discordant and disorderly motion – and brought it from disorder to order, since he judged this every way better than that. Now he that is best might not and may not affect anything but that which is most beautiful. So he considered and discovered that, whole for whole, of things visible nothing without understanding, and further that understanding cannot arise anywhere without soul. Moved by this consideration, he framed understanding within soul and soul within body, as so made the fabric of the universe, to the end that the work of his fashioning might be in its kind most beauteous and best . . .

[31b–32b] Being bodily, that which has come to be must be visible and tangible. Without fire nothing visible can come to be, nothing tangible without solidity, nothing solid without earth: whence God, in the beginning of his fashioning, made the body of the universe of fire and earth. Now two terms cannot be fairly wrought together without a third; there must be a bond between them to bring them together. The fairest of all bonds is that which makes itself and the terms it binds together most utterly one, and this is most perfectly effected by a progression . . .

Now if the body of the universe could have been a plane without depth, one middle term would have sufficed to bind together its companions and itself. But in fact the world was to be a solid, and solids must always be conjoined not by one middle term, but by two. So God inserted water and air between fire and earth, and made them all, as far as was possible, proportional to one another, air being to water as fire to air, and water to earth as air to water. Thus was compacted and constructed a visible and tangible heaven.

[49b–d] . . . consider what we have currently named water: we see it, as we fancy, becoming stones and earth by solidification, and again wind and air by liquefaction and disintegration, air becoming fire by inflammation and fire, in its turn, taking the form of air again by coalescence and extinction and air, once more, as it closes together in condensation becoming cloud and mist, water distilling from them, as they are 'felted' still closer; and earth and stones coming from water again, and all these, as it seems passing into one another by cyclical transformation. Then, since none of them thus wears a constant aspect, of which of them can one say with confident assurance that it is this *something* or not other without blushing for himself? Or none of them all; far the safest rule in speaking of them is the following. Whenever we see a thing changing, fire for example, we must, in every case, call fire not *this* but *this-like*, and water again, not *this* but always this-*like* . . .

Source: Taylor, A.E. (trans.), *Plato: Timaeus*, Methuen and Co. Ltd, 1929, pp. 27, 28–29, 48.

ARISTOTLE'S *METAPHYSICS*, BK 5, CH. 4 ON THE VARIOUS MEANINGS OF 'NATURE' (*a.* 322 BC)   **Document 3**

Literally meaning 'after the Physics ("nature")', Aristotle intended Metaphysics *to be studied after his* libri naturales. *Averroes' commentaries on* Metaphysics *(c. 1198) were important in bringing this text to the attention of the medieval world as were the partial translations of James of Venice (fl. 1136–1148) and William de Moerbeke (d. 1286). In contradistinction to Plato who had equated nature with the 'realm of forms', producing a relatively static view of nature, here Aristotle emphasises the importance of motion, and by so doing equates nature with change.*

'Nature' means in one sense, the genesis of growing things and in another, that immanent thing [a seed] from which a growing thing first begins to grow. [It is] the source for which the first primary motion of every natural object is induced in that object as such . . . Again 'nature' means the primary stuff, shapeless and unchangeable from its own potency, of which any natural object consists of these 'natures', the primary material persisting. It is in this sense that men call the elements of natural objects the 'nature', some call it fire, others earth or air or water, others something else similar, others some of these, and others all of them. Again in another sense 'nature' means the substance of natural objects; as in the case of those who say that 'nature' is the primary composition of a thing . . .

. . . as regards these things which exist or are produced by nature, although that from which they naturally are produced or exist is already present, we say that they have not their nature yet unless they have their form and shape . . . Indeed from this sense of 'nature', by an extension of meaning, every essence in general is called 'nature', because the nature of anything is a kind of essence.

From what has been said, then, the primary and proper sense of 'nature' is the essence of those things which contain in themselves as such a source of motion; for the matter is called 'nature' because it is capable of receiving the nature, and the processes of generation and growth are called 'nature' because they are motions derived from it. And nature in this sense is the source of motion in natural objects, which is somehow inherent in them, either potentially or actually.

Source: Tredennick, H. (trans.), *Aristotle, The Metaphysics, Books I–IX*, William Heinemann, 1947, pp. 219–33. Reprinted by permission of the publishers and the Trustees of the Loeb Classical Library from ARISTOTLE: VOLUME XVII, METAPHYSICS, Loeb Classical Library Volume 271, translated by H. Tredennick, pp. 219, 221, 223, 225, 227, 229, 231, 233, Cambridge, Mass.: Harvard University Press, 1933. Loeb Classical Library ® is a registered trademark of the President and Fellows of Harvard College.

Document 4   *PHYSIOLOGUS* ON THE PARTRIDGE (SECOND–FOURTH CENTURY)

Described as second only to the Bible in terms of its influence on medieval thinking, the precise origins of this work – later substantially expanded by bestiarists (see Document 17) – are still debated. The impact of its allegorical content, however, is not in doubt. This short discussion of the partridge stands as an archetypal example of how the behaviour of certain animals was used by the author of Physiologus *to provide guidance for leading a Christian life.*

Jeremiah said of the partridge, 'The partridge cried out, gathering the brood which she did not hatch.' [Jer. 17:11] The partridge warms the eggs of other birds, labouring over them and nourishing them. When the chicks have grown up and begin to fly, however, each kind flees away to its own parents and leaves the partridge by herself.

Thus the devil seizes the stock of little ones but, when they reach the fullness of age, they come to Christ and the Church, and the Devil proves a fool. If today one has evil ways, tomorrow he will become sober. Flee the devil, that is the partridge, and you will come to your rightful parents, the prophets and apostles.

Source: Curley, M.J. (trans.), *Physiologus*, Texas University Press, 1979, pp. 46–7.

Document 5   ST AUGUSTINE OF HIPPO, *DE GENESI AD LITTERAM* (*ON THE LITERAL MEANING OF GENESIS*) ON THE RELATIONSHIP BETWEEN CHRISTIAN AND NON-CHRISTIAN CONCEPTIONS OF THE COSMOS (*a*. 430)

The writings of the Church Fathers, and in particular their discussion of the Biblical story of Creation (Hexaemeron literature), provided the grounding for the Christianisation of the natural philosophy inherited from Classical Greece. In this extract St Augustine can be seen to be opening the way to finding common ground between the different traditions.

There is knowledge to be had, after all, about the earth, about the sky, about the other elements of this world, about the movements and revolutions or even the magnitude and distances of the constellations, about the predictable eclipses of moon and sun, about the cycles of years and seasons, about the nature of animals, fruits, stones, and everything else of this kind. And it frequently happens that even non-Christians will have knowledge of this sort in a way that they can substantiate with scientific arguments or experiments. Now it is quite disgraceful and disastrous, something to be on one's guard against at all costs, that they should ever hear Christians spouting what they claim our Christian literature has to say on these topics, and talking such nonsense that they can scarcely contain their laughter when they see them to be *toto caelo*, as the saying goes, wide of the mark. And what is so vexing is not that misguided people should be laughed at, as that our authors should be assumed by outsiders to have held such views and, to the great detriment of those about whose salvation we are so concerned, should be written off and consigned to the waste paper basket as so many ignoramuses.

Whenever, you see, they catch some members of the Christian community making mistakes on a subject which they know inside out, and defending their hollow opinions on the authority of our books, on what grounds are they going to trust those books on the resurrection of the dead and the hope of eternal life and the kingdom of heaven, when they suppose they include any number of mistakes and fallacies on matters which they themselves have been able to master either by experiment or by the surest of calculations? It is impossible to say what trouble and grief such rash, self-assured know-alls cause the more cautious and experienced brothers and sisters. Whenever they find themselves challenged and taken to task for some shaky and false theory of theirs by people who do not recognize the authority of our books, they try to defend what they have aired with the most frivolous temerity and patent falsehood by bringing forward these same sacred books to justify it. Or they even quote from memory many things said in them which they imagine will provide them with valid evidence, not understanding either what they are saying, or the matters on which they are asserting themselves [1 Tim 1:7].

Source: Hill, E. (ed. and trans.), *St Augustine, On Genesis*, Augustine Heritage Institute, 2002, pp. 186–7.

ISIDORE OF SEVILLE'S *DE NATURA RERUM* (*ON THE NATURE OF THINGS*), **Document 6**
CH. 11, 'THE ELEMENTS OF THE WORLD' (c. 612)

This chapter draws directly from Plato's Timaeus (Document 2) *and St Ambrose's* Hexaemeron, *a theological treatise dealing with the six days of Creation. When Bede later reworked Isidore's treatise he did not follow this version, instead substituting Pliny the Elder's conception of the elements drawn directly from pseudo-Isidore's* Liber de ordine creaturarum *'The Book on the Orders of Creatures', an Irish cosmology (Kendall and Wallis, 2010: 75–6, 138).*

There are four elements in the world: fire, air, water and earth. This is their nature: fire is thin, pointed and mobile; air mobile, pointed and thick; water thick, blunt and mobile; earth thick, blunt and immobile. Moreover they mix thus: earth . . . is linked by its thickness and bluntness to water; then water is associated with air by its thickness and mobility; air in its turn is lined to fire by their shared characteristics of sharpness and mobility; as for earth and fire, they are separated from one another, but united by the two intermediary elements, air and water . . .

Moreover here are the terms by which Ambrose distinguished the same elements, according to the qualities which permit them to mix by virtue of certain natural affinities: the earth, he said, is dry and cold, water cold and wet; air is hot and moist, fire hot and dry. It is because of the tendencies for these sensitive qualities to unite that all things mix one with another. In effect, earth being dry and cold is united with water by the cold quality which belongs to both and water because of its humidity in turn to the air, for the air is humid. Thus water, being of two sorts, cold and wet, is able to combine respectively with earth and air, that which it has which is cold with the earth, and that which is moist with the air.

Air, itself also an intermediary between the two elements that are naturally at odds with each other, that is between water and fire, reconciles these elements, for it is united with water because of its moisture and with fire because of its heat. Equally fire being hot and dry is reattached to air by its heat, but its dryness aligns and unite it closely with earth, and so it is that by this circle, comparable to people dancing in unison, that the elements arrange themselves in a harmonious alliance . . .

Source: Translated from Fontaine, J. (trans.), *Isidore of Seville, De natura rerum: Traité de la nature*, Bibliothèque de l'Ecole des Hautes Etudes Hispaniques, 28, 1960, pp. 213–16.

Document 7   EXTRACTS FROM THE *QUR'AN* (610–632)

The Qur'an, the divine revelations of Mohammed, is infused throughout with images drawn directly from the natural (divinely created) world. These short extracts reveal how the idea of 'the book of nature' formed a key concept in Moslem thought. Islam's holy text positively encourages and celebrates the study of nature explaining why the natural sciences have always been central to Islamic scholarship, and why they were so quickly embraced in the early middle ages.

[*Surah* 2. *Al-Baqara* (The Cow): 164] In the creation of the heavens and the earth, in the alternation of night and day; in the ships that sail the ocean with cargoes beneficial to man; in the water which God sends down from the sky and with which He revives the earth after its death, dispersing over it all manner of beasts; in the disposal of the winds, and in the clouds that are driven between sky and earth: surely in these there are signs for rational men.

[*Surah 6. Al-An'am* (Cattle, Livestock): 59] He has the keys of all that is hidden: none know them but He. He has knowledge of all that land and sea contain: every leaf that falls is known to Him. There is no grain in the darkest bowel of the earth, nor anything green or seared, but is recorded in a glorious Book [of nature].

[*Surah 45. Al-Jathiyya* (Crouching): 4–6] Surely in the heavens and the earth there are signs for the faithful; in your own creation, and in the beasts He scatters far and near, signs for true believers; in the alternation of night and day, in the sustenance God sends down from heaven with which He resurrects the earth after its death, and in the marshalling of the winds, signs for men of understanding.

Source: Dawood, N.J. (trans.), *The Koran*, Penguin, rev. edn, 2003, pp. 26, 98, 350.

AL-JĀHIZ, *KITĀB AL-HAYAWAN* (*BOOK OF ANIMALS*) ON DIFFERENCES   **Document 8**
BETWEEN SCHOLARLY AND POPULAR QUESTIONING OF NATURAL
PHENOMENA (*c.* 800–850)

This extract pinpoints the gulf that existed between scholarly and popular interpretation and analysis. It reminds us to be extremely careful in using the surviving sources, most of which reflect elite or educated views on nature, and to be aware that these need not necessarily reflect attitudes or ideas shared by the masses.

The masses doubt less than the elites because they do not suspend their judgement before giving their approval, or accept other possibilities and also because they never question themselves. Among them there are two attitudes: total adherence without restriction; or total rejection. They do not entertain a third option, the state of doubt, which itself comprises many degrees, a sliding scale of good or bad opinion regarding the causes of things and matters of considerable import. This group of people, for the most part, have abandoned the suspension of judgement when faced with specious arguments and have set aside scholarly research which has sought the truth. They have completely neglected this sane attitude; for them, there is only 'yes' and 'no'. Occasionally their 'no' descends into anger and their 'yes' becomes associated with satisfaction. Freedom has lost its function. The memory of the indefensible and the forbidden is dead. To speak of 'ugly' or 'beautiful' is one thing that the masses refuse.

Source: Translated from Souami, L. (ed.), *Jâhiz, Le Cadi et la Mouche*, Sindbad, 1988, pp. 75–6.

Document 9   AL-JĀHIZ, *KITĀB AL-HAYAWAN* (*BOOK OF ANIMALS*) ON THE NUISANCE OF
FLIES (*c.* 800–850)

*This book is full of anecdotes and observations on animal behaviour. It reveals
the much greater realism of Arabic writers in their treatment of nature than
contemporary writers in the Latin west for whom convention and received
wisdom appear to be more important.*

Personally, I have had occasion to suffer the mistreatment of flies. I was
wandering on the banks of the Al-Mubārak [River Basra]; I reached the lodg-
ings of Ar-Rabī. I was unable to hitch a ride on the back of a mule. I crossed
a meadow of high grass, dry and dense vegetation where there were flies in
abundance. A few of them came to land on my eyes. I shooed them away,
but they returned to land in the corners of my eyelids. I wafted my hands
more frenetically; they scattered but only as long as my movements and
gesticulations remained vigorous: flies such as these that live in the marsh
grasses and orchards have a bite second to none. They returned to the charge;
me too. In the last offensive I used my sleeve to chase them from my face.
But their attack continued uninterrupted. During all this time, I sped up in
the hope that I might put distance between them and me. When they came
back again I lifted my veil over my head to counter them since my sleeve had
been found inadequate. But they swarmed all over me once more and I could
find no alterative strategy than to run. I raced a good distance. Since my childhood I have never practised such gymnastics. I met a man from Al-Andalus
who asked me 'What has happened to you Abū 'Uthmān? Has something grave
occurred?' – 'Yes', I replied, 'the gravest thing of all.' I just wanted to find an
escape from a situation where the flies had become my sovereign overlords.

Source: Translated from Souami, L. (ed. and trans.), *Jāhiz, Le Cadi et la Mouche*, Sindbad, 1988, pp. 311–12.

Document 10   DICUIL, *LIBER DE MENSURA ORBIS TERRAE* (*BOOK OF THE MEASUREMENT OF
THE SPHERE OF THE EARTH*) ON ICELAND (825)

*An Irish monk, Dicuil's scholarship led him to the Carolingian schools. This
account of Iceland, derived from fellow monks who had travelled there in 795,
represents one of the few corrections to the received geographical wisdom of
Classical writers dating to the early middle ages. The authors Dicuil identified
as being mistaken were Pliny the Elder, Isidore of Seville, Priscian, and Solinus.*

It is now thirty years since clerics, who had lived on the island [Iceland] from
the first of February to the first of August, told me that not only at the summer
solstice, but in the days round about it, the sun setting in the evening hides

itself as though behind a small hill in such a way that there was no darkness in that very small space of time, and a man could do whatever he wished as though the sun were there, even remove lice from his shirt, and if they had been on a mountain-top perhaps the sun would never have been hidden from them.

. . . Therefore those [Classical] authors are wrong and give wrong information, who have written that the sea will be solid about Thule, and that day without nights continues right through from the vernal to the autumnal equinox, and that vice versa night continues uninterrupted from the autumnal to the vernal equinox, since these men voyaged at the natural time of great cold, and entered the island and remaining on it had day and night alternately except for a period of the solstice. But one day's sail north of that they did find the sea frozen over.

Source: Tierney, J.J. (ed.), *Dicuili, Liber de Mensura Orbis Terrae*, The Dublin Institute for Advanced Studies, 1967, p. 75.

JOHN SCOTUS ERIUGENA, *PERIPHYSEON* OR *DE DIVISIONE NATURAE* (*THE* **Document 11**
DIVISION OF NATURE), BK 3, ll. 3257–77, ON THE STRUCTURE OF THE
UNIVERSE (860)

In this short except Eriugena outlines his model – borrowed from Martianus Capella – of a geoheliocentric universe. The idea was not generally accepted. However, the discussion is also infused with the elemental complexions of the various planetary bodies which enjoyed more universal acceptance.

Therefore that planet which is called by the name of Saturn, since it is in the neighbourhood of the harmonious motions of the stars, is said to be cold and pale, whereas the body of the Sun, since it possesses the middle region of the world – for, as the philosophers affirm, the distance from the Earth to the Sun is the same as that from the Sun to the stars – is understood to occupy a kind of midway position . . . it [the Sun] is seen to be of shining colour, and this colour is intermediate between pale and ruddy, since it receives into the even temper of its own brightness a part of the paleness of the cold stars above and a part of the ruddiness of the hot bodies below. But the planets which revolve about it change their colours in accordance with the qualities of the regions they are traversing. I mean Jupiter and Mars, Venus and Mercury, which always pursue their orbits around the Sun, as Plato teaches in the *Timaeus*; and therefore when they are above the Sun they show a bright face, but when below a ruddy face.

Source: Sheldon-Williams, I.P. (trans.) revised by O'Meara, J.J., *Eriugena, Periphyseon (The Division of Nature)*, Bellarmin, 1987, pp. 327–8.

Document 12   CAPTAIN BUZURG IBN SHAHRIYA OF RAMHORMUZ, *AJAIB AL-HIND*
(*THE BOOK OF THE WONDERS OF INDIA*) ON THE HERMAPHRODITIC
HARE (*c.* 950–1000)

This work is a compilation of sailors' tales collected in the second half of the
tenth century that circulated in Khuzistan east of Iraq. Relating to a large area
encompassing East Africa, Arabia, the Persian Gulf, India, Ceylon, China,
Malaya, Sumatra and Java, they demonstrate the wide trading contacts that
the Islamic world enjoyed in Asia. This well-known tale of the hermaphroditic
hare shows that the veracity of stories of this kind, whilst happily recounted,
might also be questioned.

. . . in one of the Waqwaq Islands there is an animal like a hare, which can
change its sex, both male and female. At least this is what the people of
Sarandib say, according to what my informant learnt from an Indian. I do
not know what to say about it. They also say that the hare changes sex. In
my opinion that is ridiculous.

Source: Freeman-Grenville, G.S.P. (trans.), *Capt. Buzurg ibn Shahriyar of Ramhormuz,*
The Book of the Wonders of India, East-West Publications, 1981, p. 102.

Document 13   AVICENNA, *DANISHNAMA-I 'ALA'I* (*THE BOOK OF SCIENTIFIC KNOWLEDGE*)
ON THE SENSES (*a.* 1037)

A prolific writer and precociously talented scholar, Ibn Sina, known in the
west as Avicenna, contributed to the advancement of knowledge across the
natural sciences and medicine. His natural philosophy blended Neoplatonism
with Aristotelian ideas. Alongside his discussion of the working of the external
senses presented here, Avicenna also posited seven internal senses – a common
sense, retentive, animal and human imagination, an estimative capacity,
memory, and the ability to process information.

The perception of touch is self-evident; it consists of being put in contact
with heat, cold, humidity, dryness, hardness or softness, that which is rough
or polished, weighty or light. In instances where the touched object does not
modify the state of the organ which touches it, either by its qualities or con-
tours, the organ will not perceive it. Those organs of touch are the skin and
muscles. It is nerves which provide the skin and muscles with their faculty
to perceive.

Scent is produced through the intermediary of a body which carries
odours or which mixes with smelly vapours, and which as a consequence of
its subtlety passes through the nostrils to the lower part of the brain – to the

two protuberances which point to the brain and which resemble nipples. The body in question is like air (or like water for aquatic animals). It is certainly not necessary for odorant particles to be spread only by vapour in order for animals to perceive a smell, since it is clear that this vapour would only be able to spread them a certain distance. If odour only resulted upon its transformation into vapour even animals with an acute sense of smell would only be able to perceive it over a distance of fifty or one hundred parasangs (150 to 300 miles). Yet the Greeks related that in ancient times the smell of cadavers resulting from one of their wars drew scavenging birds, never previously seen in their towns or close by, from our towns [in Iraq] to theirs; now the shortest distance that these birds could have flown is two hundred parasangs (600 miles). Consequently, it is clear that air transported this odour and not vapour.

Hearing consists of perceiving sound. This originates from undulations of air resulting from a sudden shock of the kind made when two bodies smash together, the undulation being thrown out at a powerful and rapid speed; alternatively air breaks out from the interior of an object producing a rapid movement which creates a ripple and which spreads out quickly over a wide area. When this reaches the ear, the air which is found inside the ear succumbs to the same turbulence because of the cavity in which it is created; this undulation stimulates the auditory nerve.

As for taste, here is the cause. Humidity which is created on the tongue perceives the flavour of the object and impregnates the tongue in such a way that the lingual nerve is awakened.

Source: Translated from Achena, M. and Massé, H. (trans.), *Avicenne, Le Livre de Science*, Les Belles Lettres/Unesco, 1986, pp. 56–7.

AL-BIRUNĪ, *KITĀB-AL-SAYDANAH FI'T-TIBB (BOOK ON PHARMACY AND MATERIA MEDICA)* ON BARLEY (a. 1048)   **Document 14**

One of the greatest medieval Arabic scholars, the writings of al-Birunī span the natural sciences. In this extract the long-lasting importance of earlier writers such as Dioscorides and Galen is evident. The detailed anatomical descriptions of barley provided by the ninth-century scholar Abu Hanīfah are far superior to anything written in the Latin west at this period.

Sha'ir [barley] . . . Dioscorides says: 'The best is white and clear, slightly less nutritious than wheat. The barley that is clear exceeds the other barley varieties in nutrition. It is useful for felons [inflammations] and furuncles [boils], and against irritation and sourness in the throat. The same thing could be said of the wheat bran also, but its sieved bran is superior to that of barley. It is a diuretic and a galactogogue [promoter of lactation] if drunk by women together with aniseed.' The principal characteristic of barley is purification, but it generates flatus and flatuence all the same. It is deleterious to the stomach but is a maturative for pustules, felons, and furuncles.

Galens says: 'Barley is a refrigerant and dessicative, but still it possesses slight heat. As a dessicative, it is slightly in excess of the flour of the peeled broad bean. In other characteristics it is similar to broad bean in external uses. Broad bean, if cooked and eaten, is a flatuent, since every part of it is more nutritious than that of barley, and for this reason it is more nutritious than barley. Since both these seeds are slightly beyond the medium temperament, people tend to eat them with different foods, just as the medicines of one kind are mixed with those of another. Barley gruel is more dessicative than barley itself.'

Abu Hanīfah says: 'There are many varieties of barley. The Arab variety is white. Its ears have two sides, broad, with large grains. They are larger than those of the Iraqi barley – and this variety is the most excellent. The grain of the Ethiopian variety is black and so are its ears. It comprises two sides and it is very scabrous. It is not eaten because of its rough surface but useful for spots on the body.

The ear of the red kind is two-sided and its bread is good. The boughs of the *ju'rah* variety are thick as are its clusters and ears; its clusters are smaller than those of the poppy, and are many sided. The grain is big, long, and white. The same thing goes for the ears and hay. The barley variety is slender and suffers from blight. It is very green and fresh and yields good bread.'

Source: Said, H.M. (ed. and trans.), *Al-Biruni's Book on Pharmacy and Materia Medica*, Pakistan Series of Central Asian Studies, 2 vols, Rashid Sons, 1973, I, pp. 353–4.

Document 15   *PHYSIOLOGUS* ASCRIBED TO THEOBALD, ABBOT OF MONTE CASSINO, 'CONCERNING THE ANT' (1022–1085)

This metrical Physiologus *was considerably shorter than the prose versions from which it was derived. It became a standard school book and was heavily glossed. These annotations directed readers to the underlying meaning of the text: here summer and winter are used as metaphors for life and death; the avoidance of barley symbolised the rejection of evil and acceptance of good; and the division of the grain an image deployed to evoke the twin Christian duties to love God and their earthly neighbours.*

Now to us all by its work the ant should afford an example
Since all the food that it needs is carried home in its mouth

And in its actions, to us often indicates spiritual matters.
(Which since the Jew does not love) of these, he stands the accused.
Seeking for safety, against the frosts of the winter approaching,
Long as the earth has its heat, it never ceases to work.
Then brothers, while we have time, let us copy the ant in its labours.
Lest at the end of all time we hear the doom of our Judge.
Seeking for grain, the ant, if it finds barley, rejects it.
Thus should a man try to find law which is new, not the old.
But least the grain should sprout in the rain, when wetted with moisture
Then being useless for food, there should be nothing to eat.
Each prudent ant divides in two parts all the grain it has gathered.
Thus showing clearly one law which in its way has two paths.
One which seems of the earth, yet is turning our thoughts towards heaven
This now feeds the soul, yet too the body is fed.
Let this one be our guide, so thus we be guarded from famine.
At the last judgement of all, surely our winter of time.

Source: Rendell, A.W. (trans.), *Physiologus: a Metrical Bestiary of Twelve Chapters by Bishop Theobald*, John & Edward Bumpus Ltd, 1928, pp. 68–9.

BAUDRI OF BOURGUEIL, *TO COUNTESS ADELA*, ll. 1042–1064, ON   **Document 16**
ASTRONOMY (*a.* 1130)

This long allegorical poem addressed to William I's daughter Adela, describes the rich decorations adorning her (presumably fictitious) bedchamber and including a tapestry thought to be based on the Bayeux Tapestry, a mosaic mappa mundi *on the floor, and a detailed picture of the night sky on the ceiling. These interior decorations provide the basis upon which Baudri provides a summary of the curriculum of the seven liberal arts as taught at the beginning of the twelfth century. Astronomy formed part of the* quadrivium *together with arithmetics, geometry and music.*

Not far away from her [Lady Philosophy], two more disciples stood,
The first one, with outstretched arm, seemed to touch the sky with her stylus;
Labelling, as it seemed, each of the stars with its name.
And her stylus was huge – a whole ell – which suited her purpose,
Marking the poles of the sky with a simple device.
Why the sun is in retrograde, why the moon moves faster,
She could explain these things, using her eloquent comb;
Why it is that the sun moves so slowly around its orbit
Or what the cyclical moon's monthly shape-shifting means.

Learnedly she sang of Arcturus, Hyades, the Pleiads;
How many stars are in each of the zodiac's signs;
How far Septentio is removed from the East, the sunrise;
In what celestial part lies the mid-point of the sky;
How many ells the Northeast is away from the source of the south wind;
Or how many degrees separate these two points;
How many stars there are, their orbits, the night-sky's seasons;
Many a man she has turned into an expert on stars.
Some stars' movements are straight, while others move obliquely;
Thus would she reason and teach, trusting in rational proof.
Also, she'd show her students the five zones that make up the heavens,
The wintry regions she'd show, both of the solstices too,
And the two regions fit for man, wretched thing, to inhabit:
Frigid the other two, torrid with heat the fifth.

Source: Otter, M. (trans.), 'Baudri of Bourgueil: "To Countess Adela"', *Journal of Medieval Latin*, 11, 2001, pp. 91–2.

Document 17   *BESTIARY* ON THE PARTRIDGE (TWELFTH CENTURY)

This bestiary entry can be compared with Physiologus *(Document 4), showing how later treatment built upon and expanded on earlier core ideas. This entry contains considerably more detail regarding the natural behaviour of the bird, but the allegorical use to which it was put remained undiminished. (For metrical bestiaries see Document 21.)*

The partridge gets its name from its call. It is a cunning and unclean bird. For the males mount each other and forget their sex in the grip of their lust. They are so treacherous that one bird steals another's eggs; but this betrayal is altogether fruitless. For as soon as the young hear their true mother's voice, their natural impulse is to leave their foster-mother and return to their true mother.

The devil imitates their example, trying to rob the eternal Creator of His offspring, and if he succeeds in gathering round a few fools who do not know what they are doing, he nourishes them with carnal delights. But as soon as they hear Christ's voice, they spread their spiritual wings and commend themselves to Christ.

Partridges equip their nests with elaborate defences. They clothe their dwelling with thorn twigs, so that any animal which attacks them is held back by the sharpness of the brambles. The partridge covers its eggs with dust, and returns to its nest by different ways lest it should give away its whereabouts. The females often carry off their young elsewhere to deceive the males, who very frequently attack the young if the females pay too much attention to them. They fight at mating time, and the loser must submit to sexual intercourse like a female. The females are so lustful that the scent of the males borne on the wind will make them pregnant. If a man approaches their nest, the mothers will come out and pretend to be wounded in their feet or wings, so that they move slowly and appear to be easy to catch. By this trick they manage to hold off attackers and delude them into moving away from the nest. The young are equally cautious: when they are afraid of being discovered, they fall on their backs and lift little pieces of earth in their claws and defend themselves by concealing themselves so well that they lie hidden from detection.

Source: Barber, R. (trans.), *Bestiary*, Boydell Press, 1999, pp. 151–3.

WILLIAM OF CONCHES, *DRAGMATICON (DIALOGUES ON NATURAL PHILOSOPHY)*, BK 6, CH. 22 ON SMELL (1147–1149)   **Document 18**

Works such as William of Conches' Dragmaticon, written as the Latin west was 'rediscovering' Aristotelian texts, help us to trace how ideas on nature began to develop in their wake. The work is written as a dialogue between the 'philosopher' (William himself) and Geoffrey Plantagenet, duke of Normandy and count of Anjou. William was a tutor to Geoffrey's sons. Here William provides an early example of smell discussed in essentially Aristotelian terms. (see also Document 13).

Listen briefly to what remains to be said about the other senses. In material bodies there is a certain quality called smell. Air assumes the qualities of things it touches and especially shape, colour, smell, taste, cold, heat, harshness, smoothness (if it does not assume the very qualities identical [with itself] it nevertheless assumes some [qualities] virtually identical [with itself]). Therefore when air touches an apple, it assumes the smell that is in that apple; entering the nostrils with this smell, it reaches all the way to a certain orifice common to the mouth and nostrils. There small pieces of flesh, which extend from the brain, hang down rather like small teats. They are penetrated by a certain nerve leaving the brain, through which the soul sends that part of the aforementioned instrument which is more related to this quality [of smell] than to the others all the way to the aforementioned place. This part, receiving itself into itself the aforementioned smell, represents it to the soul in the logistic cell.

Source: Ronca, I. and Curr, M. (trans.), *William of Conches, A Dialogue on Natural Philosophy (Dragmaticon Philosophiae)*, Notre Dame Texts in Medieval Culture, 2, Notre Dame University Press, 1997, p. 165.

Document 19   HILDEGARD OF BINGEN, *PHYSICA* (*NATURAL SCIENCES*) ON GEMSTONES
(1151–1158)

*Hildegard of Bingen was one of the most original thinkers of the middle ages.
This is visible in her discussion of the formation of precious stones. Some
elements of the account accord with more mainstream opinions: these include
the central role played by the sun in their creation; and where they could be
found. Other ideas, such as the foam generated by the boiling rivers, are not
encountered in other contemporary works on this subject.*

Precious stones and gems arise in the East and in those regions where the sun
is especially hot. For the mountains that are in those zones contain a very high
temperature like that of fire because of the sun's heat. The rivers in those regions
flow and boil continuously because of the sun's excessive heat. Occasionally,
a flood gushes forth from those rivers and, swelling, flows upward toward
those burning mountains. When the same mountains, burning because of the
sun's heat, are touched by those rivers, they hiss wherever the water touches
fire or the rivers splash their foam, like fiery iron or fiery stone when water
is poured on it. In that place the foam sticks like a burdock. In three or four
days it hardens into stone.

But after the flood of these waters subsides so that the waters return again
to their streambed, the foam which had clung in several places to the mountains becomes thoroughly dry, depending on the various hours of the day
and the temperature of those hours. And, depending on the temperature of
those hours, they acquire their colours and their virtues. As they dry they
harden into precious stones. Then from various places they loosen like fish
scales and fall into the sand.

When the flood of those running streams rise again, the rivers carry off
many stones and conduct them to other countries, where they are found by
men. The mountains I mentioned – on which gems of such quality and number are born in this manner – glitter like the light of day.

Source: Throop, P. (trans.), *Hildegard von Bingen's Physica*, Healing Arts, 1998, pp. 137–8.

Document 20   RABBI PETACHIA OF RATISBON, *TRAVELS* ON THE FLYING CAMEL (1170–1187)

*The role of travellers in extending the horizons of the medieval natural world
cannot be underestimated. Some of the stories they brought back, like this one,
must have appealed to the popular image of exotic lands.*

Baghdad: There he was shown a flying camel. It is low, and its legs are slender; and if anyone wishes to ride on it he must tie himself to it lest he should

fall off. The rider traverses in one day the ground over which a man on foot would have taken fifteen. It would be possible to go even swifter if the rider could only stand it. In one second the flying camel gallops a mile.

Source: Adler, E.N. (trans.), *Jewish Travellers in the Middle Ages*, Dover Publications Inc., 1987, p. 80.

EXTRACTS FROM THE ANGLO-NORMAN AND FRENCH BESTIARIES OF **Document 21**
PHILIPPE OF THAON, ll. 307–48 (*c.* 1120) AND GERVAISE, ll. 282–304
(*c.* 1200) CONCERNING THE IDRUS AND THE CROCODILE

These two short extracts remind us that bestiaries (see Document 17) were not written as sourcebooks for natural history but as allegorical texts to illustrate theological matters. Presented in verse form, the bestiaries of Philippe de Thaon and Gervaise differ from contemporary prose bestiaries not only in their format but in their treatment of these two animals. Whilst it is clear that Philippe and Gervaise drew upon Pliny the Elder's Naturalis historia *as the source for the behaviour of the Idrus or Ichneumon (Bk 8, 35–8) – it is omitted from Isidore of Seville's* Eytmologiae *– the model for these entries was ulti-mately* Physiologus *(Document 4). By so doing, their allegorical content is more developed than many prose bestiaries which simply provide a summary of the appearance and character traits of these two animals.*

Gervaise, *Bestiaire*

That renowned beast the Idrus
Is found on the river Nile.
There is another beast, here, of which there are many,
The crocodile, which it much detests;
Always with its mouth gaping open
Moreover so wide that it is not a tight squeeze.
When the Idrus finds it sleeping
It immediately rolls in the mud
So that it is better able to wriggle
And pass into the beast without detection.
It enters into the body by the mouth,
Kills it and then forces itself out.
The crocodile has the semblance of death
And signifies hell.
The Idrus stands for Jesus Christ
Who restores life to us from death.
Because God suffered death

That death would be vanquished for all.
Hell broken and disrupted
Know all of you this demonstration of faith
The prophecy is fulfilled:
'Death', said God 'will kill me.'
'Hell', He said, 'will be defeated by me.'

Source: Translated from Meyer, P. (ed.), 'Le Bestiaire de Gervaise', *Romania*, 1, 1872, pp. 420–43.

Philippe of Thaon, *Bestiaire*

Idrus is a beast and swims with a strange force;
It resembles a snake, it lives on an island
And Physiologus says, that the Idrus
Willingly is on an island, it much detests the crocodile,
By cunning it seeks its death when it sleeps with his mouth open,
When it sees one, it puts itself into the mire,
When it is covered in mud and slimy,
And when it can strain and cover its mouth,
Then it comes to the crocodile where he sleeps on the island,
And puts itself in its mouth little by little,
Now hear, what a wonder! The crocodile awakes,
And is so greedy that he swallows it alive;
The Idrus enters into its body, the bowel of his belly
And cuts, and separates, and slays him by this means,
Then it comes out alive from his body, and bringing with it [the crocodile's]
    bowels.
This is the allegory, it signifies much.
The Idrus in truth signifies God:
God for our redemption took incarnation,
Which became from dust, and dust into mud,
Of mud came slime, and of flesh we have skin,
God was clothed with flesh, whereby Satan was vanquished,
Why should I go on telling it by another similitude?
God vanquished the Devil by a fit similitude.
The Crocodile signifies the Devil in this life;
When he sleeps with his mouth open, then he represents hell and death;
Hell rests with its mouth open, not closed;
When the Son of God took humanity,
He took up God and swallowed him alive;
That is, he entered hell, and threw out his own people,
According to his godhead, not in humanity;
Thus of hell he was the death, by such circumstance he saved us,

He entered hell alive and alive he returned from hell,
He threw the good out of hell, the bad he left there.
And Physiologus says that the Crocodile
Is bred in the water of the Nile, and is a very vile beast
Four feet has the beast, and is of a very fierce kind;
He lives on land and water, as Isidore says,
Twelve yards long is found the largest;
It has great teeth and claws, hard is the skin that it has;
It will not be burst by stone, however hard it shall be struck;
If it can devour a man, when it has eaten him it cries.

Source: Wright, T., *Popular Treatises on Science Written During the Middle Ages in Anglo-Saxon, Anglo-Norman and English*, R. & J.E. Taylor, 1841, pp. 85–6.

THE OWL: HUGH OF FOUILLOY'S *DE AVIBUS* (*ON BIRDS*) (*c.* 1132–1152)   **Document 22**
AND THE ANONYMOUS *THE OWL AND THE NIGHTINGALE*, ll. 56–100
(LATE TWELFTH CENTURY)

Hugh of Fouilloy dedicated his moralising book to the lay brothers at his priory. The book is divided into two parts: the first deals with the dove, the hawk, the turtledove and the sparrow; the second part contains 23 chapters each treating a separate bird. The standard sources for the period – Physiologus, Isidore of Seville's Etymologiae, *Rabanus Maurus'* De natura rerum, *and the Hexaemeron literature of the Church doctors – are all used. The Owl and the Nightingale is a late twelfth-century poem. The poet has clearly observed these birds in their natural habitat and is very familiar with their behavioural traits. This is thus a relatively precocious example of the naturalism that would become more common by the end of the thirteenth century.*

Hugh of Fouilloy

It [the owl] is said to be a filthy bird, because the place where it lives is befouled with its dung, because a sinner by the example of his wayward action dishonours those with whom he lives. It is a bird laden with plumage, that is, with an excess of flesh and weakness of mind, but truly constrained by a heavy indolence. It is constrained by idleness and heavy indolence, because sinners are idle and indolent in the doing of good deeds. It lingers day and night among the tombs, for the sinner enjoys the stench of human flesh. Furthermore, it lives in caves, nor does the sinner emerge through confession, but hates the light of truth.

Source: Clark, W.B. (trans.), *The Medieval Book of Birds: Hugh of Fouilloy's Avarium*, Medieval and Renaissance Texts and Studies, 80, 1992, p. 219.

The Owl and the Nightingale

So long as I [nightingale] can safely hide
And shield myself against the cold
In quiet within this hedge's fold
I neither attend to what you [owl] say,
Nor hear your threatenings with dismay.
I know how cruelly you attack
Small birds who cannot fight you back;
At every opportunity
You peck and tear them wantonly.
And that is why all birds detest you,
Screeching and crying as they chase
And mob you till you leave the place.
Even the tiniest of the tits
Would gladly tear you into bits!
For you are loathsome through and through
And wholly hateful to the view:
Your neck is thick, your body squat,
Your head much bigger than the lot.
Your eyes are black as coal, and broad
As if they had been daubed in woad.
You glare as if you'd gorge on such
As come within your talons' clutch.
Your beak is hooked and sharp and strong,
A buckled awl, its shape all wrong.
With it you gabble loud and long,
And that is what you call your song.
Then, with your claws you threaten to slash
And pound my body to a mash.
The frog that sits by the mill-house wheel
Would make a far more natural meal.
And snails and mice and such foul brood
Appear to be your proper food.
You perch by day and fly by night
And that's not natural or right.
Most foul you are and most unclean:
Your nest shows clearly what I mean,
For there you rear your noisome brood
On dirty putrefying food;
And you know what they do with it:

They foul themselves chin-deep and sit
Amid the muck as if quite blind,
Which brings this pithy saying to mind:
'Ill fortune take that thing unblest,
The bird who fouls his own nest.'

Source: Stone, B. (trans.), *The Owl and the Nightingale, Cleanness, St Erkenwald*, Penguin, 1971, pp. 182–4.

FARID AL-DIN 'ATTAR, *MANTIQ AL-TAIR* (*THE CONFERENCE OF THE BIRDS*)   **Document 23**
ON THE SPIDER (*c.* 1130–*c.* 1229)

Writers in the Latin west rarely provided realistic descriptions of the everyday workings of nature in the twelfth century such as this beautifully observed Persian poem on the spider. This short verse is thus representative of wider cultural differences in the treatment of nature visible in contemporary Christian and Islamic literature.

You've seen an active spider work – he seems
To spend his life in self-communing dreams
In fact the web he spins is evidence
That he's endowed with some far-sighted sense
He drapes a corner with his cunning snare
And waits until a fly's entangled there
Then dashes out and sucks the meagre blood
Of his bewildered, buzzing, dying food.
He'll dry the carcass then, and live off it
For days, consuming bit by tasty bit
Until the owner of the house one day
Will reach up casually to knock away
The cunning spider's home – and with her broom
She clears both fly and spider from the room
Such is the world, and one who feeds there is
A fly trapped by that spider's subtleties.

Source: Darbani, A. and Davis, D. (trans.), *Farid al-din 'Attar, The Conference of the Birds*, Penguin, 1984, pp. 107–8.

Document 24   BARTHOLOMEW THE ENGLISHMAN, *DE PROPRIETATIBUS RERUM* (*ON THE PROPERTIES OF THINGS*), BK 14, CHS 9 and 10 ON THE MOUNTAINS OF ETHIOPIA AND MOUNT ETNA (*a*. 1240)

Bartholomew's encyclopaedia enjoyed considerable popularity and was translated into a number of languages. In these two entries Bartholomew reveals his reliance upon earlier authorities, so too his lack of originality, but there is nothing odd in this, for this was the scholarly method of the period. They reveal the continued fascination for distant lands and their fauna as well as natural phenomena much closer to home (see also Document 25).

The mountains of Ethiopia

There are seven mountains of Ethiopia and it is said that amongst them is the mountain of Athlaus. As Isidore said in book 14 chapter 4, western Ethiopia is hilly, gravelly and waste in the middle and eastward, and stretches from the west side of Mount Athal to the ends of Egypt and it bordered on the west by the sea of Occian and in the north by the river Nile. In the mountains and plains of this land there are many people with weirdly shaped faces and horrible in physique. This land is also full of wild and cruel beasts, serpents and adders. There is the rhinoceros, that is the unicorn, a beast with one horn. There are camels and pards. There are cocatrices and enormous dragons from whose brains precious stones are taken. Here can be found the gems hyacinth and chrysoprase. Here cinnamon can be gathered. Many wild and fierce beasts breed here: dragons, ostriches, elephants and apes. This is taken from Isidore. Also it is said that between Cerene and Ethiopia is a well that quenches the heat of day and warms in the coolness of the night against the usual nature of water found in other springs.

Mount Etna

Etna is a hill on the island of Sicily from which emanates fire and brimstone as if it were hell, as Isidore said in book 14, chapter 7. It is said that the cavities on its southeastern side are full of brimstone and that wide caves stretch from here to the seas where they meet waves and produce wind, and this wind blows out the brimstone and creates fire. Also out of this hill comes bright burning smoke that covers the land as Isidore said. Also it is said that often a certain figure appears on this hill, and people thereabout regularly hear groaning and complaining voices, lamentation, sorrow and woe. Therefore many believe that this is a place of pain and that souls are tormented therein. But I do not affirm that. But it seems that Saint Gregory believed this in his *Dialogues*.

Source: Rendered into modern English from Seymour, M.C. *et al.* (eds), *On the Properties of Things: John Trevisa's Translation of Bartholomæus Anglicus De Proprietatibus Rerum*, 3 vols, Clarendon Press, 1975, pp. 700–1.

GAUTHIER OF METZ, *THE MYRROUR OF THE WORLD*, PT 2, CH. 4 ON   **Document 25**
INDE (*c.* 1245)

The remarkable popularity of this short treatise on the quadrivium, geography, and the workings of the natural world is exemplified by the fact that it was printed by William Caxton in 1481, two and a half centuries after it was first written. The text reproduced here, dealing with the the islands of the Far East is representative of how Europeans viewed these distant lands.

Here speaking of Inde and the things found therein
The Indes are isolated by the great sea which surrounds them. There is an island called Probane where there are ten cities and plenty of towns, and where every year there are two summers and two winters. As a result it is so temperate that there is always verdure and the trees are always in flower, leaf and fruit. And there are plentiful supplies of gold and silver and much more besides. There are great mountains of gold and of precious stones and other riches. But no man dare approach the island because of the dragons and because of the wild gryffons (which have the bodies of lions) that fly here and which would easily be able to carry away an armed man sitting on his horse when he sees him with his claws and talons. There are still plenty of other places that are so delectable, so sweet and so spiritual as this, such that if a someone were there they would say that it was indeed paradise.

Source: Rendered into modern English from Prior, O.H. (ed.), *Caxton's Mirrour of the World*, Early English Texts Society, Old Series, 110, 1913, pp. 69–70.

MATTHEW PARIS, *HISTORIA ANGLORUM* (*HISTORY OF THE ENGLISH*) ON   **Document 26**
UNSEASONABLE WEATHER (*c.* 1274)

Here is presented Paris' account of the weather in 1239 in the abbreviated version of his Chronica Majora. *Matthew Paris makes much of the weather elsewhere in his works particularly when it led to inundation and the destruction of villages, livestock and crops. (See also Documents 30 and 32.)*

The latter part of this year was cloudy and rainy, until the spring had passed, whence all confidence in the crops failed; and during two or more of the summer months, the weather was beyond measure and unusually dry and hot; as autumn, however, approached it became moist and rainy by which the crops were wonderfully restored, fresh plants springing up in place of those that had withered; and there was a great abundance of corn. At the end of the autumn, however, those who delayed their reaping were deprived of their crops; for such deluges of rain fell, that the straw as well as the grain rotted; and this unnatural autumn, which was considered generally to be a dry and cold season, generated various kinds of dangerous diseases; so that the temperature was with difficulty maintained, and no one remembered ever to have seen so many afflicted with the quartan fever.

Source: Giles, J. (trans.), *Matthew Paris' English History*, vol. 1, Henry G. Bohn, 1852, p. 158.

Document 27   *SENESCHAUCY* CH. 7 ON THE DUTIES OF THE COWHERD (*a.* 1276)

Seneschaucy, written in Anglo-Norman, deals with the day-to-day management of manorial estates and estate accounting. The duties of all the manorial officers are dealt with in individual chapters. The concern for the care of livestock that is shown here is ultimately aimed at protecting valuable manorial assets rather than anything more humane.

Here begins the office of the cowherd

The cowherd ought to know and understand his work. He ought to keep his cows well and know how to feed the calves until they are fully weaned. He ought to see that he has fine and big bulls, well matched, near the cows to mate when they will. No cow ought to suckle her young or be milked after Michaelmas to make cheese of 'after yield', for such suckling and such 'after yield' make the cows grow thin and lose strength; it makes them mate later next year, the milk will be less because of it and the calf smaller and poorer.

He ought to see that his cattle are as well fed and kept in winter and summer as he will wish to answer for. No cow or any farm animal ought to be flayed before it has been inspected and an investigation made into the cause of its death. No fire or candle ought to be taken into the cowshed except as aforesaid.

Every year it should be arranged that from each vaccary the old cows, and those with bad teeth are drafted and that the barren cows and the worthless heifers which do not thrive are drafted and put for fattening on good pasture and then sold as aforesaid. During the summer season the cowherd ought to put the cows and the other cattle every night into a fold, well strewn with litter or fern, as has been said before. He himself ought then to lie there during the nights.

Source: Oshinsky, D. (trans.), *Walter of Henley and other Treatises on Estate Management and Accounting*, Clarendon Press, 1971, pp. 283–5.

ALBERTUS MAGNUS, *DE NATURA LOCORUM* (*ON THE NATURE OF PLACES*)   **Document 28**
ll. 43–62 ON PLANETARY INFLUENCE (*a.* 1280)

In this extract, Albertus Magnus lays out the widely accepted notion that rays emitted from the stars and planets possessed powers to influence everything in the terrestrial sphere. Even minute differences in the angle at which these rays hit the ground would affect how these worked on and within the particular bodies with which they came into contact.

If anyone wished to understand all the natures and properties of particular places, he would know that there is not a point in them that does not have a special property from the virtue of the stars, . . . for the circle of the horizon is varied in relation to each point of the habitation of animals, plants, and stones; and the entire orientation of the heavens . . . is varied in relation to the varying circle of the horizon. For which cause their natures, properties, customs, actions and species, which seem to be generated in the same perceptible place, are varied, to such an extent that diverse properties and customs are attributed to twins' seeds, both for brute animals and for men, from this different orientation. And this is reasonable because it has been learned that the heavens pour forth formative virtues into everything that exists. Moreover, it mostly pours them forth by means of rays emitted by the light of the stars, and therefore it follows that each pattern and angle of rays causes different virtues in things below.

Source: Rutkin, H.D., 'Astrology', in *The Cambridge History of Science, vol. 3: Early Modern* Science, eds K. Park and L. Daston, Cambridge University Press, 2006, p. 547.

ALBERTUS MAGNUS, *DE MINERALIBUS* (*ON MINERALS*) ON SILVER (*a.* 1280)   **Document 29**

In this remarkable section of his work on minerals, Albertus reveals how he moved beyond received knowledge by visiting sites, talking to those with practical knowledge of metal deposits, and observing these veins at close quarters. In other areas of the natural sciences too, Albertus subjected hypothesis to experimental test and by so doing helped to lay the foundations of the modern scientific method. This extract can be compared with Hildegard of Bingen's fantastic accounts of gemstone formation (Document 19) slightly more than a century earlier.

As to natural processes, I have learned by what I have seen with my own eyes that a vein flowing from a simple source was in one part pure gold, and in another silver having a stony calx mixed with it. And miners and smeltmen have told me that this very frequently happens; and therefore they are sorry when they have found gold, for the gold is near the source, and then the vein fails. Then I myself, making a careful examination found that the vessel in which the mineral was converted into gold differed from that in which it was converted into silver. For the vessel containing gold was a very hard stone – one of the kind from which fire is struck with steel – and it had the pure gold and not incorporated [with the stone], but enclosed in a hollow within it; and there was a little burned earth between the stony part and the gold. And the stone opened out with a passage into the silvery vein, traversing a black stone which was not very hard but earthy. And the black stone was fissile, the kind of stone from which slates are made for building houses. This proves, however, that from a single place which was the vessel of the mineral matter both [gold and silver] evaporated, and a difference in the purification and digestion had been responsible for the difference in the kind of metal.

Source: Wyckoff, D. (ed. and trans.), *Albertus Magnus, De Mineralibus*, Clarendon Press, 1967, pp. 200–1.

Document 30   METEOROLOGICAL OBSERVATIONS ATTRIBUTED TO ROGER BACON FOR FEBRUARY 1270

Although generally attributed to Roger Bacon, there is no hard proof that he was responsible for these weather observations. Their detailed description of weather events during the night may suggest they were written by a monk who was able to observe them as he went to the nocturnal offices. They probably relate to weather around Oxford. Their date and importance, however, are not in doubt.

From the beginning of the month the weather was rainy but pleasant enough until the 4th (inclusive). On the 4th, at the third hour, there was snow with rain and great cold and nasty, rotten weather for 2 or 3 hours. In the night there was a little frost. On the 5th the frost was stronger and it was a clear day, and on the night of the 6th it was very frosty and cold, but that day, the 6th, there was a strong southerly wind in the morning and the frost melted; yet it was colder that day than before, and very cloudy, though it did not rain. On the 7th it was pleasant and clear, and on the 8th until the seventh hour it really rained . . .

Source: Long, C., 'The oldest European weather diary?', *Weather*, 29, 1974, p. 236.

MARCO POLO, *DIVISAMENT DOU MONDE* (*DIVISION OF THE WORLD*), BK 3,   **Document 31**
CH. 9 CONCERNING PYGMIES (1298)

Marco Polo's travel account, written together with the romance writer Rustichello of Pisa, provides detailed descriptions of his extended journeying in Asia. They appear to mix fact with fiction, indeed some now question whether Polo actually travelled to China. Undoubtedly, however, this work caught the public imagination, being quickly translated into several European languages. In this extract Polo and his co-author appear to debunk long-held views regarding pygmies, one of the monstrous races.

Of the Island of Java Minor
It should be known that what is reported respecting the dried bodies of diminutive human creatures, or pigmies, brought from India, is an idle tale, such men being manufactured in this island in the following manner. The country produces a species of monkey, of a tolerable size, and having a countenance resembling that of a man. Those persons who make it their business to catch them, shave off the hair, leaving it only about the chin, and those other parts where it naturally grows on the human body. They then dry and preserve them with camphor and other drugs; and having prepared them in such a mode that they have exactly the appearance of little men, they put them into wooden boxes, and sell them to trading people, who carry them to all parts of the world. But this is merely an imposition. Neither in India, nor in any other country, however wild, have pigmies been found of a form so diminutive as these exhibit.

Source: Komroff, M. (ed.), *The Travels of Marco Polo (the Venetian) Revised from Marsden's Translation*, Liveright, 1982, p. 276.

METEOROLOGICAL OBSERVATIONS OF WILLIAM MERLE (1344)   **Document 32**

William Merle has been identified as Rector of Drigby in Lincolnshire and Fellow of Merton College, Oxford. He kept records of the weather over a seven-year period between 1337 and 1344. Early observations appear rather sketchy but his observations became ever more detailed over time. This entry for June 1340 is typical of the kinds of weather events he noted. They relate both to Lincolnshire and Oxfordshire.

In June there was great heat and light rain on the 2nd, and on the 11th there was rain, but less than on the 2nd. From the 13th onwards there was moderate wind occasionally throughout the remainder of the month, and it was very strong on the 14th, and stronger on the 23rd than on the 14th, but much of the heat was lessened thereby. Yet the heat was occasionally, but not often, as great as in the first half of the month. In the week after the 13th there was rain occasionally, but very little, for there was never enough to hinder the workers in the hay-fields. It is to be noted that the rain which fell from the beginning of February till the middle of May did not penetrate much; and in the year of Christ 1331 it happened likewise.

Source: Symons, G.J. (ed.), *Willelmum Merle, Consideraciones Temperiei pro 7 Annis*, Edward Standford, 1891.

Document 33   *MANDEVILLE'S TRAVELS* ON MONSTROUS RACES (*c.* 1360)

Sir John Mandeville's Travels *purport to be a factual account of an actual journey made to the Holy Land and beyond. They are evidently fictitious. Nevertheless they serve to show how the wider world was perceived by contemporary Europeans, places of mystery and wonder.*

. . . in those isles [possibly the Andaman Islands] are many manners of folk of divers conditions. In one of them is a manner of folk of great stature, as they were giants, horrible and foul to the sight; and they have but one eye, and this is in midst the forehead. They eat raw flesh and raw fish. In another isle are foul men of figure without heads, and they have eyes in either shoulder one, and their mouths are round shaped like a horseshoe, y-midst their breasts. In another isle are men without heads; and their eyes and their mouths are behind their shoulders. In another isle is a manner of folk that has a plat face, without nose or eyes; but they have two small holes instead of eyes, and they have a plat mouth, lipless. In another isle are foul men that have the overlip so great that, when they sleep in the sun, they cover all the visage with that lip. In another isle are folk of little stature, as they were dwarfs; and they are somewhat more than pigmies. They have no mouth, but they have instead of their mouth a little hole, and therefore, when they shall eat, them behoves suck it with a reed or a pipe . . . In another isle are folk whose ears are so long that they hang down to their knees, In another isle are folk that have feet like horse, and on them they will run so swift that they will overtake wild beasts and slay them to their meat through swiftness of foot . . .

Source: Letts, M. (trans.), *Mandeville's Travels: Texts and Translations*, Hakluyt Society, series 2, 101, 1953, pp. 141–2.

EDWARD OF NORWICH, *THE MASTER OF GAME* ON GREYHOUNDS   **Document 34**
(1406–1413)

Edward wrote this treatise, essentially a translation of Gaston Phoebus' Livre de Chasse, whilst in prison. A number of original chapters were added together with telling inserts demonstrating differences between English and French hunting methods and their knowledge or otherwise of the animals they chased. In this extract is seen the considerable eye for detail required by huntsmen wishing to pick or to breed the best hunting hounds.

The good greyhound should be of middle size, neither too big nor too little, and then he is good for all beasts. If he were too big he is nought for small beasts, and if he were too little he were nought for the great beasts. Nevertheless whoso can maintain both, it is good that he have both of the great and of the small, and of the middle size. A greyhound should have a long head and somewhat large made, resembling the making of a pike. A good large mouth and good seizers the one against the other, so that the nether jaw pass not the upper, nor that the upper pass not the nether. Their eyes are red or black as those of a sparrow hawk, the ears small and high in the manner of a serpent, the neck great and long bowed like a swan's neck, his chest great and open, the hair under his chin hanging down in the manner of a lion. His shoulders as a roebuck, the forelegs straight and great enough and not too high in the legs, the feet straight and round as a cat, great claws, long head as a cow hanging down.

The bones and the joints of the chine great and hard like the chine of a hart. And if his chine be a little high it is better than if it were flat. A little pintel and little bullocks, and well trussed near the ars, small womb, the hocks straight and not bent as of an ox, a cat's tail making a ring at the end and not too high, the two bones of the chine behind broad of a large palm's breadth or more.

Source: Baillie-Grohman, W.A. and Baillie-Grohman, F.N. (eds), *Edward of Norwich, The Master of Game*, Pennsylvania University Press, 2005, pp. 113–14.

THE SECRETE OF SECRETES, 'ON THE CONDITION OF MAN'   **Document 35**
(FIFTEENTH-CENTURY VERSION)

The Secretum secretorum, *a miscellany of observations on the natural world and the nature of man was an extremely popular text, going through many redactions during the middle ages. The origins of this text are unknown but an Arabic translation ascribed to al-Bitriq was circulating as early as the ninth century. In this extract, each facet of human behaviour is likened to an animal counterpart, the whole piece, as it is stated, reinforcing the notion of Man as microcosm.*

Understand well that the most glorious God created never a wiser creature than Man. And He never set in other beasts what He set in Man, and you will find no other custom or manner other than those found in Man. For he is as bold as a lion, fearful as a hare, large as a cock, niggardly as a dog, hard and stern as a crow, meek as a turtle, malicious as a lioness, private and tame as a dove, rough and guileful as a fox, simple and meek as a lamb, swift and light as a doe or pricket, slow as a bear, precious and dear as an elephant, vile and dull as an ass, rebellious and noisy as a lion cub, meek and humble as a peahen, wicked as a stork, dumb as a fish, reasonable as an angel, lecherous and malicious as an owl, profitable as a horse, nervous as a mouse. And universally there is no animal, vegetable or mineral, no star or planet, no sign nor celestial host that has any property other than that found in Man. And therefore *Homo* is called the little world.

Source: Rendered into modern English from Manzalaoui, M.A. (ed.), *Secretum Secretorum. Nine English Versions*, Early English Text Society, Old Series, 276, 1977, pp. 80–1.

References

Primary sources

Many works on medieval natural science and philosophy are now available in English translation. Essential reading is Grant, *A Source Book in Medieval Science* which provides complete translations and extended extracts of the most important texts. These have purposely not been reiterated in the Documents Section which should be thought of simply as a complementary collection to the more comprehensive treatment provided by Grant. Key extracts of other late antique and medieval writings on nature have been collected by Torrance, *Encompassing Nature: A Source Book*, especially chapters 13 to 15.

The key English translations of medieval texts – in chronological order of their originals – are Barney *et al.*, *The Etymologies of Isidore of Seville*; Kendall and Wallis, *Bede, On the Nature of Things and On Times*; Sheldon-Williams, *Eriugena, Periphyseon*; Van Ardsall, *Medieval Herbal Remedies: The Old English Herbarium and Anglo-Saxon Medicine*; Sachau, *Alberuni's India*; Rendell, *Physiologus*; Burnett, *Adelard of Bath, Conversations with his Nephew*; Barber, *Bestiary*; Clark, *The Medieval Book of Birds*; Ronca and Curr, *William of Conches, Dragmaticon*; Throop, *Hildegard von Bingen's Physica*; Thorndike, *The Sphere of Sacrobosco and its Commentators*; Wood and Fyfe, *The Art of Falconry by Frederick II of Hohenstaufen*; Bodenheimer, *Rabbi Gershon Ben Shlomoh d'Arles, The Gate of Heaven*; Kitchell and Resnik, *Albertus Magnus, On Animals*; Tilmann, *An Appraisal of the Geographical Works of Albertus Magnus*; Wyckoff, *Albertus Magnus, De Mineralibus*. Middle English editions include Manzalaoui, *Secretum Secretorum*; Prior, *Caxton's Mirrour of the World*; and Seymour *et al.*, *On the Properties of Things*.

Useful bibliographical references to printed editions of medieval primary sources in Latin and other languages, arranged thematically, are provided by contributors to Mantello and Rigg, *Medieval Latin: An Introduction and Bibliographical Guide*.

Secondary literature

The classic treatment of western natural philosophy remains Glacken, *Traces on the Rhodian Shore*. The first two volumes of Thorndike, *A History of Magic and Experimental Science*, if old, remain a treasure trove of information and usefully provide biographical accounts for many of the major figures in the study of the medieval nature. Despite its focus on the early modern period, Thomas, *Man and Nature* contains much that is of interest for the medieval historian and should be read. Lindberg, *Science in the Middle Ages* continues to offer a good introduction to many aspects of the medieval natural sciences especially Stannard's contribution on 'Natural History'. More recent assessments of key themes and particular thinkers are concisely laid out in individual entries in Glick *et al.* (eds), *Medieval Science, Technology, and Medicine*. Three edited volumes – Salisbury, *The Medieval World of Nature*; Hanawalt and Kiser, *Engaging with Nature*; and Ridyard and Benson, *Man and Nature in the Middle Ages* – offer a wealth of perspectives on the medieval natural world even if their coverage is rather idiosyncratic. Environmental historians will find much of interest in Radkau, *Nature and Power* and cultural and theological historians likewise in Bartlett, *The Natural and the Supernatural in the Middle Ages*. For an introduction to Islamic attitudes to nature refer to Nasr, *An Introduction to Islamic Cosmological Doctrines* and Turner, *Science in Medieval Islam*. For Judaic perspectives see Harvey (ed.), *The Medieval Hebrew Encyclopedias of Science and Philosophy* and Zonta, 'Mineralogy, botany and zoology in medieval Hebrew encyclopaedias'.

References

Achena, M. and Massé, H. (trans.), *Avicenne, Le Livre de Science*, Les Belles Lettres/Unesco, 1986.

Adler, E.N. (ed.), *Jewish Travellers in the Middle Ages: 19 Firsthand Accounts*, Dover Publications Inc., 1987.

Alexander, D., *Saints and Animals in the Middle Ages*, Boydell, 2008.

Alexandre, P., *Le Climat en Europe au Moyen Age: Contribution à l'Histoire des Variations Climatiques de 1000 à 1425, d'Après les Sources Narrative de l'Europe Occidentale*, Ecole des Hautes Etudes en Science Sociales, 1987.

Allott, S. (trans.), *Alcuin of York* c. AD 732 to 804: His Life and Letters, William Sessions, 1974.

Almond, R., *Medieval Hunting*, Sutton, 2003.

Anderson, E., 'The seasons of the year in Old English', *Anglo-Saxon England*, 26, 1996.

Anderson, W. (trans.), *The Consolation of Philosophy*, Centaur Press, 1963.

Angremy, A., 'La Mappemonde de Pierre de Beauvais', *Romania*, 104, 1983.

Anon. (trans.), *Fitz-Stephen's Description of the City of London*, B. White, 1772.

Arano, L.C. (trans.), *The Medieval Health Handbook: Tacuinum Sanitatis*, Barrie & Jenkins, 1976.

Arikha, N., *Passions and Tempers: A History of the Humours*, Ecco, 2007.

Astill, G. and Langdon, J. (eds), *Medieval Farming and Technology. The Impact of Agricultural Change in Northwest Europe*, Brill, 1997.

Backhouse, J., *The Lindisfarne Gospels*, Phaidon, 1981.

Backhouse, J., *The Bedford Hours: Medieval Manuscripts in the British Library*, New Amsterdam Press, 1991.

Baillie-Grohman, W.A. and Baillie-Grohman, F.N. (eds), *Edward of Norwich, The Master of Game*, Pennsylvania University Press, 2005.

Balme, D.M. (trans.), *Aristotle, History of Animals, Books VII–X*, Harvard University Press, 1991.

Barber, R. (trans.), *Bestiary: Being an English Version of the Bodleian Library, Oxford M.S. Bodley 764*, Boydell Press, 1999.

Barney, S.A., Lewis, W.J., Beach, J.A. and Bergof, O. (trans.), *The Etymologies of Isidore of Seville*, Cambridge University Press, 2006.

Bartlett, R., *The Natural and the Supernatural in the Middle Ages*, Cambridge University Press, 2008.

Baxter, R., *Bestiaries and Their Users in the Middle Ages*, Sutton, 1998.

Benton, J.R., *The Medieval Menagerie: Animals in the Art of the Middle Ages*, Abbeville Press, 1992.

Berger, M., *Hildegard of Bingen, On Natural Philosophy and Medicine*, D.S. Brewer, 1999.

Berman, C., 'Agriculture', in *Medieval France: An Encyclopaedia*, eds W.W. Kilber, G.A. Zinn, J. Bell Henneman and L. Earp, Routledge, 1995.

Best, M.R. and Brightman, F.H. (eds), *The Book of Secrets of Albertus Magnus*, Red Wheel/Wieser, 2000.

Betts, H., *Johannes Scotus Erigena: A Study in Mediaeval Philosophy*, Russell & Russell, 1964.

Biggam, C.P. (ed.), *From Earth to Art: The Many Aspects of the Plant-World in Anglo-Saxon England*, Costerus, New Series, 148, 2003.

Biller, P., 'Cathars and the material world', in *God's Bounty? The Churches and the Natural World*, Studies in Church History, 46, eds P. Clarke and T. Claydon, Boydell & Brewer, 2010.

Blake, M. (trans.), *Aelfric's De Temporibus Anni*, D.S. Brewer, 2009.

Bloch, M., *French Rural History. An Essay on its Basic Characteristics*, Routledge & Kegan Paul, 1966.

Blume, D., 'Children of the planets: the popularization of astrology in the 15th century', in *Il Sole e la Luna*, Micrologus 12, 2004.

Bodenheimer, F.S. (trans.), *Rabbi Gershon Ben Shlomoh d'Arles, The Gate of Heaven (Shaar ha-Shamayim)*, Kiryath Sepher, 1953.

Bodenheimer, F.S. and Rabinowitz, A. (trans.), *Timotheus of Gaza, On Animals: Fragments of a Byzantine Paraphrase of an Animal-Book of the 5th Century AD*, Collections de Travaux de l'Academie Internationale d'Histoire des Sciences, 3, Brill, 1948.

Boese, H. (ed.), *Thomas Cantimpratensis, Liber de natura rerum*, De Gruyter, 1973.

Bolens, L., 'De l'idéologie Aristotelicienne à l'empirisme médiévale: les sols dans l'agronomie Hispano-Arabe', *Annales*, 30:5, 1975.

Boudet, J.-C., 'Astrology', in *Medieval Science, Technology, and Medicine: An Encyclopedia*, eds T.F. Glick, S.J. Livesey and F. Wallis, Routledge, 2005.

Bradley, S.A. (ed. and trans.), *Anglo-Saxon Poetry*, J.M. Dent, 2003.

Brimblecombe, P., 'Meteorological service in fifteenth-century Sandwich', *Environment and History*, 1:2, 1995.

Burnett, C. (ed.), *Adelard of Bath: An English Scientist and Arabist of the Early Twelfth Century*, Warburg Institute Surveys and Texts, 14, Warburg Institute, 1987.

Burnett, C., 'Astrology', in *Medieval Latin: An Introduction and Bibliographical Guide*, eds F.A.C. Mantello and A.G. Rigg, Catholic University of America Press, 1996.

Burnett, C. (trans.), *Adelard of Bath: Conversations with his Nephew: On the Same and the Different, Questions on Natural Science, and On Birds*, Cambridge University Press, 1998.

Burrow, J.A., *Ages of Man. A Study in Medieval Writing and Thought*, Clarendon Press, 1986.

Bynum, W., 'The Great Chain of Being after forty years: an appraisal', *Journal of Historical Science*, 13, 1973.

Camille, M., *Mirror in Parchment: The Luttrell Psalter and the Making of Medieval England*, Reaktion, 1998.

Campion, N., *The History of Western Astrology*, vol. 2: *The Medieval and Early Modern Worlds*, Continuum, 2009.

Cannan, F., 'The myths of medieval heraldry', *Nottingham Medieval Studies*, 47, 2003.

Capuano, T.M., '*Capitols singulars deles llauors que deuras sembrar*: a late medieval planting guide for the Spanish Levant', *Catalan Review*, 12, 1998.

Carey, H.M., 'Astrological medicine and the medieval English folded almanac', *Social History of Medicine*, 17:3, 2004.

Carmody, F.J. (trans.), *Brunetto Latino, Li Livres dou Tresor*, Berkeley University Press, 1948.

Chadwick, H. (trans.), *Origen, Contra Celsum*, Cambridge University Press, 1980.

Chardonnens, L.S., *Anglo-Saxon Prognostics, 900–1100. Studies and Texts*, Brill, 2007.

Cheyette, F.L., 'The disappearance of the ancient landscape and the climatic anomaly of the early Middle Ages: a question to be pursued', *Early Medieval Europe*, 16:2, 2008.

Chiesa, P. (intro.), *The Travels of Friar Oderic*, Wm. B. Eerdmans Publishing Co., 2002.

Clagett, M. (trans.), 'The compatibility of the Earth's diurnal rotation with astronomical phenomena', in *A Source Book in Medieval Science*, ed. E. Grant, Harvard University Press, 1974.

Clark, T. and Derhalli, M. (trans.), *Al-Mansur's Book On Hunting*, Aris and Phillips, 2001.

Clark, W.B. (trans.), *The Medieval Book of Birds: Hugh of Fouilloy's Avarium*, Medieval and Renaissance Texts and Studies, 80, 1992.

Clark, W.B., *A Medieval Book of Beasts: The Second-Family Bestiary*, Boydell, 2006.

Clarke, C., *Literary Landscapes and the Idea of England, 700–1400*, Cambridge University Press, 2006.

Clément-Mullet, J.-J. (trans.), *Ibn al-'Awwâm, Le Livre de l'Agriculture*, Actes Sud/Sindbad, 2000.

Cockayne, T.O., *Leechdoms, Wortcunning and Starcraft of Early England*, Longman *et al.*, 2 vols, 1864.

Cohen, E., 'Animals in medieval perceptions: the image of the ubiquitous other', in *Animals and Human Society: Changing Perspectives*, eds A. Manning and J. Serpell, Routledge, 1994.

Colgrave, B. and Mynors, R. (trans.), *Bede's Ecclesiastical History of the English People*, Clarendon Press, 1992.

Collins, B. (trans.), *Absan al-Taqāsīm fī Ma'rifat al-Aqālīm al-Muqaddasī, The Best Division for Knowledge of the Regions*, Garnet Publishing, 2001.

Cook, A.S. and Pitman, J.H. (trans.), *The Old English Physiologus*, Yale Studies in English, 63, 1821.

Coolman, B.T., *The Theology of Hugh of St. Victor*, Cambridge University Press, 2010.

Corbin, H., *Avicenna and the Visionary Recital*, trans. W.R. Trask, Pantheon Books, 1960.

Corcoran, T.H. (trans.), *Seneca, Naturales Quaestiones*, 2 vols, William Heinemann, 1971–2.

Corner, G.W. (trans.), 'Anatomical demonstration at Salerno (*The Anatomy of the Pig*)', in *A Source Book in Medieval Science*, ed. E. Grant, Harvard University Press, 1974a.

Corner, G.W. (trans.), 'A scholastic anatomy: *The Anatomy of Master Nicolas*', in *A Source Book in Medieval Science*, ed. E. Grant, Harvard University Press, 1974b.

Coupland, G.W., 'An attack upon astrology', in *A Source Book in Medieval Science*, ed. E. Grant, Harvard University Press, 1974.

Crawford, S.J. (trans.), *Byrhtferth's Manual*, English Text Society, Original Series, 177, Oxford University Press, 1929.

Crossley-Holland, K. (trans.), *The Exeter Book Riddles*, Penguin, rev. edn, 1993.

Cummins, J., *The Hound and the Hawk: The Art of Medieval Hunting*, Phoenix Press, 1988.

Curley, M.J. (trans.), *Physiologus*, Texas University Press, 1979.

Dalby, A. (trans.), *Geoponika: Farm Work. A Modern Translation of the Roman and Byzantine Farming Handbook*, Prospect Books, 2011.

Dales, R.C., 'Marius "On the elements" and the twelfth-century science of matter', *Viator*, 3, 1972.

Danielsson, B. (ed.), *William Twiti, The Art of Hunting, 1327*, Almqvist and Wiksell International, 1977.

Darbani, A. and Davis, D. (trans.), *Farid al-din 'Attar, The Conference of the Birds*, Penguin, 1984.

Davies, R.T., *Medieval English Lyrics: A Critical Anthology*, Faber and Faber, 1965.

Dawood, N.J. (trans.), *The Koran*, Penguin, rev. edn, 2003.

Dendle, P. and Touwaide, A. (eds), *Health and Healing from the Medieval Garden*, Routledge, 2008.

Druce, G.C., 'The elephant in medieval legend and art', *Journal of the Royal Archaeological Institute*, 76, 1919.

Duby, G., *Rural Economy and Country Life in the Medieval West*, trans. C. Postan, Edward Arnold, 1968.

Duby, G., *The Early Growth of the European Economy. Warriors and Peasants from the Seventh to the Twelfth Century*, trans. H.B. Clarke, Cornell University Press, 1978.

Duff, J.W. and Duff, A. (eds and trans.), *Minor Latin Poets*, rev. edn, William Heinemann, 1935.

Dufournet, J., *Les Très Riches Heures du Duc de Berry*, Bibliothèque de l'Image, 1995.

Dutton, P.E., 'Thunder and hail over the Carolingian countryside', in *Agriculture in the Middle Ages. Technology, Practice and Representation*, ed. D. Sweeney, Pennsylvania University Press, 1995a.

Dutton, P.E., 'The materialization of nature and of quaternary man in the early twelfth century', in *Man and Nature in the Middle Ages*, eds S.J. Ridyard and R.G. Benson, Sewanee Mediaeval Studies, 6, University of the South Press, 1995b.

Dutton, P.E., *Carolingian Civilisation: A Reader*, Broadview Press, 1999.

Dyer, C., *Making a Living in the Middle Ages: The People of Britain 850–1520*, Yale University Press, 2002.

Eichholz, D. (trans.), *Theophrastus, De Lapidibus*, Clarendon Press, 1965.

Evans, J. and Serjeantson, M.S. (eds and trans.), *English Mediaeval Lapidaries*, Early English Text Society, Original Series, 190, 1933.

Fathers of the Dominican Province (trans.), *Thomas Aquinas, Summa Theologica*, Hayes Barton Press, 2006.

Fisher, C., *The Medieval Flower Book*, British Library, 2007.

Flores, N.C., 'The mirror of nature distorted: the medieval artist's dilemma in depicting animals', in *The Medieval World of Nature: A Book of Essays*, ed. J.E. Salisbury, Garland Medieval Casebooks, 5, 1993.

Fontaine, J. (trans.), *Isidore of Seville, De Natura Rerum: Traité de la Nature*, Bibliothèque de l'École des Hautes Études Hispaniques, 28, Paris, 1960.

Fox, H.S.A., 'Approaches to the adoption of the midland system', in *The Origins of Open-Field Agriculture*, ed. T. Rowley, Rowman and Littlefield, 1981.

Frazer, J., *The Golden Bough*, Wordsworth, 1993.

Freeman-Grenville, G.S.P. (trans.), *Captain Buzurg ibn Shahriyar of Ramhormuz, The Book of the Wonders of India: Mainland, Sea and Islands*, East-West Publications, 1981.

Freitag, B., *Sheela-na-gigs: Unravelling an Enigma*, Routledge, 2004.

French, R., 'Foretelling the future: Arabic astrology and English medicine in the twelfth century', *Isis*, 87, 1996.

Friedländer, M. (trans.), *Moses Maimonides, The Guide for the Perplexed*, Routledge & Kegan Paul, 1903.

Friedman, J.B., *The Monstrous Races in Medieval Art and Thought*, Harvard University Press, 1981.

Friedman, J.B., 'Harry the Haywarde and Talbat his dog: an illustrated girdle book from Worcestershire', in *Art into Life: Collected Papers from the Kress Art Museum Medieval Symposia*, eds C.G. Fisher and K.L. Scott, Michigan State University Press, 1995.

Garmondsway, G.C. (trans.), *Aelfric's Colloquy*, Exeter University Press, 1991.

Gelling, M., *Place-Names in the Landscape. The Geographical Roots of Britain's Place-Names*, J.M. Dent, 1993.

Giles, J.A. (trans.), *Matthew Paris' English History from the year 1235 to 1273*, 3 vols, Henry G. Bohn, 1852–1854.

Giles, J.A. (ed.), *William of Malmesbury. Chronicle of the Kings of England*, trans. J. Sharpe, George Bell and Sons, 1904.

Ginzburg, C., *The Cheese and the Worms. The Cosmos of a Sixteenth-Century Miller*, trans. J. and A. Tedeschi, Johns Hopkins University Press, 1992.

Glacken, C.J., *Traces on the Rhodian Shore: Nature and Culture in Western Thought from Ancient Times to the End of the Eighteenth Century*, University of California Press, 1967.

Glick, T.F., *Islamic and Christian Spain in the Early Middle Ages*, Brill, 2005.

Glick, T.F., Livesey, S.J. and Wallis, F. (eds), *Medieval Science, Technology, and Medicine: An Encyclopedia*, Routledge, 2005.

Goldstein, B.R. (trans.), *Al-Biṭrūjī, On the Principles of Astronomy*, 2 vols, Yale University Press, 1971.

Grant, E. (ed.), *A Source Book in Medieval Science*, Harvard University Press, 1974a.

Grant, E. (trans.), 'The image or representation of the world (The image or representation of the world (*Ymago mundi*)', in *A Source Book in Medieval Science*, ed. E. Grant, Harvard University Press, 1974b.

Grant, E., *Planets, Stars, and Orbs: The Medieval Cosmos, 1200–1687*, Cambridge University Press, 1996.

Green, M., *Animals in Celtic Life and Myth*, Routledge, 1998.

Guthrie, W.K.C. (trans.), *Aristotle, On the Heavens*, William Heinemann, 1953.

Haberman, J. (trans.), *The Microcosm of Joseph ibn Saddiq*, Rosemount, 2003.

Hackett, J., 'Nature: diverse medieval interpretations', in *Medieval Science, Technology, and Medicine: An Encyclopedia*, eds T.F. Glick, S.J. Livesey and F. Wallis, Routledge, 2005.

Hanawalt, B.A. and Kiser, L.J. (eds), *Engaging with Nature: Essays on the Natural World in Medieval and Early Modern Europe*, Notre Dame University Press, 2008.

Harvey, P.D.A., *Manorial Records of Cuxham, Oxfordshire, circa 1200–1399*, Oxfordshire Record Society, 50, 1976.

Harvey, P.D.A., *Mappa Mundi: The Hereford World Map*, Hereford Cathedral and British Library, 1996.

Harvey, S. (ed.), *The Medieval Hebrew Encyclopedias of Science and Philosophy*, Amsterdam Studies in Jewish Thought, Kluwer Academic Publishers, 2000.

Hassig, D., *The Mark of the Beast: The Medieval Bestiary in Art, Life, and Literature*, Garland, 1999.

Helminski, C.A. (ed.), *The Book of Nature: A Sourcebook of Spiritual Perspectives on Nature and the Environment*, The Book Foundation, 2006.

Hicks, C., *Animals in Early Medieval Art*, Edinburgh University Press, 1993.

Hill, D.R., *Islamic Science and Engineering*, Edinburgh University Press, 1993.

Hoage, R.J. and Deiss, W.A., *New Worlds, New Animals. From Menagerie to Zoological Park in the Nineteenth Century*, Johns Hopkins University Press, 1996.

Hoffmann, R.C., *Fishers' Craft and Lettered Art: Tracts on Fishing from the End of the Middle Ages*, Toronto University Press, 1997.

Holmyard, E.J. and Mandeville, D.C. (trans.), 'On the formation of stones and mountains', in *A Source Book in Medieval Science*, ed. E. Grant, Harvard University Press, 1974.

Hoppenbrouwers, P., 'Agricultural production and technology in the Nether-lands, *c.* 1000–1500', in *Medieval Farming and Technology. The Impact of Agricultural Change in Northwest Europe*, eds G. Astill and J. Langdon, Brill, 1997.

Hunt, T., *Plant-Names of Medieval England*, Brewer, 1989.

Hutchinson, G.E., 'Attitudes toward nature in medieval England: the Alphonso and Bird Psalters', *Isis*, 65, 1974.

Jackson, B. (trans.), *The Nine Homilies of the Hexaemeron and the Letters of Saint Basil the Great, Archbishop of Caesarea*, The Nicene and Post-Nicene Fathers, second series, 8, 1894.

James, B.S. (trans.), *The Letters of St Bernard of Clairvaux*, Sutton, 1998.

James, J., *The Music of the Spheres: Music, Science and the Natural Order of the Universe*, Grove Press, 1995.

Janko, R., 'Empedocles, "On Nature" I 233–364: a new reconstruction of "P. Strasb. Gr." Inv. 1665–6', *Zeitschrift für Papyrologie und Epigraphik*, 150, 2004.

Joachim, H.H. (trans.), 'De generatione et corruptione', in *The Works of Aristotle*, vol. 2, ed. W.D. Ross, Clarendon Press, 1930.

Jones, P.M., *Medieval Medicine in Illuminated Manuscripts*, British Library, 1998.

Jones, R., 'Directional names in the early medieval landscape', in *Sense of Place in Anglo-Saxon England*, eds R. Jones and S. Semple, Shaun Tyas, 2012.

Jones, R. and Page, M., *Medieval Villages in an English Landscape: Beginnings and Ends*, Windgather Press, 2006.

Jones, W.J.S. (trans.), *Hippocrates IV*, William Heinemann, 1943.

Kay, S., *The Romance of the Rose*, Critical Guides to French Texts, 110, 1995.

Kemp, S., 'A medieval controversy about odor', *Journal of the History of the Behavioural Sciences*, 33:3, 1997.

Kendall, C.B. and Wallis, F. (trans.), *Bede, On the Nature of Things and On Times*, Translated Texts for Historians, 56, Liverpool University Press, 2010.

Kington, J., *Climate and Weather,* Collins, 2010.

Kitchell, K.F. and Resnik, I.M. (trans.), *Albertus Magnus, On Animals. A Medieval Summa Zoologica*, Johns Hopkins University Press, 1999.

Kitson, P.E., 'Lapidary traditions in Anglo-Saxon England. Part II: Bede's *Explanatio Apocalysis* and related works', *Anglo-Saxon England*, 12, 1983.

Kline, N.R., *Maps of Medieval Thought: The Hereford Paradigm*, Boydell, 2001.

Klingender, F.D., *Animals in Art and Thought: To the End of the Middle Ages*, Routledge & Kegan Paul, 1971.

Komroff, M. (ed.), *The Travels of Marco Polo (the Venetian) Revised from Marsden's Translation*, Liveright, 1982.

Lamb, H.H., *Climate, History and the Modern World*, 2nd edn, Routledge, 1995.

LaMonte, J.L. (ed.), *Gregory of Tours, Selections from the Minor Works*, Pennsylvania University Press, 1949.

Lawn, B. (ed.), *The Prose Salernitan Questions: Edited from a Bodleian Manuscript (Auct. F.3.10)*, Auctores Britannici Medii Aevi, 5, Oxford University Press, 1979.

Lawson, R.P. (trans.), *The Song of Songs: Commentaries and Homilies*, Longmans, Green and Co., 1957.

Lee, H.D.P. (trans.), *Aristotle, Meteorologia*, William Heinemann, 1952.

Leonard, W.E., *The Fragments of Empedocles*, Open Court Publications, 1908.

Le Roy Ladurie, E., *Montaillou. Cathars and Catholics in a French Village 1294–1324*, trans. B. Bray, Scolar Press, 1978.

Letts, M. (trans.), *Mandeville's Travels: Texts and Translations*, Hakluyt Society, Series 2, 101, 1953.

Levey, M., 'Arabic mineralogy of the tenth century', *Chymia*, 12, 1967.

Lewis, C., Mitchell-Fox, P. and Dyer, C., *Village, Hamlet and Field. Changing Medieval Settlements in Central England*, Windgather Press, 2001.

Lewis, C.S., *Studies in Words*, Cambridge University Press, 1967.

Lewis, S., *The Art of Matthew Paris in the* Chronica Majora, Scolar Press, 1987.

Lewit, T., 'Pigs, presses and pastoralism: farming in the fifth to sixth centuries AD', *Early Medieval* Europe, 17:1, 2009.

Lindberg, D.C. (ed.), *Science in the Middle Ages*, Chicago University Press, 1978.

Lindberg, D.C., 'The transmission of Greek and Arabic learning to the West', in *Science in the Middle Ages*, ed. D.C. Lindberg, Chicago University Press, 1978.

Long, C., 'The oldest European weather diary?', *Weather*, 29, 1974.

Long, P.O., 'Mining and ore processing', in *Medieval Latin: An Introduction and Bibliographical Guide*, eds F.A.C. Mantello and A.G. Rigg, Catholic University of America Press, 1999.

Lovejoy, A.O., *The Great Chain of Being: The Study of the History of an Idea*, Harvard University Press, 1976.

Mair, A.W. (trans.), *Collections: English and Greek*, William Heinemann, 1928.

Malone, K., 'King Alfred's north: a study in mediaeval geography', *Speculum*, 5:2, 1930.

Mantello, F.A.C. and Rigg, A.G. (eds), *Medieval Latin: An Introduction and Bibliographical Guide*, Catholic University of America Press, 1996.

Manzalaoui, M.A. (ed.), *Secretum Secretorum. Nine English Versions*, Early English Text Society, Old Series, 276, 1977.

Marcus, R. (trans.), *Philo, On the Creation; Allegorical Interpretation*, Harvard University Press, 1987.

Marshall, E. (trans.), *Bede, The Explanation of the Apocalypse*, James Parker and Co., 1878.

Marvin, W.P., *Hunting Law and Ritual in Medieval English Literature*, D.S. Brewer, 2006.

McCluskey, S., *Astronomies and Cultures in Early Medieval Europe*, Cambridge University Press, 1998.

Merton, T. (ed.), *The Wisdom of the Desert: Sayings from the Desert Fathers of the Fourth Century*, New Directions, 1961.

Meyer, P. (ed.), 'Le Bestiaire de Gervaise', *Romania*, 1, 1872.

Migne, J.-P. (ed.), *Opera Omnia Alani de Insulis*, Patrologiae Latina, 210, Garnier & Migne, 1855.

Migne, J.-P. (ed.), *S. Joannes Chrysostom*, Patrologiae Graeca, 49, Migne, 1862.

Moffat, D.M. (trans.), *The Complaint of Nature*, Yale Studies in English, 36, Yale, 1908.

Mommsen, T. (ed.), *C. Iulii Solini, Collectanea Rerum Memorabilum*, Berolini and Weidmannos, 1958.

Monat, P. (trans.), *Marbode, Poème des Pierres Précieuses*, Atopia, 1996.

Munkler, M., 'Experiencing strangeness: monstrous peoples on the edge of the Earth as depicted on medieval *Mappae Mundi*', *The Medieval History Journal*, 5:2, 2002.

Murdoch, J.A., 'The development and criticism of atomism in the later middle ages', in *A Source Book in Medieval Science*, ed. E. Grant, Harvard University Press, 1974.

Murray, H., *The Travels of Marco Polo*, Oliver & Boyd, 1845.

Myrdal, J., 'The agricultural transformation of Sweden, 1000–1300', in *Medieval Farming and Technology. The Impact of Agricultural Change in Northwest Europe*, eds G. Astill and J. Landgon, Brill, 1997.

Nasr, S.H., *An Introduction to Islamic Cosmological Doctrines*, New York University Press, 1993.

Nelson, W. (trans.), *A Fifteenth Century School Book, from a Manuscript in the British Museum (Ms. Arundel 249)*, Clarendon Press, 1956.

Newman, M., 'Christian cosmology in Hildegard of Bingen's illuminations', *Logos*, 5:1, 2002.

Nichols, S., Kablitz, A. and Calhoun, A., *Rethinking the Medieval Senses: Heritage, Fascinations, Frames*, Johns Hopkins University Press, 2008.

Obrist, B., 'Wind diagrams and medieval cosmology', *Speculum*, 72, 1997.

O'Connor, T. and Sykes, N.J. (eds), *Extinctions and Invasions: A Social History of British Fauna*, Windgather, 2010.

Offord, M.Y. (ed.), *The Parlement of the Thre Ages*, Early English Texts Society, Old Series, 246, 1959.

Ogden, M. (ed.), *The Cyrurie of Guy de Chauliac*, Early English Texts Society, Old Series, 265, 1971.

Oggins, R.S., 'Falconry and medieval views of nature', in *The Medieval World of Nature*, ed. J.E. Salisbury, Garland Publishing, 1993.

O'Meara, J.J. (trans.), *The History and Topography of Ireland*, Penguin, 1982.

Osbaldeston, T.A. (trans.), *Dioscorides, De Material Medica*, Ibidis Press, 2000.

Oshinsky, D. (trans.), *Walter of Henley and other Treatises on Estate Management and Accounting*, Clarendon Press, 1971.

Otte, J.K., 'The life and writings of Alfredus Anglicus', *Viator*, 3, 1972.

Otte, J.K., 'The role of Alfred of Sarashel (Alfredus Anglicus) and his commentary on the *Metheora* in the reacquisition of Aristotle', *Viator*, 7, 1976.

Otter, M. (trans.), 'Baudri of Bourgueil: "To Countess Adela"', *Journal of Medieval Latin*, 11, 2001.

Owen, T. (trans.), *The Fourteen Books of Palladius Rutilius Taurus Æmilianus, On Agriculture*, J. White, 1807.

Page, S., *Astrology in Medieval Manuscripts*, British Library, 2002.

Park, K., 'The meaning of natural diversity: Marco Polo on the "Division" of the World', in *Texts and Contexts in Ancient and Medieval Science*, eds E. Sylla and M. McVaugh, Brill, 1997.

Park, K., 'Nature in person: medieval and renaissance allegories and emblems', in *The Moral Authority of Nature*, eds L. Daston and F. Vidal, Chicago University Press, 2004.

Pasnau, R., 'Human nature', in *The Cambridge Companion to Medieval Philosophy*, ed. A.S. McGrade, Cambridge University Press, 2003.

Payne, A., *Medieval Beasts*, New Amsterdam Books, 1990.

Pearsall, D.A. and Salter, E., *Landscapes and Seasons of the Medieval World*, Elek, 1973.

Pedersen, O., 'Astronomy', in *Science in the Middle Ages*, ed. D.C. Lindberg, Chicago University Press, 1978.

Pedersen, O., 'The origins of the *Theoretica Planetarum*', *Journal for the History of Astronomy*, 12, 1981.

Pettit, E. (ed. and trans.), *Anglo-Saxon Remedies, Charms, and Prayers from British Library Ms Harley 585: The Lacnunga*, 2 vols, Edwin Mellen Press, 2001.

Pfeiffer, F. (ed.), *Konrad von Megenberg, Das Buch der Natur*, Karl Aue, 1861.

Pfister, C., Luterbacher, J., Schwartz-Zanetti, G. and Wegmann, M., 'Winter air temperatures in the Middle Ages (AD 750–1300)', *The Holocene*, 8, 1998.

Phillips, A.A. and Willcock, M.M. (eds and trans.), *Xenophon, On Hunting*, Aris and Phillips, 1999.

Pilgrim, S. and Pretty, J. (eds), *Nature and Culture: Rebuilding Lost Connections*, Earthscan, 2010.

Poulsen, B., 'Agricultural technology in medieval Denmark', in *Medieval Farming and Technology. The Impact of Agricultural Change in Northwest Europe*, eds G. Astill and J. Landgon, Brill, 1997.

Price, B.B., 'The physical astronomy and astrology of Albertus Magnus', in *Albertus Magnus and the Sciences*, ed. J.A. Weisheipl, Pontifical Institute of Mediaeval Studies, 1980.

Prior, O.H. (ed.), *Caxton's Mirrour of the World*, Early English Texts Society, Old Series, 110, 1913.

Rackham, H. (trans.), *Pliny, Natural History, vol. 1: Preface and Books I–II*, William Heinemann, 1949.

Rackham, H. (trans.), *Pliny, Natural History, vol. 6: Books XX–XXIII*, William Heinemann, 1951.

Rackham, O., *Trees and Woodland in the British Landscape. The Complete History of Britain's Trees, Woods and Hedgerows*, J.M. Dent, 1993.

Radkau, J., *Nature and Power: A Global History of the Environment*, Cambridge University Press, 2002.

Raffel, B. and Olsen, A.H. (eds and trans.), *Poems and Prose from the Old English*, Yale University Press, 1998.

Reeds, K.M., 'Albert on the natural philosophy of plant life', in *Albertus Magnus and the Sciences*, ed. J.A. Weisheipl, Pontifical Institute of Mediaeval Studies, 1980.

Reeds, K.M., *Botany in Medieval and Renaissance Universities*, Garland, 1991.

Reeves, C., *Pleasures and Pastimes in Medieval England*, Sutton, 1995.

Rendell, A.W. (trans.), *Physiologus: A Metrical Bestiary of Twelve Chapters by Bishop Theobald*, John & Edward Bumpus, 1928.

Resl, B. (ed.), *A Cultural History of Animals in the Medieval Age*, Berg, 2007.

Riddle, J.M., 'Marbode of Rennes' (1035–1123) "De lapidibus" considered as a medical treatise, with text, commentary and C.W. King's translation together with text and translation of Marbode's minor works on stones', *Sudhoffs Archiv*, 20, 1977.

Riddle, J.M. and Mulholland, J.A., 'Albert on stones and minerals', in *Albertus Magnus and the Sciences*, ed. J.A. Weisheipl, Pontifical Institute of Mediaeval Studies, 1980.

Ridyard, S.J. and Benson, R.G. (eds), *Man and Nature in the Middle Ages*, University of the South Press, 1995.

Robbins, F.E. (trans.), *Ptolemy, Tetrabiblos*, William Heinemann, 1948.

Robbins, R.H., 'English almanacks of the fifteenth century', *Philological Quarterly*, 18, 1939.

Roberts, B. and Wrathmell, S., *An Atlas of Rural Settlement in England*, English Heritage, 2000.

Rodrigues, L.J., *Anglo-Saxon Verse Charms, Maxims, and Heroic Legends*, Anglo-Saxon Books, 1993.

Ronca, I. and Curr, M. (trans.), *William of Conches, A Dialogue on Natural Philosophy* (Dragmaticon Philosophiae), Notre Dame Texts in Medieval Culture, 2, Notre Dame University Press, 1997.

Rothwell, H. (ed.), *English Historical Documents 1189–1327*, Eyre and Spottiswoode, 1975.

Rouse, W.H.D. (trans.), *Lucretius, De Rerum Natura*, William Heinemann, 1953.

Rutkin, H.D., 'Astrology', in *The Cambridge History of Science, vol. 3: Early Modern Science*, eds K. Park and L. Daston, Cambridge University Press, 2006.

Sachau, E.C. (trans.), *Alberuni's India: An Account of the Religion, Philosophy, Literature, Geography, Chronology, Astronomy, Customs, Laws and Astrology of India about AD 1030*, 2 vols, Kegan Paul, Trenche, Trüber and Co., 1910.

Said, H.M. (ed. and trans.), *Al-Biruni's Book on Pharmacy and Materia Medica*, Pakistan Series of Central Asian Studies, 2 vols, Rashid Sons, 1973.

Said, H.M. (trans.), *Al-Beruni's Book of Mineralogy*, Pakistan Hijra Council, 1989.

Salisbury, E. (ed.), *The Trials and Joys of Marriage*, Rochester University Press, 2002.

Salisbury, J.E. (ed.), *The Medieval World of Nature: A Book of Essays*, Garland Medieval Casebooks, 5, Garland, 1993.

Salisbury, J.E., 'Human beasts and bestial humans in the middle ages', in *Becoming Beast*, eds J. Ham and M. Senior, Routledge, 1996.

Salisbury, J.E., *The Beast Within: Animals in the Middle Ages*, 2nd rev. edn, Routledge, 2010.

Salzman, L.F., 'Some Sussex miracles', *Sussex Archaeological Collections*, 66, 1925.

Sandler, L.F., *The Psalter of Robert de Lisle in the British Library*, British Library, 1999.

Scafi, A., *Mapping Paradise: A History of Heaven on Earth*, British Library, 2006.

Schipper, W., 'Rabanus Maurus and his sources', in *Schooling and Society: The Ordering and Recording of Knowledge in the Western Middle Ages*, eds A.A. MacDonald and M.W. Twomey, Peeters, 2004.

Schipperges, H., *Hildegard of Bingen: Healing and the Nature of the Cosmos*, Markus Weiner, 1997.

Sears, E., *The Ages of Man: Medieval Interpretations of the Life Cycle*, Princeton University Press, 1986.

Serini, E., *History of the Italian Agricultural Landscape*, trans. R. Burr Litchfield, Princeton University Press, 1997.

Seymour, M.C. *et al.* (eds), *On the Properties of Things: John Trevisa's Translation of Bartholomæus Anglicus De Proprietatibus Rerum*, 3 vols, Clarendon Press, 1975.

Sheldon-Williams, I.P. (trans.), revised by O'Meara, J.J., *Eriugena, Periphyseon (The Division of Nature)*, Bellarmin, 1987.

Sheridan, J.J. (trans.), *Alan of Lille, The Plaint of Nature*, Pontifical Institute of Mediaeval Studies, 1980.

Singer, C. (trans.), 'Anatomy based on human dissection: *The Anatomy of Mundinus*', in *A Source Book in Medieval Science*, ed. E. Grant, Harvard University Press, 1974.

Skeat, W.W. (ed.), *Aelfric's Lives of Saints*, 2 vols, Kegan Paul, Trench, Trübner and Co., 1900.

Sorrell, R.D., *St Francis of Assisi and Nature: Tradition and Innovation in Western Christian Attitudes toward the Environment*, Oxford University Press, 1988.

Souami, L. (ed. and trans.), *Jâhiz, Le Cadi et la Mouche*, Sindbad, 1988.

Sowerby, B., *The Wakefield Second Shepherds' Play: From the Towneley Cycle – Modernised Edition*, Trafford Publishing, 2010.

Stahl, W.H. (trans.), *Commentary on the Dream of Scipio by Macrobius*, Columbia University Press, 1990.

Stahl, W.H., Johnson, R. with Burge, E.L. (trans.), *Martianus Capella and the Seven Liberal Arts, vol. 2, The Marriage of Philosophy and Mercury*, Columbia University Press, 1977.

Stange, E. (ed. and trans.), *De Encyklopädie des Arnoldus Saxo*, Erfurt, 1905–7.

Stannard, J., 'Pliny and Roman botany', *Isis*, 56:4, 1965.

Stannard, J., 'Albertus Magnus and medieval herbalism', in *Albertus Magnus and the Sciences*, ed. J.A. Weisheipl, Pontifical Institute of Mediaeval Studies, 1980.

Stone, B. (trans.), *The Owl and the Nightingale, Cleanness, St Erkenwald*, Penguin, 1971.

Storey, R.L., *Chronology of the Medieval World 800 to 1491*, Barrie and Jenkins, 1973.

Swanton, M.J. (ed. and trans.), *The Anglo-Saxon Chronicle*, rev. edn, Phoenix, 2000.

Sykes, N.J., *The Norman Conquest: A Zooarchaeological Perspective*, British Archaeological Reports, International Series, 1656, 2007.

Symons, G.J. (ed.), *Willelmum Merle, Consideraciones Temperiei pro 7 Annis*, Edward Standford, 1891.

Talbot, C.H., *Medicine in Medieval England*, Oldbourne, 1967.

Taylor, A.E. (trans.), *Plato: Timaeus and Critias*, Methuen and Co., 1929.

Taylor, J., *An Atlas of Roman Rural Settlement in England*, Council for British Archaeology Research Reports, 151, 2007.

Terral, J.-F. and Durand, A., 'Bio-archaeological evidence of olive tree (*Olea europaea* L.) irrigation during the middle ages in southern France and north eastern Spain', *Journal of Archaeological Science*, 33:5, 2006.

Thomas, K., *Man and Nature: Changing Attitudes in England 1500–1800*, Penguin, 1984.

Thomas, P.D., 'The Tower of London's royal menagerie', *History Today*, 46:8, 1996.

Thompson, D.W. (trans.), *Aristotle, Historia animalium*, Clarendon Press, 1910.

Thorndike, L., *A History of Magic and Experimental Science*, 8 vols, Columbia University Press, 1929.

Thorndike, L. (trans.), *The Sphere of Sacrobosco and its Commentators*, Chicago University Press, 1949.

Throop, P. (trans.), *Hildegarde von Bingen's Physica*, Healing Arts Press, 1998.

Tierney, J.J. (ed.), *Dicuili, Liber de Mensura Orbis Terrae*, The Dublin Institute for Advanced Studies, 1967.

Tilander, G. (ed.), *Les Livres de Roy Modus et de la Royne Ratio*, 2 vols, Didot, 1932.

Tilander, G. (ed.), 'La Venérie de Twiti', *Cynegetica*, 2, 1956.

Tilander, G. (ed.), 'La Chace dou Cerf', *Cynegetica*, 7, 1960.

Tilmann, J.P., *An Appraisal of the Geographical Works of Albertus Magnus and His Contribution to Geographical Thought*, Ann Arbor, 1971.

Toomer, G.J. (trans.), *Ptolemy's Almagest*, Duckworth, 1984.

Torrance, R.M. (ed.), *Encompassing Nature: A Source Book. Nature and Culture from Ancient Times to the Modern World*, Counterpoint, 1999.

Tredennick, H. (trans.), *Aristotle, Metaphysics, Books X–XIV*, William Heinemann, 1947.

Tredwell, K.A., 'Theoretica planetarum', in *Medieval Science, Technology, and Medicine: An Encyclopedia*, eds T.F. Glick, S.J. Livesey, and F. Wallis, Routledge, 2005.

Turner, H.R., *Science in Medieval Islam: An Illustrated Introduction*, Texas University Press, 1995.

Turtledove, H. (trans.), *The Chronicle of Theophanes: Anni Mundi 6095–6305 (AD 602–813)*, Pennsylvania University Press, 1982.

Tzanaki, R., *Mandeville's Medieval Audiences: A Study on the Reception of the Book of Sir John Mandeville (1371–1550)*, Ashgate, 2003.

Van Ardsall, A., *Medieval Herbal Remedies: The Old English Herbarium and Anglo-Saxon Medicine*, Routledge, 2002.

Van den Abeele, B., *La Fauconnerie au Moyen Age*, Klincksieck, 1994.

Varty, K., *Reynard the Fox: A Study of the Fox in Medieval English Art*, Leicester University Press, 1967.

Vincent of Beauvais, *Speculum Maius*, Germann Liechtenstein, 1494.

Voigts, L.E., 'Plants and planets: linking the vegetable with the celestial in late medieval texts', in *Health and Healing from the Medieval Garden*, eds P. Dendle and A. Touwaide, Boydell, 2008.

Von Erhardt-Siebold, E. and Von Erhardt, R., *The Astronomy of Johannes Scotus Eriugena*, Williams & Wilkins Co., 1940.

Wallis, F. (trans.), *Bede, The Reckoning of Time*, Translated Texts for Historians, 29, Liverpool University Press, 1999.

Walsh, G.G. (trans.), *St Augustine, The City of God*, Catholic University of America Press, 1963.

Walsh, P.G. (trans.), *Boethius, The Consolation of Philosophy*, Clarendon Press, 1999.

Walshe, M.O'C. (trans.), *Meister Eckhart: Sermons and Treatises*, vol. 2, Element Books, 1981.

Warner, G. (intro.), *Queen Mary's Psalter Miniatures and Drawings by an English Artist of the 14th century Reproduced from Royal MS. 2B. VII in the British Museum*, British Museum, 1912.

Weisheipl, J.A., 'Curriculum of the arts faculty at Oxford in the early fourteenth century', *Mediaeval Studies*, 26, 1964.

Weisheipl, J.A. (ed.), *Albertus Magnus and the Sciences*, Pontifical Institute of Mediaeval Studies, 1980.

Wetherbee, W. (trans.), *The Cosmographia of Bernardus Silvestris*, Columbia University Press, 1973.

White, T.H. (trans.), *The Book of Beasts Being a Translation from a Latin Bestiary of the Twelfth Century*, Jonathan Cape, 1954.

Wicksteed, P.H. and Cornford, F.M. (trans.), *Aristotle, The Physics*, vol. 1, William Heinemann, 1929.

Williams, M., 'Dark ages and dark areas: global deforestation in the deep past', *Journal of Historical Geography*, 26:1, 2000.

Williams, R., *Keywords: A Vocabulary of Culture and Society*, Croom Helm, 1976.

Williamson, T., *Shaping Medieval Landscapes. Settlement, Society, Environment*, Windgather Press, 2003.

Wippel, J.C., 'The Paris condemnations of 1270 and 1277', in *A Companion to Philosophy in the Middle Ages*, eds J.J.E. Garcia and T.B. Noone, Blackwell, 2003.

Wood, C.A. and Fyfe, F.M. (eds and trans.), *The Art of Falconry by Frederick II of Hohenstaufen*, Stanford University Press, 1943.

Wood, F., *Did Marco Polo Go to China?*, Westview Press, 1998.

Woodward, D., 'Reality, symbolism, time, and space in medieval world maps', *Annals of the Association of American Geographers*, 75:4, 1985.

Woolgar, C., *The Senses in Late Medieval England*, Yale University Press, 2006.

Wright, R.R. (trans.), *Al-Biruni, Elements of Astrology*, Luzac, 1934.

Wright, T., *Popular Treatises on Science Written During the Middle Ages in Anglo-Saxon, Anglo-Norman and English*, R. & J.E. Taylor, 1841.

Wright, T. (ed.), *Alexander Neckam, De naturis rerum et De laudibus divinae sapientiae*, Longman, Roberts & Green, 1863.

Wyckoff, D. (ed. and trans.), *Albertus Magnus, De Mineralibus*, Clarendon Press, 1967.

Yalden, D., *The History of British Mammals*, Poyser, 1999.

Youngs, D., *The Life-Cycle in Western Europe, c. 1300–c. 1500*, Manchester University Press, 2006.

Yule, H. (trans.), *The Wonders of the East by Friar Jordanus*, Hakluyt Society, 1863.

Zonk, M., 'The place of the senses', in *Rethinking the Medieval Senses*, eds S. Nichols, A. Kablitz and A. Calhoun, Johns Hopkins University Press, 2008.

Zonta, M., 'Mineralogy, botany and zoology in medieval Hebrew encyclopae-dias', *Arabic Sciences and Philosophy*, 6, 1996.

Index

Aachen 83

Aaron 99–100

Aberdeen Bestiary 46, 67, 77

Abrahamic religions 7

Abu Ma'Shar 26; *Abbreviations to the Introduction to Astrology* 26; *Great Introduction to Astronomy* 26

Abu-Yusuf, Rabbi 50, 96

Abyssinia 57

Adelard of Bath 6, 26, 34, 43, 70, 71, 80, 90, 97; *De avibus tractatus* 80; *Quaestiones naturales* 6

Aden 57

Aelfric, abbot of Eynsham 28, 35, 38, 47; *Colloquy* 38; *De temporibus anni* 47

aeromancy 35

Africa 50, 55, 56, 57, 60

Ages of Man 67–68, 72

Agincourt, battle of 37

Agnes dei 74

Agobard, bishop of Lyons 41

agriculture 18, 34, 47, 48–53, 64, 98

agronomy 85, 88, 103

air 41–42, 43, 44, 65, 70, 86, 89, 108

air, element 12–18, 19, 90, 106

Al-Andalus 50, 54, 57, 96

Al-Asma'ī 80; *Kitāb al-Khail* 80

Al-Bakri 54; *Kitāb al-Masālik w-al-Mamālik* 54

Al-Bata'ih 39

Al-Batrīq 18

Al-Battani 26; *De motu stellarum* 26

Al-Birunī 39, 55, 57, 59, 98, 103, 105; *Book of Minerals* 105; *Ta'rikh al-Hind* 59; *The Sum of Knowledge about Precious Stones* 103

Al-Bitruji 31–32

Al-Farhini 26; *De scientia astrorum* 26

Al-Jāhiz 84

Al-Kafi 80

Al-Khawarizmi 26; *Astrological Tables* 26

Al-Mansur 80

Al-Muqaddasī 27, 39, 57, 96

Al-Rahman III, Caliph 7

Al-Rashid, Harun 83

Al-Razi 93, 98

Alan of Lille 5, 21; *De planctu natura* 21; *Liber in distinctionibus dictionum theologicalium* 5

Albertus Magnus 25, 30, 31, 33, 63, 64, 71, 72, 82, 88–89, 90, 94, 95, 103, 105; *De mineralibus* 103, 105; *De vegetabilibus* 88, 94; *On Animals* 72

alchemy 101, 103

Alcuin of York 27

ale 75

Aleppo 96

Alexandria 76

Alfred the Great, king of England 78

Alfredus of Sarashel 11, 88; *De plantis* 88

alluvium 51

almanacs 33, 66

Alps 83, 96

Alsace 96

Ambrose, Saint 6, 109

amphibians 76, 77; crocodile 76, 106; frogs 42

Anatoli, Jacob 7

anatomy 8, 20, 64–65, 66, 68, 72, 80, 88, 110

angels 13, 62

Anglicus, Robertus 53

Anglo-Saxon Chronicle 38, 47, 78

animals (*see also* amphibians, birds, fish, insects, mammals, reptiles) 8, 10, 11, 13, 21, 23, 39, 53, 62, 63, 64, 69, 73–84, 87, 88, 92, 100, 108, 111; beasts of the chase 76; breeding of 51; diseases 80, 81; extinction of 79; wild animals 23, 73, 77, 78

Anthony, Saint 108

Antipodes 57, 106

aphrodisiacs 92

aquaducts 50

Aquinas, Thomas 22, 31, 107; *Summa theologica* 31

Arabia 39

Arabian Nights 98

Arabic texts 7, 9, 20, 33, 93, 110

arable 49

archaeological evidence 49

Ardennes 96

Aristarchus of Samos 31

Aristotle 4, 7, 10–11, 14, 16–17, 22, 23, 25, 30, 31, 32, 33, 41, 43, 48, 62, 63, 70, 71, 81, 88, 91, 100, 101, 102, 103, 107, 110; Aristotelian philosophy 4, 10, 14, 15, 22, 32, 33, 62–63, 67, 70, 81, 82, 101, 102, 107, 110; *De anima* 10; *De animalibus* 11, 63, 81; *De caelo* 10, 14; *De generatione animalium* 11; *De generatione et corruptione* 10, 14, 16–17; *De motu animalium* 11; *De partibus animalium* 11; *De progressu animalium* 11; *De vegetabilibus* 11; *Historia animalium* 22–23 *Libri naturalis* 10; *Metaphysica* 4–5; *Meteorologica* 10, 101; *Parva naturalia* 10–11; *Physica* 10, 23,

Arnold of Saxony 5, 100; *De finibus rerum* 100; *De floribus naturalium rerum* 5

aromatics 91

artistic representations of nature 78, 83, 84, 92, 95, 110

Asia 48, 55, 56, 58, 59, 60

assarting 51

astrolabes 26, 34

astrology 22, 25–36, 65, 66, 67; elections 33, 34; interrogations 33, 34; judicial astrology 34; nativities 33, 34; revolutions 33, 34, 40

astronomy 25–36

atmosphere 4, 21, 25, 42, 43

Atomism 23–24

Augustine of Hippo, Saint 6, 63, 67; *De civitate dei* 63

Augustinians 6

Averroes 103

Avicenna 18, 20, 70, 71, 93, 100, 102, 103, 105; *Al-Qānūn fi al-Tibb* 18, 20

Avignon 75

bacon 75

Bacon, Roger 37, 71

Baghdad 83

Balkans 96

Bartholomew the Englishman 5, 6, 10, 14, 16, 17, 18, 36, 41, 45, 65, 67, 68, 71, 86, 87–88, 93, 100; *De proprietatibus rerum* 5–6, 14, 100

Basil, Saint 6, 108–109; *Hexaemeron* 108

Basra 20

Bassus, Cassianus 85

Bathelemy Mini of Siena 95; *Tractatus de herbis* 95

Bayeux Tapestry 75

bear-baiting 73

Beauchamp, earls of Warwick 75

Bede 5, 6, 9–10, 11, 13, 15, 27, 29, 30, 40, 43, 45, 53, 96, 100; *De natura rerum* 5, 9–10, 13; *De temporibus* 9–10; *De temporum rationale* 9, 29; *Ecclesiastical History* 53; *Explanatio apocalypsis* 100

Beirut 96

bellatores 111

Benedictines 6, 92

Beowulf 47

Bern 77

Bernard of Clairvaux, Saint 8

bestiaries 23, 46, 76–78, 82, 84, 91, 94, 100, 111

Bhātal 39

Bible 7, 76, 99–100, 109, 113; Exodus 99–100; Genesis 7, 35, 62; Job 107–108; New Testament 108; Old Testament 7, 76, 107; Psalms 7; Revelation 100; Romans 108; Song of Songs 108; Wisdom 107

bile 18, 19

birds 13, 21, 38, 59, 74, 75, 76, 77, 80, 82, 83, 108; barnacle geese 81–82; birds of prey 80, 83; chickens 75, 76; cockerels 69; cranes 53; cuckoo 112; ducks 76; eagles 69, 74, 77; falcons 75; geese 75, 76; hawks 53, 80; kites 53; owls 60; parrots 73; puffins 74; swans 75; vultures 69, 98; water fowl 75

Black Sea 38

bladder 43

blood 18, 19, 58, 69, 81

blood-letting 66

Boethius 20, 21, 23, 30; *Consolatio philosophiae* 20, 21, 23

Bonatti, Guido 34

Bonaventa, Saint 109 *Liber astronomicus* 34

bones 73

Books of Hours 74, 111

Borneo 59

Bosphorus 39

botany 78, 85, 91, 94, 95

bowels 43

Brahmânda 27

bread 52

Brethren of Purity 20, 72, 89, 101, 102, 103; *Ikhwan al-Safa* 20

Britain 48, 52, 96
brontology 40
bull-baiting 73
Burchard of Worms 41
Buridan, John 32; *The Compatibility of the Earth's Diurnal Rotation with Astronomical Phenomena* 32
butchery 80
Byrhtferth of Ramsey 15–16, 47; *Enchiridion* 15–16, 47
Byzantium 57, 85

cadavers 17
Calcidius 12, 20, 26
Cancer, Tropic of 57
cannibals 59
Canterbury 67
Capitols singulars deles llauors que deuras sembrar 87
Capricorn, Tropic of 57
cardinal points 15, 16, 38, 39, 46, 55, 64, 72, 86
Carpathian mountains 96
Cassy, Lady 75
Cathars 6
Cato 85
caves 44, 101–102
celestial bodies (*see also* planets, stars) 10, 14, 25, 27, 28, 30, 33, 34, 41, 66, 89, 90, 112
celestial sphere 4, 14, 65
cereals 19, 39, 48, 51, 52, 75, 85, 91; barley 51, 52, 87; corn 50, 52; oats 52; rye 52, 87; sorghum 87; spelt 87; wheat 48, 51
Chain of Being 10, 22–23, 62–63
champion land 53
Charlemagne 27, 79, 83; *Capitulare de Villis* 79
Charles of Anjou, king of Naples and Sicily 81
charms 81, 85
Chartres, 'school' of 6, 21
Chaucer, Geoffrey 34; *Wife of Bath* 34
Childeric 74
China 59, 73
choler 18, 64
Christianity 27, 107; Church 4, 6, 34, 59, 64; Church fathers 6; scholarship 20, 25, 55, 63, 107
Christmas 40
Chrysostom, John 6, 109
Circa instans 93
clayland 48, 51
climate 50, 52
climatic zones 39, 56, 57, 64, 90, 104; temperate zone 39, 56, 57, 64, 90; fiery zone 39, 56, 97; frigid zone 56
clouds 41, 42, 43, 44, 45

cochineal 50
cock-fighting 73
Cockaigne, land of 98
Coilon 39
cold 37, 38, 42, 43, 45, 57, 64, 101, 102
cold, elemental quality 14–17, 19, 42, 65, 66, 70, 86, 89, 90, 93, 94, 103, 104, 106
Columella 85
colour 53–54, 64, 94, 99, 100, 102, 104
Columbum 60
comets 25, 106
common sense 70
complexions (*see* humours and temperaments)
Computus 29
Constantine the African 18, 68
Constantinople 39
constellations 33
Copernicus 31
Corbie 59
Cordova 7
cosmology 15, 22, 31, 33, 35, 58
cosmos 21, 22, 66, 107
Creation 35, 62, 107, 108, 109
crops (*see also* cereals) 41, 45, 51, 52, 53
cryptozoology (*see also* 'mythical creatures') 58, 74, 77
Cuthbert, Saint 15, 74
Cuxham 75
cynegetic literature 80
Cynewulf 76

Damigero 98
Daniel of Morley 14, 34; *Philosophia* 14
De utilitatibus astrolabii 26
De viribus herbarum 93
Dead Sea 96
Deerhurst 75
deferents 31
Demiurge 20
demography 49–50, 52
Denmark 52
dew 41–42, 89, 98
Dicuil 54; *De mensura orbis terrae* 54
diet 19
disease (*see also* illnesses) 52
Dioscorides 18, 41, 91, 93, 99, 100, 107; *De materia medica* 18, 91, 99; *Dioscorides alphabeticus* 91
dissection 68
diuretics 92
divination 34, 35
domestic animals (*see* birds, mammals)

Dominicans 5
Don, river 55
drainage 51, 52
dry, elemental quality 14–17, 43, 45, 65, 66, 86, 89, 90, 93, 103, 104, 106
dung 73, 77, 87, 88
dust 72

Eagle Tower 75
earth, 72, 86, 89, 93, 95, 97, 101, 108
earth, element 12–18, 19, 88, 89, 90, 103, 106
earthquakes 45
Easter 29, 47
Ebstorf world map 58
eccentrics 29, 30
Eckhart, Meister 109
eclipses 5, 28, 32, 112
Edward III, king of England 75
Edward, duke of Norwich 79, 84; *The Master of Game* 80, 84
eggs 17
Egyptian texts 76
elements (*see also* earth, water, air, fire, hot, cold, dry, moist) 10, 12–18, 19, 23, 35, 42, 67, 86, 87, 88, 89, 97, 102, 106, 107, 110; theory of 10, 12–18, 24, 41; qualities 14–17, 18, 34, 67, 86, 93, 104
emotion 62
emparkment 79, 83
Empedocles 12; *Physis* 12
encyclopaedias 5–6, 7, 19, 67, 68, 72, 77, 86, 91, 100, 103, 109
England 9, 41, 49, 50, 75, 78, 79, 83, 90, 96
Enlightenment 22
Epicureanism 5
equants 31
epicycles 31, 32
Equator 39, 44, 45, 57
equinoxes 16, 33, 57, 86
Eriugena, John Scotus 3–4, 5, 29, 30; *De divisione nature* 29; *Periphyseon* 29
Erzgebirge 96, 103
Est, Richard 75
ether, element 14, 21
Ethiopia 64
Eudoxus 30
Eugene 26
Eustace, Saint 74
Exeter Book 49

falconry 81
famines 33, 52
fat 73

feathers 73
fenland 48
Finland 52
Fioretti 74
fire, element 12–18, 19, 43, 90, 97, 106
Firmament 21, 28
fish 13, 21, 38, 42, 76, 77, 79, 108, 110; mullet 74
floods 33, 112
flowers 53; Dragon Arum 94; Great white convolvulus; Madonna lily 91; marigold 81; roses 87, 95; water lily 89
fog 41
folklore 47, 81, 85, 98
Forest Charter 79
forests (*see also* woodland) 53, 79
Forests 51, 78–79
fossils 103
France 9, 38, 48–49, 51, 54, 75, 90, 99
Francis of Assisi, St 74, 107
Franciscans 6, 59
Frederick II, Holy Roman Emperor 7, 80, 81, 83; *De arte venandi cum avibus* 80, 84
free will 62
Frieberg 96, 97
frost 37, 65, 112
fruit (*see also* trees) 17, 50, 85, 86, 88, 89, 90; apples 95; bananas 50; citrus fruits 50; grapes 48, 90, 95; melons 87; mulberries 90; pomegranates 90; watermelons 50
Fuller brooch 69

Galen 18–19, 68, 93, 107; *Megnategni* 18; *Pantegni* 93
Gauthier of Metz 6, 26, 42; *L'image du monde* 6
Galippus 7
gases 17
Geber 101
gemstones (*see* precious stones)
gender 45; female 46, 65, 94, 98; male 46, 65, 94, 98
Genesis B 38
genitalia 64
geocentricism 27
geography 54–60
geology 103, 105
Geoponika 85, 86, 104
Geographica 54
geoheliocentrism 29–30
geomancy 34
Gerald of Wales 82
Gerard of Cremona 7, 14, 26
Germany 9, 26, 51, 97

Gershon ben Shlomah 7, 42, 90, 103; *Sha'ar ha-Shamayim* 7
Ghawr 96
Glastonbury 95
Gloucestershire 75
Gnosticism 20
God 4, 13, 21, 27, 28, 34, 63, 66, 76, 108, 109
Gog and Magog 58, 59
Goslar 96
grands défrichements 51
grassland 49
Grattius 80
Greek scholarship 7; texts 7, 20, 25, 76, 98
Gregory of Tours 26; *De cursibus ecclesiasticis* 26
Grosseteste, Robert 71
Gubbio 74
Guido of Pisa 54
Guy of Chauliac 68; *Chirugia magna* 68

hail 38, 41, 42–43, 45
hair 64, 69, 72
Ham, son of Noah 56
Haram 39
harmony of the spheres 29–30
Harrison, William 53
harvest 39, 46, 47, 52
Harz mountains 96
hawking 68
heat 39, 42, 43, 44, 57, 58, 64, 86, 97, 101, 102, 103
hearing 71, 94
heathland 52
Hebraic texts 7, 9, 76, 110
heliocentrism 31
Henry I, king of England 83
Henry II, king of England 34
Henry III, king of England 79, 83
Henry IV, king of England 75
Henry of Ferrières 80; *Les Livres du Roy Modus et de la Royne Ratio* 80
herbals 19, 23, 78, 90–95
Herbarius Apulei Platonicus 92
herbs 8, 85, 91, 92, 93; coriander 91, 94; dill 81, 94; fennel 81, 91–94; lovage 81, 94; rue 87; sage 87
Hereford *mappa mundi* 58
Hermann Contractus 26
Hermann the Dalmatian 26
hibernation 92
Higden, Ranulf 60; *Polychronicon* 60
Hildegard of Bingen 5, 6, 17–18, 19, 22, 27, 34, 66, 67, 81, 94, 97; *Causae et curae* 17–18; *Physica* 5, 17, 94, 97
Hindus 20, 27, 55, 59

Hippocrates 18–19, 64, 67, 107; *Aphorisma* 18; *Prognostica* 18; *Regimen* 18
Honorius of Autun 54, 58; *Imago mundi* 54, 58
horoscopes 33, 34, 112
hot, elemental quality 14–17, 19, 42, 45, 66, 70, 86, 87, 88, 89, 90, 93, 94, 104, 106
Hubert of Liège, Saint 74
Hugh of Fouilloy 77; *Avarium* 77
Hugh of St Victor 109; *De tribus diebus* 109
Hulwān 39
human body 18–19, 21, 22, 46, 64, 65–69, 72; abdomen 66; ankles 66; arms 66, 94; back 94; bladder 65, 91; bones 68, 72; bowels 92; brain 69, 71, 72; breastbone 69; chest 66, 93; ears 65, 66, 70, 71, 92; eyes 21, 64, 70, 71, 77, 91, 99; face 64, 72; feet 66, 70, 72, 94; fingers 64, 66, 68; flesh 68, 72; gall 69; genitalia 66; hands 64, 68, 70, 94, 99; head 20, 66, 69; heart 66, 68, 69; hips 66; intestines 72; kidneys 69, 91, 92; knees 66, 94; liver 68–69, 99; lungs 68; mouth 70, 71; muscles 70; nerves 71, 72; nose 70; nostrils 69, 71; neck 66, 94; ribs 69; sinews 68; skin 70; skull 69; spleen 65, 69; stomach 68, 92, 94; thighs 66; throat 66; tongue 71; veins 68
humans 8, 10, 17–18, 62–72, 106; life cycle 15, 16, 19, 66; temperaments 15
humidity 40, 45, 71
humours (*see also* choler, melancholy, phlegm, sanguine) 18–19, 23, 33, 45–46, 64, 66, 67, 86, 94; theory of, 18–19, 23
hunger 37–38
Hunt of Venus 74
hunting 68, 74, 78–80, 84

Ibn al-'Awwām 86, 104; *Kitāb al-Filāha* 86
Ibn al-Mundhir al-Baitār 81; *Kitāb al-Nāsirī* 81
Ibn Butlan 46; *Tacuinum Sanitatis* 46, 93
Ibn Hawqal 54; *Sūrat al-'Ard* 54
Ibn Rushd (Averroes) 7, 23
Ibn Shahriyar, Buzurg 59, 98
Ibn Wahshiyya 86; *Nabatean Agriculture* 86
Ibn Zakariyya 98
icebergs 38–39
Iceland 54
illnesses 19, 46, 91–92; asthma 92; bites 91, 94; bleary-eyes 46; boils 92; cancer 65; catarrh 65; consumption 65; croup 92; diarrhoea 92; dropsy 65, 92; eye disease 99; fever 46, 99; fistula 65; flux 46, 65; gout 65; impotence 92; insomnia 94; leprosy 65; morphew 65; nausea 92; palsy 65; phthisic 65; quartan fever 64, 65; stones 92; tumours 92; water retention 99; worms 91

immortality 62
India 39, 48, 50, 55, 57, 58, 59, 60, 64; literature
    25, 76
Indravēdi 39
infants 45, 63
Ingelheim 83
Ingham 75
insects 23, 76, 77; ants 39, 77; bees 23, 39, 53, 73,
    74, 77; cicadas 74; fleas 40, 112; flies 23, 84, 112;
    silkworms 50
intellect 20, 23, 62, 63
internal organs 65–66, 68
Iraq 20
Ireland 54, 73
irrigation 50, 52
Isabella, sister of Henry III 83
Isidore, bishop of Seville 5, 6, 9, 10, 13, 15,
    18–19, 25, 28, 29, 40, 43, 54, 59, 67, 76,
    96, 99; De natura rerum 5, 15, 28;
    Etymologiae sive origines 5, 9, 29,
    76, 99
Islam 26, 107
Islamic world 7, 8, 26, 50, 63, 79, 82, 93, 96, 101,
    103
Israeli ben Solomon 93
Italy 6, 9, 48, 54, 75, 96,

Jaber ben Hayyān 101, 102, 103
James of Venice 10
Japhet, son of Noah 56
Java 59
Jerome, Saint 6
Jerusalem 95
John of Sacrobosco 33; Tractatus de sphaera 33
John of Seville 26
Jordanus, Friar 39, 59–60
Joseph ibn Saddiq 21; Olam kaṭan 21
Judah ben Solomon ha-Cohen 7; Midrash
    ha-Hokhmah 7
Judaic theological traditions 4, 6, 108
Jewish scholarship 7, 8, 20, 21, 55, 107; Hebraic
    texts 7, 9, 76, 110
Julian calendar 29
Jutland 52

Karakorum 59
Kashmīr 39, 98
Khozars, king of the 50
Khuzistan 59
kinematics 30, 32
Konrad of Megenburg 6, 110; Das buch der natur 6,
    110

La Chace dou Cerf 80
laboratores 111
labours of the months 47
Lady and the Unicorn tapestry 70, 75
Lambert of St Omer 54, 56; Liber floridus 54
lapidaries 91, 99–101
Latin scholarship 7, 64, 71; texts 9, 34
Latin west 7, 9, 12, 14, 20, 23, 48, 71, 82, 85, 103,
    104, 110
Latini, Brunetto 6; Li livres dou tresor 6
Lausanne 34, 35
Le Viste family 75
leather 73
Leopold of Austria 65; Compilatio de astrorum scientia
    65
Levita, Abuteus 7
lightning 40, 41, 43, 45
lime 17, 42
Lindesfarne 74
locus amoenus 95
Loire 93
London 83
Longthorpe Tower 67, 69, 75
Louis IX, king of France 83
Low Countries 96
Lucretius 5; De rerum natura 5
luminary period 28
Lyons 41

Macer floridus 93
Macrobius 20, 26, 56, 57; Commentarii in somnium
    Scipionis 20, 26, 56
macrocosm 15, 19–22, 23
Magna Carta 79
Magonia 41
mammals 76, 77, 82; asses 81; badgers 53, 77, 81;
    bats 60; bears 75, 78, 79, 83; beavers 82; boars
    69, 75, 78; camels 60, 83; cats 73; cattle 38, 48,
    52, 73, 75, 76, 77, 81; cheetahs 83; deer 78, 79;
    dogs 73, 74, 75, 76, 77, 80, 91; dromedaries 83;
    elephants 60, 77, 83; fallow deer 79; foxes 53, 78;
    giraffes 83; hares 74, 76; hedgehogs 75; horses 50,
    60, 68, 73, 75, 76, 77, 80, 81; hyenas 83; leopards
    75, 83; lions 74, 77, 83; lynxes 83; marten 78;
    mice 77; moles 77; monkeys 69, 73, 83; mules 73;
    otters 79; oxen 39, 60, 73, 74; panthers 76–77,
    83; pigs 48, 51, 52, 68, 75; polar bears 83; rabbits
    53; red deer 74, 75, 78; roe deer 78; sheep 50, 51,
    52, 73, 77, 81, 98; seals 74; squirrels 73; weasels
    8, 82, 107; wolves 38, 53, 74, 79
Mandeville, Sir John 60, 98
Manichaeism 20

manure 52, 104

maps 55–58, 61; Beatus maps 57; Cotton Tiberius map 57; *Mappa mundi* 35, 58, 98; quadripartite maps 57; T-O maps 55, 56, 57; Y-O maps 56; zonal maps 56

Marbode, bishop of Rennes 99, 100; *Liber lapidum seu de gemmis* 99

Marius 13–14

marl 88

marshland 48, 52, 53

Martianus Capella 27, 29, 30, 56; *De nuptiis Philologiae et Mercurii* 27

mathematics 4, 27, 31, 32, 33

Maurus of Salerno 68; *Anatomia* 68

Maurus, Rabanus 5, 6, 29; *De naturis rerum* 5; *De universo* 5, 29

Mazdaism 20

meadows 51, 53, 79, 109

meat 17, 73

Mecca 26

medicine 8, 18, 26, 33, 34, 66, 81, 85, 90, 9–93, 94, 95, 99

Medieval Warm Period 50

Mediterranean 37, 48, 55, 83, 104

melancholy 18, 64, 65, 94

memory 69

menageries 83

menstruation 92

Merle, William 37, 39–40

mermaids 59

Meseta 96

Mesopotamia 57, 86

metallurgy 103

metals 8, 10, 23, 50, 53, 96–105, 110; antimony 102; copper 50, 96, 101, 102; gold 50, 96, 97, 101, 102; iron 50, 96, 97, 102; lead 96, 101, 102; mercury 101–102, 103; precious metals 23; silver 50, 96, 97, 99, 101, 102; steel 97; tin 50, 96, 101; zinc 96

metaphysics 4–5, 19, 31

meteorology 10, 25, 37–47

microcosm 15, 19–22, 23, 62

milk 13–14, 73, 76

Milky Way 25, 36

minerals 10, 23, 76, 88, 96–105, 111; alum 102; calcite 102; gypsum 102; iron sulphate 102; saltpetre 102; sulphur 50, 96, 101–102, 103; natron 102; vitriols 102

mines 96, 103

Mirror on Astronomy 34

mist 40

Mohammed 108

moist, elemental quality 14–17, 19, 43, 45, 66, 86, 90, 93, 103, 104, 106

moisture 44, 45, 86, 89, 90, 101

Mondino de'Luzzi 68; *Anatomia* 68

Mongols 59

monsoons 39

monstrous races 35, 58, 59, 60, 61, 63–64; Antipodes 63; Cyclopes 63; Cynocephalae/dogheads 59, 63–64; Essendones 58; Hermaphrodites 63; Monocoli 58–59; Pygmies 63; Sciapods 63; Scythians 58; Turks 58

Montaillou 54

Monte Cassino 76

Montereale 54

Montpellier 8

months 16, 35, 79, 87; March 80, 87; May 79, 80; November 86

moon 4, 5, 21, 27, 28, 29, 32, 40, 41, 65–66, 67, 86–87, 102, 112; lunar cycle 29; man in the moon 36

mortality 37–38, 62

morphology 88

Moses Maimonides 19; *Dalālat al-Hā'irīn* 19

Moses of Palermo 81; *De curationibus infirmatatum aequorum* 81

Moslem scholarship 7, 8, 14, 20, 23, 25, 55, 57, 58, 71, 80, 81, 89, 98, 107

Moslem theological traditions 6, 9, 108

mountains 50, 51, 72, 96, 102, 103

Mozarabs 7, 26

mud 72

'mythical' creatures 58, 60; bonnacons 58, 77; dragons 58, 60; griffins 58, 75, 77; manticores 58; tigolopes 58; unicorns 70, 75

Naples 81

natural world, concept of 3, 62

nature, concept of 3–5

Near East 26

Neckam, Alexander 5, 6, 8, 11, 36; *De naturis rerum* 5, 11

necromancy 34

Nemesianus 80

Neoplatonists 4, 110

Neoplatonism 7, 14, 20, 21, 22

Netherlands 52

Nicholas of Damascus 11, 88; *De plantis* 11, 88

Nicolas the Physician 68; *Anatomia magistri Nicholai Physici* 68

Nijmegen 83

Nile, river 55, 106

Noah 56

Norfolk 75
Norman Conquest 37, 78
Normandy 53, 75, 78
Northamptonshire 53, 67
Norway 52, 83
Norwell 53–54
Nottinghamshire 54
Nully 51
numerology 21, 67, 108

oceans 45, 55, 57, 59, 72, 97; Atlantic 82; currents
    44, 57
Oderic of Pordenone 59; *Description of the East* 59
Odo of Meung 93
oil 50, 99
open fields 50–51
Oppian 80
oratores 111
Oresme, Nicolas 34–36
Origen 108; *Contra celsum* 108
Orosius 54; *Historiae adversum paganos* 54
Oxford 39
Oxfordshire 75, 83

paganism 108
palaeoenvironmental evidence 49
Palermo 80
Palestine 96
Palladius 85
Paradise 98
Paris 34
Paris, Matthew 83
Parlement of the Thre Ages 80
pasture 51, 52, 53, 109
peasants 8, 24, 34, 36, 37, 40, 47, 75, 86–87, 98,
    104–105, 109, 111, 112; attitudes to nature 8–9,
    54
peatland 52
pedology 103
Percy, earls of Northumberland 75
Persia 20, 59; literature 25
Peterborough 67, 78
pets 73, 75
Philo 108; *De opficio mundi* 108
phlegm 18, 19, 64
Phoebus, Gaston 79, 80; *Livre de Chasse* 79, 80
physics 4, 5
Physiologus 76, 77, 82, 100
physiology 63, 66, 68, 88
Pierre of Ailly 57; *Imago mundi* 57
Pierre of Beauvais 27, 54, 58; *Mappemonde* 27, 54, 58

Pietro di Crescenti 85, 104; *Opus ruralium
    commodorum* 85
Pisanello 74; *The Vision of St Eustace* 74
place-names 49, 51, 53, 78
Placidus 74
Placitus, Sextus 81; *Medicina de quadrupedibus* 81
plague 33, 52, 106
planets 4, 10, 21, 22, 26, 28, 30, 31, 32, 34, 65, 66,
    102, 112; Mars 28, 29, 32, 66, 102; Mercury 28,
    29, 32, 66; Jupiter 28, 29, 32, 66, 102; precession
    27, 32, 33; planetary periods 28; planetary stations
    27, 28, 29, 31, 32; retrogradation 27, 29, 31, 32,
    65; Saturn 26, 29, 32, 65–66, 67, 102; Venus 28,
    29, 66, 102
plant anatomy: bark 88; buds 86, 89; bulbs 86;
    flowers 85, 86, 88, 89, 94; leaves 86, 88, 89, 91,
    94; pith 88; roots 86, 88, 89, 91, 107; sap 87, 89;
    stamens 91; stems 88, 89, 91, 94; seeds 86, 89,
    91, 94
plants 8, 10, 11, 19, 23, 53, 72, 76, 85–95, 107,
    111; cotton 50; Crocus 50; croton oil 41;
    defoliation 88; germination 86; gourds 87;
    Henbane 41; mandrake 94, 106; nettles 81,
    92–93; osiers 93; poisonous plants 92; planting 85
Platearius, Mattheaus 93; *De medicines simplicibus* 93
Plato 4, 7, 12, 19, 20, 22, 28, 30, 90, 107, 110;
    Philibus 20; Platonic philosophy 4, 7, 12–13, 14,
    15, 30, 32, 43, 48, 62, 70, 107, 108, 110; *Timaeus*
    12–13, 19, 20, 26
Plato of Tivoli 26
Pliny the Elder 5, 26, 27, 29, 39, 54, 76, 85, 91, 92,
    93, 96, 98, 100, 107; *Naturalis historia* 5, 26, 76,
    85, 91, 98
Plotinus 20; *Enneads* 20
ploughs 49, 50, 52, 53, 88
Poland 52
polar regions 45, 57
Polo, Maffeo 59
Polo, Marco 39, 59, 98; *Travels* 59
Polo, Nicolò 59
Polybus 19; *De humoribus* 19; *De natura hominis* 19
polyptyques 51
precious stones 59, 60, 96, 97, 98; adamant 100;
    agate 100; amber 96; amethyst 100; beryl 99, 100;
    carbuncle 60, 100; carnelian 102; chalcedony 100;
    chrysolite 100, 102; chrysophrase 100; crystal 50,
    96, 102; diamonds 98, 102; emerald 100; hyacinth
    100, 102; Indian stone 100; jasper 99, 100; jet 96;
    ligurius 100; onyx 100; opal 102; pearl 100; rain
    stones 98; ruby 102; sapphire 100; sardius 100;
    sardonyx 100; topaz 100; turquoise 102

pregnancy 99
pre-Socratic philosophy 4, 12
Prester John 59, 98
Prime mover 4, 22, 31, 32
prognostication 40
psalters 67, 74; Bird Psalter 74; Luttrell Psalter 74; Queen Mary Psalter 74
Pseudo-Apuleius 92, 93
Ptolemy 26, 29, 30–31, 32, 33, 56, 65, 67; *Almagest* 26, 30; *Planisphere* 26; *Tetrabiblos (Quadripartitum)* 26, 33, 67
pyromancy 35
Pythagoras 21, 67, 108

Quadrivium 25
quadrupeds 77, 81
quarries 96
quintessence, element 14, 30
Qur'an 108, 113

rain 39, 40, 41–42, 43, 50, 72, 89, 102
rainbows 41, 106
rationality 62–63, 64
Ratramnus 59
Ravenna 54, 83
reason 62–63, 69, 107
reptiles 76, 77; snakes 59, 75, 92, 98, 110
Reynard the Fox 74
Richard II, king of England 75
Richard of Chichester, Saint 74
Richard of Holdingham 58
rice 50
Rig veda 20
Rimbert 59
rivers 50, 57, 72, 79, 103
Robert de Lisle 67
Roger of Hereford 34
Roger of Salerno 68; *Practica chirugia* 68
Roman de la Rose 95
rotae 15, 45, 55
Ruffinus 95
Ruffus, Jordanus 81; *De medicina equorum* 81

Salerno 6, 7, 8, 18, 68, 93
sand 52, 60
Sandwich 40
salt 40, 81, 96–97, 102
salt marsh 52
sanguine 18, 64
Saxony, Lower 96
scala naturae 23, 62, 77, 88

Scandinavia 52, 59
Scottus, Michael 7, 81
sea creatures 77
seasons 15, 16, 19, 35, 44, 46–47, 50, 53, 64, 67, 79, 97, 107, 112; autumn 16, 19, 46, 72, 86; spring 16, 19, 38, 40, 46, 72, 86; summer 16, 19, 39, 40, 42, 43, 46, 57, 72, 86, 87; winter 16, 19, 38, 39, 40, 42, 43, 46, 57, 72, 86
Secretum secretorum 65, 66
Seine, river 38
Seneca 6; *Naturales quaestiones* 6
senses (*see also* hearing, sight, smell, taste, touch) 62, 69–72
shells 82
Shem, son of Noah 56
Shem-Tor ibn Falaquera 7; *De'ot ha-filisofim* 7
shepherds 37, 38, 54
shooting stars 25
Sicily 7, 26, 54, 79, 81
sight 71–72, 91, 92, 106, 109
signatures 94
Silverstone 53
Silvester, Bernard 21, 22, 23; *Cosmographia* 21, 23; *De mundi universitate* 21
Sind 57
Sisibut, king of Spain 5
smell 53, 60, 63, 65, 70–71, 76, 92, 104
smoke 17
snails 53
snakes (*see* reptiles)
snow 38, 41, 43, 45
soils 19, 46, 54, 72, 87, 97, 103, 111
Solinus 58, 59, 98, 100; *Collectenea rerm memorabilium* 58
solstices 16, 57, 107
soul 10, 20, 21, 23, 62, 64, 68, 71, 88, 110; sensible soul 88; vegetative soul 88, 89
sound 53, 63
South China Sea 59
Speculum astronomiae 31
Spain 5, 6, 9, 26, 50, 54, 96, 104
spices 59
spiders 69
springs 50, 53
stalactites 102
stalagmites 102
Stapleton, Sir Bryan 75
stars 4, 8, 10, 21, 25, 26, 27, 28, 30, 32, 33, 34, 36, 72, 107; Arcton 36; Pole star 36; Septemtri 36
steam 17
Stoicism 6, 20, 108

stones (*see also* precious stones) 8, 10, 23, 43, 106, 110; formation of 97–98; gravel 87; loadstones 106; magnet 100; marble 50, 96; porphyry 50, 96; sandstone 96
storm-makers 41
Strabo 54
Strabo, Walahfrid 92–93; *Hortulus* 92
sublunary sphere (*see* terrestrial sphere)
suet 73
sugar cane 50, 90
Sumatra 59
Sunda archipelago 57
superlunary sphere (*see* celestial sphere)
superstitions 41
Sun 5, 14, 21, 27, 28, 29, 31, 32, 33, 38, 39, 40, 41, 42, 43, 44, 57, 58, 66, 87, 97, 101, 102, 112
supernatural world, concept of 3
surgery 68
Sussex 74
Sutton Hoo 74–75
Sweden 52
Switzerland 35
Syria 96

Tanais, river 55
taste 17, 70, 71, 90, 91, 92, 104
temperaments (*see also* choler, melancholy, phlegm, sanguine) 15, 18, 33, 64, 66
Tempier, bishop of Paris 34
Terraconta 58
terrestrial sphere 4, 14, 65
texture 17, 54, 104
The Ballad of the Tyrannical Husband 76
The Phoenix 47
The Plants and their Children 34, 65
The Seafarer 47
Theobald, abbot of Monte Cassino 76
Theobaldus-Physiologus 76
Theodore of Antioch 7
Theophanes the Confessor 38
Theophrastus 91, 100; *De causis plantarum* 91; *De historia plantarum* 91; *De lapidibus* 100
Theoretica planetarum 32
Thomas of Cantimpré 5, 6, 100, 110; *De natura rerum* 5, 100, 110
Thracia 39
thunder 40, 41, 43, 45, 71, 72
tides 29, 112
timekeeping 26
Timotheus of Gaza 41, 63
Toledo 7

touch 70
Tower of London 83
Tractatus de quarternario 64
transhumance 51
translation of texts 7, 10, 11, 14, 18, 22, 26, 30, 33, 54, 76, 79, 80, 88, 91, 92, 93, 98
trees 49, 78, 79–80, 82, 85, 86, 87, 91, 110, 111; almond 87; bay-laurel 87; deciduous 52; elder 94; figs 39, 90; lemon 86, 87; olives 39, 48, 90; orange 87; spruce 52; walnut 87
Trentino 75
Troyes 38
Twiti, William 80; *L'Art de Venerie* 80

universities 10–11, 33
urbanism 50
urine 68, 73

vapours 17, 41–42, 43, 44, 45, 68, 70, 89, 101, 103
Varro 85
vegetables 11, 23, 85, 87, 88, 91, 110, 112; artichokes 50; asparagus 93; aubergines 50; cabbage 87; celery 93; cucumber 87; garlic 86, 87; green beans 87; lettuce 87; onions 87; parsley 93; prickly lettuce 81; radish 87; spinach 50
venison and vert 78–79
vernacular texts 34, 76
veterinary science 80–81
Vices 67
Villeneuve St Georges 51
Vincent of Beauvais 6, 93, 100; *Speculum naturale* 6, 100
vines 91
vineyards 51
Virtues 67
volcanoes 112

Wace 53
Wakefield mystery plays 37, 38
Walter of Henley 87, 104; *Husbandry* 87
water 42–43, 50, 70, 86, 87, 97, 99, 101, 103
water, element 12–18, 19, 43, 88, 89, 90, 106
wax 73
weather 26, 33, 37–47, 111, 112
wetlands 49, 50, 51
William I, king of England 78
William of Conches 6, 16, 27, 42, 43, 44, 55, 57, 71, 97; *De philosophia mundi* 6; *Dragmaticon* 6, 42, 44
William of Malmesbury 83
William of Moerbeke 10

William of Rubruck 59
William of Saliceto 68; *Chirugia* 68
windmills 50
winds 15, 35, 38, 39, 41–42, 43–45, 46, 72, 86, 90,
    97, 107, 112; *Africus* 45; *Aparticus* 45; *Apeliotes* 45;
    Aquilo 45; *Auster* 45; *Circius* 45; *Corus* 45;
    Euroauster 45; *Euronotus* 45; *Favonius* 45; *Notus*
    45; *Septentio* 45; *Subsolanus* 45; *Vulturnus* 45;
    Zephyrus 45
wine 50
wood 17
woodland 48, 49, 50, 51, 52, 53, 78, 109, 111;
    wood pasture 52
Woodstock 83
wool 73

Worcestershire 40
Worms 41, 83

Xenophon 80

Yemen 57
Yugoslavia 39

zodiac 22, 30, 33, 35, 65, 74; Aries 66; Aquarius 65,
    66; Cancer 66; Capricorn 65, 66; Gemini 66; Leo
    66; Libra 66; Pisces 66; Sagittarius 66; Scorpio 66;
    Taurus 66; Virgo 66
zodiac men 22
zoology 79
Zoroastrianism 20